TITANIC THOMPSON

The Man Who Bet on
Everything

· · ·

KEVIN COOK

PICADOR

First published 2010 by W. W. Norton & Company, New York

First published in Great Britain 2011 by Picador
an imprint of Pan Macmillan, a division of Macmillan Publishers Limited
Pan Macmillan, 20 New Wharf Road, London N1 9RR
Basingstoke and Oxford
Associated companies throughout the world
www.panmacmillan.com

ISBN 978-0-330-52994-5

1 3 5 7 9 8 6 4 2

A CIP catalogue record for this book is available from
the British Library.

Printed in the UK by CPI Mackays; Chatham ME5 8TD

For Cal & Lily
always 2 p.m.

"Is it wrong to gamble, or only to lose?"
—Sky Masterson, *Guys and Dolls*

CONTENTS

PROLOGUE

HE BLEW INTO TOWN LIKE A ROGUE WIND THAT LIFTED girls' skirts and turned gamblers' pockets inside-out. Tall and thin with a bland mask of a face, he had close-set eyes that looked a little dead, at least until he offered you a bet. Then those dark eyes sparked and he smiled like he had good news.

"Are you a gambling man?" he'd ask. "Because I am."

Alvin was his name, but nobody called him that. They called him "Titanic."

Titanic Thompson—a made-up name for a self-made man who won and lost millions of dollars playing cards, dice, pool, golf, horseshoes, and anything else he could think of to bet on. He also killed five men. "But they'd all tell you they had it coming." He also married five women, each one a teenager on her wedding day. Titanic liked his women young and pretty, his cars big and fast, his suckers rich and gullible. He spent fifty years roaming America's back roads, living by his wits and reflexes, until America changed and there was no more room for such a man.

●　　●　　●

IN THE YEARS BETWEEN world wars, Titanic Thompson motored from town to town in a nickel-plated, two-ton Pierce-Arrow, the same car Babe Ruth, Franklin Roosevelt, and the shah of Persia favored. He carried his tools in the trunk: left- and right-handed golf clubs, a bowling ball, horseshoes, a shotgun, and a suitcase full of cash. During his first twenty years on the road he crossed paths with Harry Houdini, Al Capone, Howard Hughes, Minnesota Fats, and Jean Harlow. Still he managed to remain a cipher to the public. Damon Runyon wanted to write about him, but Titanic told him to forget it. He said, "Mine ain't the kind of work publicity helps." So Runyon based a character on him—Sky Masterson, the hero of *Guys and Dolls*.

Professional gamblers still talk about Titanic Thompson. They say that he threw a watermelon over a three-story building, that he pulled Capone's pants down, that he beat Ben Hogan playing golf right-handed and then turned around and beat Byron Nelson left-handed, that he survived the sinking of the *Titanic* by sneaking into a lifeboat dressed as a woman. Only the watermelon story is true. But plenty of other Titanic tales are gospel. He hunted quail by throwing rocks, knocking the birds out of the air. He tricked Capone out of five hundred dollars and double-crossed Arnold Rothstein, the crime boss who fixed the 1919 "Black Sox" World Series. He hustled country-club golfers for twenty thousand a hole while Hogan and Nelson were earning ten thousand a year. He once drove a golf ball more than five hundred yards.

There's a true story to his name too. In 1912, a few weeks after the unsinkable *Titanic* sank, taking 1,517 souls down with her, a rangy teenager in a brown suit stepped into Snow Clark's pool hall in Joplin, Missouri. He proceeded to beat every player in the place, then asked, "Who's the best cue in town?" That would be Snow, the pool players said. Snow Clark could run the table as fast as you could blink.

"Where do I find him?"

"Right over there."

Alvin from Arkansas moseyed over and introduced himself. In an Ozarks twang that sounded half-dim, he challenged the pool-hall owner to a game for five hundred dollars. That was enough to get Clark's attention. In 1912, a fellow could live for a year on that much money, or live like a prince for a couple of months, feasting on one-dollar steak dinners, with pie and ice cream on the side. Young Alvin did the latter after he ran the table on Snow Clark.

On his way out he noticed a sign Clark had posted in the window: *$200 to Any Man Who Jumps over My New Pool Table.* The table was nine feet long and four and a half feet wide. To clear it, a jumper would have to hurdle a fifty-four-inch surface that was thirty inches off the floor—an Olympic-caliber jump—before crashing down on the far side. "I can do it," Alvin said. "I can outjump a herd of bullfrogs." Clark and the others laughed. Even if the kid somehow cleared the table, he'd break his leg or arm or skull on the landing.

Alvin walked out, leaving them wondering if they had offended the boy by laughing at him. He returned ten minutes later dragging a mattress he'd bought at a fleabag hotel. He positioned the mattress beside the pool table, walked around to the other side, took a running start, and sprang into the air. According to an eyewitness, "He leaped headfirst across the table, did a flip and landed on his back on that mattress."

As Alvin collected his winnings, someone asked Snow Clark the stranger's name. "I don't rightly know, but it ought to be 'Titanic,' " Clark said. "He sinks everybody."

After his christening in that smoky poolroom, the young hustler hit the road. Ahead lay more adventures, bigger money, romance, and violence, and on that road he would invent a vocation. Titanic Thompson would be America's original proposition gambler, always on the move, one step ahead of his victims and the law.

1 OUT OF THE WOODS

HE WAS BORN ALVIN CLARENCE THOMAS IN 1892. *Thomas*, not *Thompson*, not yet. He grew up poor in a log cabin on a dirt road in the Ozarks. There was no shame in that, at least the dirt-road part of it, since there were only ten miles of paved roads in the United States. In 1892, most of the country's sixty-five million citizens lived quietly in the wide spaces between cities. But the American century was coming, bringing new and surprising events. In the year of Alvin's birth, the U.S. immigration station on Ellis Island opened, Lizzie Borden gave her parents forty whacks, and nine boys at the YMCA in Springfield, Massachusetts, played the first game of a sport called basketball (final score 1–0).

Alvin drew his first breath in Monett, Missouri. According to family lore, his father was playing poker in a saloon that night. Lee Thomas was tall with a soft voice. He got loud only when he was flush or drunk, and he was said to be both on the night his son was born, so he kept on playing, sipping from a flask of what he called his hollerin' whiskey. Lee didn't go home until the next day, Thanksgiving Day, the thirtieth Thanksgiving since President Lincoln declared it a national holiday back in 1863, and Lee wasn't at all thankful when he saw the newborn at his wife's breast. A few weeks later, on one of those winter mornings when you could see your breath indoors, he packed a cardboard satchel and went to the shelf where his wife kept her pin money in a sugar bowl. Stepping softly, he picked her last five dollars out of the bowl. His wife never saw him again.

Alvin's mother, Sarah, always said they were lucky Lee left when he did. She was still young enough to catch a man, even with a baby underfoot. Sarah wound up marrying a hog farmer who had a plot near Rogers, Arkansas, forty miles southwest of Monett. The dense Ozark Forest outside town was so deep a green it was a shade of black. Only about twelve hundred people lived in Rogers in the 1890s, most of them clustered around a double row of clapboard buildings on Walnut Street, where horse-drawn carts loaded with apples rolled to the town's only thriving business, a hulking apple-vinegar plant. The plant gave off a sour-apple reek that reminded churchgoers of Adam and Eve's sin. Empty carts rolled back the other way toward the orchards that gave Benton County its motto, "Land of the Big Red Apple."

Alvin's stepfather raised hogs and poultry on a hill beyond the orchards. Relatives grew peas and corn to feed the stock, and tended a patch of tobacco. Alvin and his mother, stepfather, two stepsisters, and two stepbrothers shared a three-room cabin. In a tin washtub in the middle of the main room, they took weekly baths in water that had been heated in a pot hung over the fire. Alvin was the youngest so he bathed last, in cool, murky water. He waited for his turn in the privy too, where spiders lurked in the summertime and unmentionable icicles hung under the seat in the winter.

They were Baptists, his new family, each one dunked in a tank at the whitewashed church in Eureka Springs on the day of his or her salvation. They feared God and tuberculosis, which was still the leading cause of death in America, so familiar that Alvin must have heard the schoolyard verse that paraphrased Shakespeare: "TB or not TB, that is the question. Consumption be done about it? Of cough not!" His stepfather and step-uncles went to church on Sunday and worked hard all week. For sport they hunted, pitched pennies, shot at targets, played checkers and dominoes and penny-ante poker. Pretty soon Sarah's kid was taking their pennies. Little Alvin could toss a coin so that it hopped once and landed flat against a wall. He could make the coin lean on the wall if he wanted. He beat everyone at checkers but loved poker most of all. A deck of cards was an extended family to him, the only friends he had. As soon as he learned the rules of poker, he began to understand percentages—the odds that governed how cards combined to form different hands. When it came to numbers, Alvin had perfect pitch.

The cards did favors for him once he tattooed them. He taught himself to cheat even with a fresh deck: Using a fingernail to put a nearly invisible nick on the cards' backs, he marked the face cards and aces he got during the first few hands of a game. He had figured out a simple system card-markers still use today: A notch or dot on a card's edge signifies a high card; a mark elsewhere means it's a low card; a middle card gets no mark. Before long the deck was practically transparent to him. While his schoolmates studied their times tables, he sat on his straw mattress running cards through his fingers, watching the notched cards' progress as he dealt poker hands to phantom opponents. His dexterity improved until he could deal from the bottom of the deck so smoothly that nobody spotted the trick. He could shuffle one-handed, flipping every other card as it passed through his hand so that half the deck was face-up and half face-down when he finished.

What he couldn't do was read. For Alvin, school was an hour's walk to a wooden prison where a boy was legally caged while squirrels, sparrows, and grown-ups went free. Sitting at a desk made him want to jump out of his skin. So he quit going to school and spent the long days fishing for catfish and bass and hunting rabbit, possum, and raccoon.

His uncles said he was one-sixteenth Indian thanks to a full-blooded Cherokee who had shinnied up his mother's side of the family tree. How else to account for his running, jumping, and shooting skills? They had all watched the boy level his .22 rifle and hit a crow between the eyes from fifty yards. They had seen him down birds without using a gun, pegging a rock at a bird and *bang*, killing it. Not every time, but enough to put quail on the table most days.

His best friend was a chocolate-brown water spaniel named Carlo that bounded through the woods with him or sat watching him chop logs, the only manual labor Alvin ever did. He always said he grew tall and strong swinging an axe in those woods, cutting timber into planks eight and a half feet long, seven inches thick, and nine inches wide, the size of railroad ties. Carlo followed as Alvin carted the planks by mule to Rogers, where a man from the Frisco Railroad inspected them and paid twenty-five cents apiece for the good ones. Alvin gave most of the money to his mother but kept a few nickels to bet with.

One bright morning he spied a man at a White River fishing hole. "I watched this dude fish with his elegant casting outfit, and I wanted it," he said decades later. The man returned to the same spot several days in a row, pulling in trout with his shiny rod and reel.

Eleven-year-old Alvin tossed a stick into the water. Carlo leaped in, swam to the stick, and brought it back.

"That's a fine fetchin' dog," the dude said.

"He'll fetch anything," Alvin boasted. "I could chuck a rock in there and he'd dive in and bring it back."

"Is that a fact?"

The man didn't believe it. He said there was no way a dog could find a particular rock in a riverbed. After some back and forth they settled on a wager—the kid's .22 rifle against the man's fishing gear.

"Boy, you got a bet."

Alvin picked up a stone. He said he couldn't lose—old Carlo'd be back with that rock in a jiffy.

But the fisherman was no all-day sucker. "Hold on, now. You better mark that rock," he said. "Mark it so I'll know it's the same one you threw in."

"OK, if you say so." Alvin scratched a big *X* on the rock and chucked it into the water. The spaniel dived in. Half a minute passed. Man and boy waited while the water settled. Leaves rustled. At last Carlo broke the surface and paddled to the riverbank.

The dog dropped the stone he had fetched. "Well, I'll be damned," the fisherman said when he saw the *X* on the rock. "That's a hell of a dog or a hell of a trick." He packed up his gear and began to leave.

Alvin stepped in front of him. "That fishing pole's mine. I won it fair and square."

The man seemed to think that was funny until he got a good look down the barrel of the boy's .22. "Pay off," Alvin said.

The fancy fellow dropped his gear. Alvin spent the rest of the summer yanking trout from the White River with the fine rod and reel he hadn't really won fair and square, since Carlo couldn't really tell one rock from another. What the fisherman didn't know was that the boy had spent hours at that spot the evening before he offered the bet, marking rocks and chucking them into the water. When he finished, the bottom of the fishing hole was littered with stones marked with *X*'s.

WITH NO MORE BOOK learning than his elders had, Alvin trained himself to outsmart them. When no one was looking, he pitched pennies at a tin cup. After hundreds of tosses he grooved a soft underhand motion. Now he could offer a crazy-sounding bet: "I can make nine out of ten from five paces"—and do it. No trick, just practice. He sat on his bed dealing poker hands until he could win with marked or unmarked decks. One trick was tipping the back of the deck upward while he dealt, bending the near corner just enough to peek. It didn't feel like cheating, really. It was more like learning what he could get away with, since the other fellows, especially Alvin's uncles, would surely do the same if they could.

Beating his cousins and uncles out of their dimes and soon their dollars did nothing for Alvin's standing with his aunts. They raised hell with his stepfather, whose opinion of the boy was low to begin with. To him, Alvin was a born conniver, just like the long-gone Lee Thomas.

When his stepfather sputtered at him, blaming Alvin's bloodline for all that was wrong with him, Alvin took it as a compliment. He never hid his disdain for the hog farmer or his longing to escape this patch of the Ozarks where the sun set early every evening on nothing much and the sour-apple reek from Rogers drifted on the wind.

He was sixteen the day he packed a satchel. "I was six-foot-one and strong as a wild razorback hog," he would recall. "There was no place for me out in the country. It was time to see what the world held for a boy of my talents."

His mother asked where he'd go. What would he do?

To town, he said. To gamble.

"Promise me something," Sarah said. "Give me your word that you'll never smoke or drink."

"I promise," Alvin said. He would keep his vow for the better part of a century while counting himself lucky that she hadn't brought up the sixth, seventh, eighth, ninth, and tenth commandments. He kissed his mother goodbye and walked downhill, with the legs of his bib overalls tucked into a new pair of boots. He had fifty cents in his pocket. It was eight miles to Rogers, a two-hour walk even for a long-legged boy in a hurry. When he hit town, he headed for the Frisco Railroad station, but rather than sit at the station he waited a couple hundred yards up the track. He climbed onto the first northbound train when no one was looking and rode the rails out of his youth.

Alvin's times were forward-looking. In 1909, Admiral Robert Peary planted Old Glory with its forty-six stars in wind-polished ice at the North Pole—or so he claimed—while workers ten thousand miles to the south shoveled a hundred thousand cubic yards of tropical mud per day, digging the Panama Canal. In Detroit, Henry Ford's new motor company had just introduced the Model T. The company's assembly lines would soon produce a Model T every three minutes, but automobiles were still a rare sight in most of the country. There were no stop signs then, so when the first two Model T Fords in Ohio arrived at the same unmarked crossroads one day, neither driver would give way, and they crashed into each other. Much of the South and Middle West was still half-wild, with traveling medicine shows rousing the dust along with tent revivals, turkey shoots, and the not-so-occasional holdup. Bank- and train-robbers Butch Cassidy and the Sundance Kid, who died that year, were celebrated as throwbacks to a more colorful century, along with homegrown outlaws like Missouri-born Jesse James.

Alvin's first stop out of Rogers was Monett, Missouri, the town of his birth. He thought he might pick up his daddy's trail there. Instead he came across a man banging a bass drum on a street corner, hawking colorful accordion maps of the United States featuring the faces of the twenty-six presidents. "One dollar apiece," called J.C. Arthur, thumping his drum. "A mere dollar for the most educated map either side of the wide Mississippi!" The country boy didn't have a dollar, but he had a proposition: He said he could sell those maps door-to-door.

Arthur looked into the gawky teenager's bland face, and like many men after him he saw no malice or deceit. In this case his trust was well placed. They struck a deal, and the apprentice proved himself right away, captivating a Monett housewife with the tale of how he had left Arkansas alone and penniless. He was looking for his daddy, he said, but in the meantime, thank the good Lord, he'd met a kind man who'd agreed to pay him a few cents' commission for selling these maps, "the finest educational maps ever seen in these parts." Before long the woman was reaching into her apron for a dollar.

From Monett, Alvin and J.C. Arthur canvassed southwest Missouri and northwest Arkansas, knocking on screen doors in Branson, Joplin, Fayetteville, and Rocky Comfort. Alvin sold more maps with his sob story than Arthur had ever sold with his drum. At each stop he asked if anyone had seen a man who "looks a bit like me, I expect, but older. Calls himself Lee Thomas." Nobody recalled seeing such a man.

In the winter of 1909 he and Arthur passed through Springfield, Missouri, Queen City of the Ozarks. Eyes wide, Alvin watched the first automobile he had ever seen, a shiny black Model T, reach a startling forty miles per hour before it got mired in a puddle. He resolved on the spot to own a car someday. And he knew he'd never get one by selling maps. A man needed to think big if he was to rise above his origins. Otherwise he might pass through the world without leaving a trace.

It didn't take long for him to learn that card rooms were like churches, brothels, and mad dogs: Every town had at least one. The card rooms were often in the stale-smelling hindquarters of a saloon, where any male of shaving age with five or ten dollars was welcome to pull up a chair. Alvin's youth was no hindrance; in fact it helped him. Poker players were glad to welcome a boy with his first bankroll in his pocket. They never expected such a young shaver to be a sharp. Not that Alvin always cheated. More often he won by reading other players' intentions on their faces or by the way they moved their chips or shifted in their chairs.

Maybe he got his watchfulness from being an unwelcome stepson in an overcrowded house, or maybe it was a genetic gift from sly, long-fingered Lee Thomas. Whatever the cause, Alvin often found himself a few dollars ahead after a dozen hands. Hours later he might be up twenty or thirty dollars, at a time when a pint of beer in the saloon out front sold for a nickel. Not that he bought any beer. Keeping his promise to his mother, he spent the same nickel on a plate of ham and beans and a glass of milk.

Other players took a liking to him. Despite his height they called Alvin a good little player. As he pushed back from the table with a shy smile, not even those who had lost to him hated him. Some of them even bought maps.

Sarah's boy blew most of his first bankroll on a three-piece suit he found in a Springfield secondhand store. He was done wearing overalls. On his next map-selling trip he hooked his thumbs in his vest pockets, doing his best to look like a riverboat gambler. Striding into the town square in tiny Franklin, Missouri, he joined a crowd gathered behind a covered wagon for an old-time medicine show. A weathered gent in a ten-gallon hat stood in the wagon, hollering down at the crowd. His hat, his hair, and his tightly trimmed goatee were as white as the fringe on his buckskin jacket. Captain Adam Bogardus was hawking a miracle medicine guaranteed to cure rheumatism, gout, crossed eyes, female woes, and other ills. He raised his arms. "Attention, please!" In a bullhorn voice, he swore he had ridden with Theodore Roosevelt's Rough Riders on the charge up San Juan Hill in far-off Cuba back in 1898, surviving by fortuitous providence to bring his miracle cure to the good people of this fine village. Bogardus finished his spiel with a bang.

"Behold!" he cried.

In one smooth motion he sailed a pie tin into the air, shouldered his Winchester, and shot it down, *bang bang.*

The people of Franklin cheered, but Alvin wasn't so impressed by a rifleman who took two shots to hit such a large target. He hung around after the show while Bogardus sold bottles of his potion. Then the boy in the secondhand suit approached the captain. "I can beat you at shooting," he said.

Bogardus bent down, cupping his ear. "What did you say, son?"

"I can outshoot you."

The captain laughed. "Son, you must be mad. I am the world's champion."

Unlike many of Bogardus's claims, that one had some truth to it. Captain Adam Henry Bogardus, a Civil War veteran, had started shooting pigeons in the days when marksmen shot live birds released from wire traps. In 1878 he performed for European royalty in Paris as "Master Manipulator of the Shot Gun and Champion Wing-Shot of the World." Later he toured with Buffalo Bill Cody and Annie Oakley. The great Bogardus staged a show of his own in New York, shooting at glass balls launched across Madison Square Garden. The glass targets resembled Christmas ornaments and exploded into shining shards when hit. Firing at top speed for six hours, pausing to cool his gun barrel in a bucket of ice, Bogardus broke 4,844 out of 5,000 targets without plugging a single spectator. He won nationwide acclaim that day, but those 5,000 shotgun blasts near his right ear cost him most of his hearing.

Thirty years later the captain walked with a limp, the result of a shotgun accident. His seventy-five-year-old trigger finger wasn't as steady as it used to be.

"There's one way to find out if I'm better than you," Alvin said. He picked a pie tin off the wagon and nailed it to a fencepost twenty paces away. He had already learned the con artist's trick of painting a target around a bullet hole to "prove" his marksmanship to the next man who passes by, but that wasn't possible with Bogardus looking over his shoulder. Nor was it necessary. Alvin returned to the wagon. Bogardus handed down his Winchester and the boy fired half a dozen times. The target was still smoking as they went to examine it. Captain Bogardus, who would be inducted into the

Trapshooting Hall of Fame in 1913, took one look and said, "Do you need a job, son?"

Alvin always claimed he had hit the pie tin six times but left only one hole—"a hole barely bigger than the first bullet." Whatever he and the captain saw, Alvin took over as the trick shooter for the Bogardus Miracle Medicine Show that day, and map man J.C. Arthur went back to banging his drum solo. The boy was learning to use other men as stepping-stones.

The medicine show toured four states, with Alvin shooting pie tins, cabbages, and tomatoes while the captain speechified from his wagon, waving his arms and quoting scripture, selling bottles of goop that cured nothing but alleviated a good deal of suffering as a blend of herbs, cocaine, and alcohol will do. Alvin introduced a new shooting feat during a circuit of the two-year-old state of Oklahoma: He flipped a silver dollar into the air and shot a hole through it. Only he and Bogardus knew that the real trick was *missing* the coin when he shot at it, since he had palmed the coin he showed the crowd and thrown one that already had a hole in the middle—and he didn't want to destroy his pre-shot silver dollar. He discovered that he could fire sideways or straight up and still fool the rubes because they were watching the coin, not the gun. He told Bogardus he had concluded that the human race was divided into two groups, the suckers and the sharps, and he was a born sharp.

His cut of their take was a few dollars per show. He added to that in poker and dice games at every stop and soon bought a brand-new suit and derby hat. Strolling through towns as far west as Tulsa, smiling and touching the bill of his derby when he passed a pretty girl, he sometimes whistled, sometimes sang. Alvin never could carry a tune, but that didn't keep him from croaking his favorite songs.

Me and my partner and my partner's friend, can pick more cotton than
*   the gin can gin . . .*

Uncle Bud, he built a house, built it 'cross the water, to keep them gamblers away from his daughter . . .

After a year with the medicine show he was itching to move on. Shaking Bogardus's hand, he leaned toward the old man's better ear to shout goodbye. As Alvin recalled it, "I said farewell to the captain and roamed around on my own for a year, living the gambler's life."

Nineteen-ten was a year of marvels in the sky. Theodore Roosevelt, the flying former president, rode an aeroplane almost a mile. The first to pilot a flying machine over Australia was an unlikely aviator named Harry Houdini. The German zeppelin *Deutschland* floated passengers from Frankfurt to Düsseldorf before crashing and burning on its ninth voyage. Halley's Comet appeared over the Northern Hemisphere, a snowball in the night sky signifying great or awful events depending on your superstition. The comet appeared a little lower each night until it slipped under the Earth, starting a seventy-six-year slingshot journey that would bring it back in 1986, while Alvin did his traveling by train and riverboat, playing ten- and twenty-dollar poker games, keeping his ears open. One night he heard about a man who claimed to be unbeatable at dice.

Joe Green, a slob in a stained undershirt, ran a barge called *Rambler* out of Marked Tree, Arkansas. Green shot dice on the deck between the crates of vegetables he hauled up and down the St. Francis River. Alvin met the boat at the Marked Tree dock and introduced himself, saying he'd heard a fine fellow named Green liked to play dice for money. Green invited him to ride along. The boy had one thing to do before they shoved off—a lingering kiss with a schoolgirl on the dock.

He won $2,000 on the next few *Rambler* runs. Green couldn't fathom his misfortune. He was "all gambler," the type who thinks his luck is bound to hold when he's up and certain to turn when he's down. He said his barge was worth $2,500 and he wanted to play for it, which is how Alvin acquired his first employee: By the time the barge returned to the dock, Green was working for the dandy-dressed boy he called the "Derby Kid."

The schoolgirl was waiting for her beau. "Nellie, come take a ride on my boat," Alvin called. She climbed aboard.

Green invited a guest of his own to join them, a bull-necked drunk named Jim Johnson, who plopped his bulk on a vegetable crate and said, "Fetch the dice, boy. We're playing craps."

They weren't two miles downriver before Alvin had him down fifty dollars. Johnson pulled a knife. "Cheater! I'll slit your throat." He shoved the youngster to the rail and with one last push sent Alvin tumbling into the river. Green and Johnson got a kick out of watching the boy splash in the muddy water. They were still laughing when he climbed back aboard, but Nellie was crying by then, clutching her torn dress.

"I'm going to keep tearing her clothes till I get what's underneath," Johnson told Alvin. "And then I'll cut your goddamned head off."

"No. You'll keep away from her."

"Will I?" Johnson reached for his knife. Alvin saw a hammer lying on the deck. He grabbed it and swung it at Johnson's head. The bigger man sagged against the rail. Alvin could have stopped right there. Instead, as he remembered, "I popped him three or four more times and it was his turn to go over the rail."

He always said the crucial difference between him and Jim Johnson was simple: "I was a strong swimmer and he couldn't swim a lick." He neglected to mention that he had been conscious when he hit the water, while Johnson was out cold thanks to those hammer pops to the head.

Deputies pulled Johnson's body from the river two days later. An unnamed witness, probably Joe Green, had alerted the Poinsett County sheriff to the crime. Alvin Thomas was arrested for murder. This being Marked Tree, a tiny river town unreachable by road, the boy was hauled into a hearing in the train depot, where the sheriff served as prosecutor, defense lawyer, and judge. There was no evidence. No witnesses testified. The verdict: guilty.

Sentencing was swift. The sheriff told Alvin he could stay in town, awaiting jail or the noose. Or he could hand the sheriff the deed to the *Rambler*, and git.

Alvin got.

Goodbye, Nellie.

He bought a new derby to replace the one he had lost when he fell overboard, then followed the St. Francis downriver until it fed into the Mississippi. When he reached a new town, he'd wander into a nickelodeon and pay five cents to see a twelve-minute travelogue showing the black-and-white wonders of New York, Paris, or Egypt. Soon there were short silent movies shown in vaudeville houses along with the usual singers and variety acts. Sometimes actors and actresses performed the movies' dialogue while the film unreeled behind them. In big cities a twelve-piece pit orchestra played along with silent movies; in small towns, a lone piano. Alvin may well have seen one of the first Pathé newsreels in New Orleans in 1911. He crossed Louisiana, heading west to rugged oil towns on the Texas-Louisiana border. "Every place I went, I asked if anybody knew Lee Thomas." One night he stepped into a card room in Oil City, Louisiana, a rowdy boomtown full of roughnecks, tough women, and loose money. As Alvin told the story for the rest of his life, "I had fifteen hundred dollars in my pocket. I saw several men playing stud poker. The dealer was tall and slim like me and had long, slender fingers that riffled the cards and laid them out neatly across the table."

"It's a cash game," the dealer said. He wore a three-piece suit with a satin vest. A diamond glimmered on his ring finger. "Twenty-five dollars to play."

Alvin peeled a few bills off his bankroll. If his heart was pounding, you couldn't tell it by looking at him.

On the first hand, the dealer showed a pair of kings. Alvin had aces. He raked in two hundred dollars, enough to buy a small house or a strong interest in an Oil City gusher.

"What did you say your name was?" the dealer asked.

"Didn't say."

They played all night. As the hours passed, the chips migrated to Alvin's side of the table. Other players went bust and headed out to get breakfast while the dealer and the kid played on. Alvin kept his eyes on the older man, watching for signs of worry or weakness or recognition, seeing only the blank gaze of a professional.

Finally the dealer stood up. "You've taken sixteen hundred dollars off me," he said. "I got a right to know your name."

"I'm Alvin Thomas," the boy said. He pushed his chips across the table. "You're my daddy, and I'm giving you your money back."

Lee Thomas blinked. Then he burst out laughing. "My own boy cleaned me out!" He came around the table to embrace his son—after scooping the chips into his pockets.

2 FUN AND GAMES

ALVIN ALWAYS LIKED TELLING PEOPLE HOW HE HAD found his father. If the stakes of the Oil City stud game and the diamonds on Lee's fingers grew in the telling, well, why not? Alvin had been retailing his life story since he sold his first map, and now the first chapter had a happy ending: Found the son of a bitch, turned the tables on him, got a hug for it. But the next part wasn't so happy.

"I stayed in Oil City awhile, playing partners with my daddy, cheating the oil-field boys out of their pay," he said. "It didn't last, though." It didn't last because Lee Thomas hadn't changed his stripes. Lee turned out to be the worst sort of hustler, not a fellow who thinks up smart ways to win but a plain cheat who stole some of his son's bankroll when he thought Alvin was asleep. So this time the boy left the man behind. "I told my daddy goodbye and never saw him again, or heard his voice."

It was the spring of 1912. The *Titanic* was settling into the North Atlantic seabed under two and a half miles of icewater. The Derby Kid was nineteen years old, no longer a boy. He had fled a farmhouse full of step-kin and used his guts and natural gifts to become

that most American creation: a self-made man. He still had plenty
to learn, but at nineteen he was the man he would be. He had no
religion, no politics, little interest in other men beyond how much
gamble they had in them, and no desire to find a safe place in the
world. He just wanted to gamble every day of his life.

He was marking cards in a roadhouse near Joplin, Missouri,
notching the edges with a pinkie nail he sharpened every day with
a file. This was the 1912 trip to Joplin that would earn him his
nickname—Titanic, the pool-table jumper who sank everybody.
But before Alvin ducked into Snow Clark's pool hall, he was cheating in a Joplin roadhouse when a man in a black coat pulled up a
chair beside him. "Son, I've been watching you play, and I think
you're going to be the best gambler in America," the man said.
Polston was his name. Mr. Polston owned a bank and played a little
poker himself, he said, "but not very well." A longtime loser at the
tables, he wanted Alvin to help him get back at the sharps who
had beaten him for years. He offered to stake the youngster "in
high-money games, high as you like." That sounded good to Alvin,
who was soon unpacking his bags in a high-raftered room in Joplin's Connor Hotel, an eight-story palace with a grand staircase of
Italian marble, a tailor shop, a barbershop, and a billiards room
where the tables had leather-mesh pockets. A grandfatherly man in
a blue uniform with brass buttons brought a vase of fresh flowers to
Alvin's room and let Alvin know that room service wasn't limited
to flowers or steak and potatoes. He could also have a girl or two
from the House of Lords if he wanted. Mr. Polston was paying.
Alvin told the old fellow he wasn't greedy; he'd never ask for two.

He took his time with Polston's friends. After a week he was
more than a thousand dollars in the hole. The banker, handing him
five thousand more, looked ill. As Alvin told the story, Mr. Polston
turned a shade of green between lime and frog when Alvin began
doubling his bets in hopes of getting even, the way suckers do.
And then, with the stakes too rich for all but the top-money poker

players in southwest Missouri, he shoved his entire pile toward the ziggurat of chips in the middle of the table. "Raise two thousand," he said—a sum equal to about forty thousand in 2010 dollars. He won that hand but lost the next. Over the following twelve hours he lost the small pots, keeping a little blood in the others' mouths. Still all the crucial hands were the same: "Raise a thousand." "Raise five thousand." By morning he had broken them all.

Polston was giddy. The banker followed his young champion back to the hotel and up to his room, going on about all the money they could make together, smiling as he put his nose to the flowers on the dresser, and asking, in a winking way, if Alvin had everything he needed. What he didn't know was that Alvin wasn't so keen on whores. It was nothing against them personally, they were working the odds like everyone else, but they tended to be twice his age. The banker's teenage daughter was more his speed. A black-haired spitfire, she had been entertaining Alvin in his hotel room while her father worked at the bank. That was why Alvin was taking so long to break the local cardplayers. He was enjoying himself. But after a couple weeks' worth of afternoons with Polston's daughter he grew bored with her. When two Joplin boys asked him along on a fishing trip, he jumped at the chance.

Beanie Benson and Hickory McCullough were decent poker players and raconteurs but lousy fishermen. They'd each toss two or three lines in the water and then get so busy drinking and telling jokes that they didn't notice when they got a bite. Alvin had to reel in what they caught. One time while Beanie and Hickory were gabbing away on the drive back to town, and Alvin was sitting in the backseat with a bucket of fish, he noticed a work crew planting a new road sign: *JOPLIN 20.* That night he hired a man to drive him back to the same spot. They dug up the sign and moved it five miles closer to town. The next time the gamblers went fishing, Alvin spent the day coddling Beanie and Hickory, baiting hooks for them and handing them drinks. On the way home he pointed at the road sign. "That sign's a lie," he told his drunken companions. "It's no twenty miles from here to Joplin."

"Sure it is. They're careful about that sort of thing," Beanie said.

"I'll bet you a hundred it's no more than fifteen miles."

"I'll bet five hundred you're wrong."

"I'll take five hundred of that," Hickory said.

Alvin said, "Boys, you got a bet."

They measured the distance on Hickory's odometer: fifteen miles. Hickory swore he was going to raise hell with the roads department.

After that, Beanie and Hickory refused to bet with Alvin. If he had offered one-to-two that he could eat sugar and flour and crap a birthday cake, they would have bought candles. It was time to move on.

He telephoned the banker's daughter to say goodbye. She wept and asked to see him one last time, for one last kiss, so he walked to Polston's house, where she took his hand and led him to the davenport. They had just finished getting naked when her father came home from work early. Alvin pulled his pants on just as the girl's mother came charging up the porch steps. Polston looked from his wife to his hysterical daughter to the half-dressed Derby Kid. He didn't want to lose the best young gambler in America. He gulped and tried to make the most of an awkward introduction.

"Alvin," he said, "I'd like you to meet my wife."

"Pleased to meet you, ma'am!" Alvin hustled down the steps and kept going until he was back in his hotel room. Leaving an envelope full of hundred-dollar bills as a thank you to Polston, he headed for the train depot, detouring only to clean out Snow Clark's poolroom and hurdle the billiard table. Emerging as Titanic Thomas, he rode a Kansas City Southern dining car out of town, watching shadows rise on the east-facing hills of Jasper County. Half an hour later the train crossed the Arkansas state line. It passed within hiking distance of Rogers and the farmhouse where he had been raised. His mother hadn't heard a word from her Alvin in two and a half years. She would have to wait a while longer because he wasn't stopping now. He didn't have enough money yet.

NEW ORLEANS, SHREVEPORT, HOT SPRINGS, Tulsa, St. Louis, Kansas City—at every stop a lean, watchful young man stepped from a train and found his way to games of cards and dice. He wore a brown suit, the sort of suit backwoods boys wore to weddings and funerals. He won a little more money than he lost except for the times when he won a lot more, and at each stop he learned something that could shift the odds in his favor, like how to mark a card without putting notches on the edges. (Crimp the high cards ever so slightly so their backs catch the light.) At each stop he learned something about human nature too. In New Orleans he encountered a French Quarter card cheat and his good-luck charm, a voodoo priest who shook a little pouch full of pebbles, red pepper, gunpowder, cat hair, a dove's blood, and a shark's tooth—a gris-gris bag—and stared evil-eyed at Titanic, who stared cross-eyed right back. In Shreveport, Titanic peered up at a brand-new skyscraper, the ten-story Commercial National Bank building, visible from any point in town. He was waiting for one of his marks, a man he had beaten at dice, poker, and horseshoes, to come out with the thousand dollars he owed him. Ti spent fifty dollars off the top on a gabardine suit a shade of green on the more conservative side of frog. In St. Louis he rode an electric streetcar from one end of town to the other and back, waving at the big-city girls. "He was fun," said a woman who knew him. "He took his hat off when he spoke to you. Alvin was slim like a willow, and he didn't walk, he *sauntered.*"

There were good reasons for the swing in his step. "Every town had a game or two—illegal, of course," he remembered. "But there are different kinds of illegal. It was usually a twenty-dollar fine to the town judge if you got caught. That was your ante for playing in his town." In each town he stopped first at the pool hall. If the pool hall was dead, a dollar in the palm of the desk clerk at the best hotel in town bought directions to a poker parlor where the buy-in might be ten dollars or a thousand depending on the town and the confidence level of the local sharps. Twenty-year-old Titanic was always the youngest player. He introduced himself as Alvin Thomas out of Rogers, Arkansas, and called the other men "sir." If another man shorted the pot or tried to slip away without settling up, the kid was the first to call him on it: "Sir, you'd better pay off."

As Ti put it, winning was harder than just winning. Shorting the pot—tossing in ten chips when you owed eleven, for instance— was only one wrinkle cheats tried. Thieves were a bigger threat: They often vultured big-money games, jumping the winners the minute they reached the street. One stud-poker player, $1,500 to the good, survived a shootout on a Kansas City sidewalk only to be tackled outside his hotel ten minutes later. He pulled his pistol and fired at his assailants, who ran away. The victor lurched into his hotel, where the doorman gave him a pat on the back—a signal to a nearby thug who then followed the winner upstairs and delivered a brass-knuckled hello to the back of his neck. The thug caught the winner as he fell, as civilized thugs did, and robbed him, but left fifty dollars in his pocket. A tip.

In 1914 Memphis mayor E. C. "Boss" Crump vowed to wipe out the road-gambling "easy riders" who rolled into his city and beat honest Memphians out of their paychecks. Titanic hit town in time to hear musician W. C. Handy lead his street-corner blues band. A spiffy black man in a brass-buttoned suit buttoned up to his chin, Handy sang,

Mista Crump don't allow no easy riders here
Mista Crump don't allow no easy riders here

I don't care what Mista Crump won't allow
I'm goin' barrelhouse anyhow.

Ti loved the blues from that day on. He went barrelhouse in Memphis saloons, staying sober with soda water on ice.

"He was like a magician. He had the hands of an artist," said the pool hustler Minnesota Fats, who was transfixed the first time he saw Ti shuffle a deck of cards. "The way he moved his eyes and fingers at the same time was liable to hypnotize you on the spot."

There was more than misdirection at work. There was also Ti's plain delight in playing games, a contagious pleasure that made others want to play too. That contagion is the seed of cons going back to William Thompson, America's original con artist, who sidled up to prosperous-looking gentlemen in New York City in the 1840s, engaged them in witty conversation, and closed by saying, "Sir, have you the confidence to trust me with your watch?" Many did, and he walked off with their watches. After the police collared the original Thompson, a jury had to decide what if anything he was guilty of. Was it a crime to gull the gullible? At the end of a trial that inspired Herman Melville's book *The Confidence Man*, the jury convicted William Thompson of larceny and entrusted him to the warden at Sing Sing.

Titanic had better luck, not that he trusted that fair-weather mistress. He trusted his instincts and a gun he bought in Tennessee, a Luger he kept in a shoulder holster. He believed in skill and positive thinking, enhanced when necessary by cheating or superior firepower. "To be a winner," he said, "a man needs to feel good about himself and have some kind of advantage."

When the action cooled in Memphis, he moved on to Hot Springs, Arkansas, where gamblers congregated at the turreted red-brick Arlington Hotel at the foot of Hot Springs Mountain. The town huddled around forty-seven natural springs whose waters had fallen as rain in the Caesars' time, percolating through the Earth's crust over the centuries until they reached red-hot fissures deep in the crust, then boiled up and bubbled out of Arkansas at a scalding 147 degrees. Some said the waters were "radioactive," a word coined three years before (by Marie Curie, who won the 1911 Nobel Prize for discovering radium and polonium: She carried glowing test tubes of the new elements in her pockets and ultimately died of exposure to them). Polio sufferers and the occasional leper made their ways to Hot Springs to dip into what they hoped would be curative baths. Each March, baseball players from the Boston Red Sox, Pittsburgh Pirates, Brooklyn Dodgers, and other clubs came to town for what they called "Springs Training." The strapping ballplayers rubbed elbows with disabled pilgrims and pale vacationers who expected the waters to cure their gout or lack of pep. Gamblers at the Arlington preyed on anyone willing to bet a dollar on cards or dice. Ti's favorite tablemates were the circus performers who wintered in town. When the circus arrived, you might see an off-duty acrobat doing a handstand on the hotel's chimney. Ti sat in on a poker game with the circus's bearded lady, who growled, "Raise twenty," in a wrestler's voice while her rubbery husband, a Mexican contortionist called "El Spheros," tucked his feet behind his ears, hugged his knees, and rolled around the hotel's wide, wooden porch like a beach ball.

Though the medical pilgrims swore by the healing power of Hot Springs' waters, some locals claimed the baths would make a man anemic, impotent, or both. Titanic, seeing no clear edge either way, avoided the spas and holed up in the hotel. There was risk there too, according to the bellboy, who said the Arlington was haunted. Ti laughed and said he'd bet any ghost it couldn't scare him. When he wasn't playing poker on the porch, he practiced card-flipping in his room. He would sit on his bed for hours at a stretch, picking the top card off a deck, holding it flat between his forefinger and middle finger, and flicking his wrist to send it spinning toward the brass doorknob ten feet away. Fifty-two cards, a hundred and four, five hundred and twenty, a thousand and forty. It was no more tedious to him than the hours he'd spent practicing while sitting on his bed in his stepfather's house, hiding from his uncles. Once his mind zeroed in on the task at hand, time moved like the cards that flew almost the same way but never exactly the same way twice, striking the doorknob at almost but not exactly the same spot. He watched them fly. He adjusted the angle of his wrist, the placement of his fingers, and flipped another hundred cards. At the end of his stay, thousands of practice flips had left a horizontal mark on the doorknob, a shiny half-inch minus sign. A minus for everyone else, a plus for him.

He practiced dice-throwing too, recording his results in a note-book he had bought in the gift shop. The purity of dice pleased him, the tumble of numbers, a vice that was already ancient when Chaucer called it "the very mother of lies and deceit, and false swearing, and blasphemy, and waste of cattle and time." The bard of Canterbury was condemning hazard, a precursor of craps that evolved from still-older games invented by the Romans. The bones a laughing pair of Roman legionnaires were said to have rolled for Jesus's cloak would have been the original astragali, four-sided chunks of bone from the heel joints of slaughtered sheep. (Astragali had been used since 3000 BCE; cubes of wood or ivory came later.) Rome's emperors were avid dicers, dating back to Julius Caesar's return from Gaul in 49 BCE. When Caesar reached the Rubicon, the river between Gaul and Italy, he made his decision to advance on Rome and destroy the republic after a roll of the dice and a vision that Fortuna, the goddess of luck, wanted him to attack. "The die is cast," he said, commanding his men to cross the Rubicon.

No Roman emperor was more of a gambler than stammering Claudius, who rolled 'em the Appian way in the first century, riding in a chariot outfitted with a dice board on rollers that kept the board steady on the bumpiest roads. Claudius may have been *tem-*

perantia itself compared to his predecessor Caligula and successor Nero, but one day the gods whispered in his ear, telling him to bet a Caesar's ransom of four hundred thousand sesterces on a single roll of the astragali. No one recorded the result, but in the end gambling history wasn't kind to Claudius. According to Seneca, the emperor died and went to Hades, where he spends eternity dropping the bones into a bottomless dice cup. He shakes the cup forever but the dice never roll.

Dice have become so familiar as keepsakes, earrings, fuzzy rearview-mirror toys, and symbols of fun or vice that it is possible to forget their original function: They are random-number generators. The polyurethane dice in today's casinos, machined within a ten-thousandth of an inch of perfect symmetry, achieve a computer-like precision. If you threw a million pairs of dice on a craps table at Caesars Palace, a task that would take two months, twenty-four hours a day, seven days a week, each side of each die would come up 16.666 percent of the time. Continue forever like a Las Vegas Claudius and the percentage zooms in ever more tightly on 16.666, with the sixes repeating forever. The Bible-thumpers of Alvin Thomas's youth would have found no coincidence in the fact that dice odds carry the Number of the Beast into infinity.

Gamblers in every era do all they can to tilt the odds. Elizabethan sharps drilled pip-sized holes in wooden dice and injected droplets of mercury to add weight to one side or the other. Shakespeare called quicksilvered dice "fulhams" for the Thames-side neighborhood where gamesters rolled such dice in hazard pits that were as raucous if not as bloody as the cockpits nearby. In cockfighting, the man with the better bird won; in hazard pits it was often the man with the doctored dice. But you don't have to load dice with mercury to shift the odds. You can shave one corner of a die to make one side come up more often than it should. You can throw a pair of cheater dice—one with fives on all six sides and one that's all sixes and twos, so that each roll is seven or eleven—if you're slick enough to palm the game dice, switch your dirty dice in for one pivotal roll, retrieve them, and switch them back out before anyone notices.

Craps evolved from hazard and probably owes its name to "crabs," an early term for snake eyes. Craps revolves around the number seven. The shooter wins if his first roll is seven or eleven. So does anyone who bets on him. He loses, along with those betting on him, if he rolls two, three, or twelve. Any other total—four, five, six, eight, nine, or ten—becomes his *point*, and now the number seven turns against the shooter. To win he must roll his point again before he craps out by throwing a seven. And since seven is the likeliest combination, coming up once in every six throws, or 16.666 percent of the time—that number again—the shooter is more likely to crap out than to match his point. Unless he tweaks the odds.

By Titanic's day a few plutocrats in upholstered gentlemen's clubs employed leather- or even mink-lined dice cups, but most players spurned dice cups as unmanly, better suited to Parcheesi. Real men cast the bones by hand, a custom that favored a fellow with the hands of a magician. Sitting in his room at the Arlington in Hot Springs, Ti made hundreds of practice throws and wrote down the results. He learned that it was best to start with the sixes kissing, one six oriented up-down and the other left-right. Then if he gave the dice a fake shake and released them stiff-wristed so that they skidded rather than tumbled, they came up seven only once in nine or ten tries rather than once in six. He was mastering an early, instinctive sort of arbitrage, creating a margin he could spin into profits. Perfecting that stiff-wristed throw might take years, but he didn't mind. "If a thing's hard to do, most folks are too lazy to do it. That puts me one up on 'em," he said.

In early evenings before the hundred-dollar buy-in poker games began, he liked to sit in a rocking chair on the Arlington's porch, watching fireflies. First one yellow dot would appear, then two or three, a dozen, twenty, more. Before long the gloaming between the porch and Hot Springs Mountain was full of them, each bug signaling the others, *Here I am.* And one night they synchronized. Ti had seen it happen when he was growing up: First a few sparked at the same instant, then more and more of the blinks matched until the last stragglers joined the chorus and they were all blinking in unison, a firefly pulse.

A traveler checking into the hotel in the spring of 1915 might have encountered a long, lean fellow idly flipping cards at an upturned derby hat on the lobby rug. The beanpole would miss more often than not, curse his luck, then try again. Tourists fresh from the bathhouses would stop to watch. Eventually a rather rude hotel guest would appear, laughing at Titanic's efforts, irking Ti so much that Ti bet the man five dollars he could flip fifty cards out of a deck into that danged hat. Fifty out of fifty-two. "Son, that's a bet," the rude man would say.

To tourists who wanted in on the action, Ti said no. He was betting "this smart alec here," not every hotel guest in west-central Arkansas. They'd offer to up the stakes—from a dollar to ten or even fifty, and give him odds. Two to one. Ten to one! Ti called them tempters and sons-of-bucks for trying to take advantage of his good nature, but agreed, he said, because he figured the Lord looks after fools. When the money was piled on a table, he got up and stretched. He cracked his knuckles. He shook out his wrist to loosen it. The tourists smiled at what appeared to be a display of nerves, when in fact he was enjoying himself. Ti paced off the distance from his chair to the derby, three long steps, and shook his head at the thought of such a vastness. Then he stepped back to his chair and sailed thirty cards in a row into the hat. Then he missed. And missed again! With no margin for error remaining, he flicked the last twenty to finish with fifty cards in the hat and two on the rug.

"That was a close one," he'd say. "Suppose I give you all another chance and try to make all fifty-two—double or nothing?" Any takers would soon owe him more than they had planned to spend all week. His average was 200 in a row; his record was 460.

He told his marks he couldn't hardly believe his luck. When they were gone, he got even with the smart alec who had started it all— his partner—who got 10 percent of the take.

Damon Runyon, chronicler of New York crooks and their molls, would tell a story about a father who sent his boy off to the city with these words: "Son, no matter how far you travel, or how smart you get, always remember this: Someday, somewhere, a guy is going to come to you and show you a nice, brand-new deck of cards on which the seal has not yet been broken. This man is going to offer to bet you that he can make the jack of spades jump out of the deck and squirt cider in your ear. Now, son, do not bet this man, for as sure as you stand there, you are going to wind up with an earful of cider." Like Runyon's trickster, Titanic would have gotten nowhere if not for a steady supply of marks lining up for their earfuls of cider. Today, when gray-haired gamblers tell Titanic stories, non-gamblers sometimes marvel less about his skills than about his enablers. How did he find so many suckers?

Two answers: time and talent. In the early twentieth century, as machines began replacing men on farms and in factories, workers fought back by forming European-style labor unions. Rural people flocked to the cities. Where did that leave the lone guns who would never join any crowd? Historian Frederick Jackson Turner had famously declared the American frontier "closed" in 1893; the wilderness was gone, every square mile mapped and policed. Turner got his details wrong—the "free land" he pined for had been stolen from Indians in the first place, and much of the West was still nearly empty—but he caught the spirit of the time. From then on, a growing population would begin to subdivide a shrinking map, and the outlaws hiding out in the creases would be hailed as the last real Americans.

Rootless road gamblers became avatars of a new generation whose parents had made heroes of gunslingers. The tales of the road gamblers of the Teens and Twenties, like the stories everyone knew about the Wild West gunmen of old, were made of both gospel and guff, but there was almost always some truth to them. Billy the Kid, who had killed four men rather than the twenty he claimed, held his fire when he entered a dark room in Fort Sumner, New Mexico, giving bartender-sheriff Pat Garrett a chance to shoot him through the heart. "Wild" Bill Hickok really was playing poker in a tavern in Deadwood, in the Dakota Territory, holding two pair, aces over eights, the day he died. Hickok was a gunslinger who hated card sharps. In one game against a card mechanic he went all-in and lost to aces he was sure had slid from the other man's sleeve. Wild Bill pulled both of his six-shooters and proposed a new rule: "I have a pair of sixes and they beat anything." He claimed that pot, but lost his life the day a sneak named Crooked Nose McCall crept up behind him and shot him in the back of the head. Since that game in 1876, Hickok's aces and eights have been called the "dead man's hand." A generation later the Derby Kid was as close as most folks would ever get to an outlaw. Brave amateurs wanted to try him. Professionals *had* to try him or lose face. Every local poker king in a wobbly saloon chair had a stake in humbling the kid who had killed big Jim Johnson on a riverboat out of Marked Tree, Arkansas.

Titanic also had a talent shared by every successful hustler. He could spot a compulsive gambler a mile away. Then as now, some people just *had* to bet and keep betting. Ti tempted them with wagers they couldn't win. But he didn't take without giving. Before taking their money, he gave them the confidence that they could beat him.

Johnson's was the only life he had taken as of 1915, though his body count would surpass Billy the Kid's before he was done. He was growing into his role as king of the road gamblers, a role that called for brass balls as well as the quick fingers and easy patter of a showman, a savant's knack for numbers, a con man's eye for others' weaknesses, and the patience of a crooked saint. Nobody had ever measured his blood pressure—he was leery of doctors, with their laudanum, leeches, and bone saws—but it must have been somewhere between the values for hibernation and coma. One of his bedmates remembered holding her thumb to his wrist. "His pulse was *so slow-w-w,*" she said. Las Vegas casino mogul Jack Binion recalls watching an older Titanic wait for the river card in a twenty-five-thousand-dollar hand: "He sat so still you'd swear he wasn't breathing. You just knew that this guy pissed ice water."

A Hot Springs schoolboy fell under Titanic's spell. Hubert Cokes, who was fourteen that year, still in short pants, saw Ti as a genius. "He could see around corners. He could do anything," Cokes recalled. "I watched Titanic bet he could throw a walnut from the porch of the Arlington Hotel to the roof of a five-story building across the street. Then he reared back and did it. Nobody knew how. When the other men threw walnuts they barely went across the street."

One Arlington Hotel guest who might have seen Ti's walnut-pitching was also a pitcher: the Boston Red Sox rookie Babe Ruth, who trained with the team in Hot Springs that year along with Red Sox stars Tris Speaker and Smoky Joe Wood. Another compulsive guest at the Arlington was eager to try Titanic. Mister Not Enough, as Ti and Cokes called him, scoffed at the dollar-ante poker played on the hotel's porch. He dared Ti to offer a bet, so Ti said he could flip fifty-two cards under a door and land at least half of them in his hat in the next room. He would flip the cards so that they skipped under the closed door and hopped into his upturned derby hat. "Not enough," said Mister Not Enough, waving a thousand dollars. "You should make them all!" They settled on fifty out of fifty-two. Mister Not Enough was gullible enough to plop onto the bed in Ti's room and count the cards as they disappeared under the door. "One, two, three, . . . fifty-one, fifty two." He opened the door, saw fifty cards in the derby and two on the floor, and said he was good and God-damned.

Later on, Titanic met young Cokes outside the hotel. He handed over a hundred-dollar bill, the first one Hubert had ever touched—the boy's pay for waiting in the next room, sticking the first fifty cards in the hat, and slipping out the window.

TITANIC STEERED CLEAR OF banker Polston's house when the gamblers' circuit brought him back to Joplin. He rented a room in a downtown boardinghouse where the seventeen-year-old chambermaid took a liking to him. Nora Trushel would make the beds in all the other rooms, then slip into Ti's bed and help him make a shambles of it. After a couple of close calls—Nora diving under the sheets while the proprietress banged on the door, asking what that noise was all about—they made love without making a sound. Then they dozed until the milkman passed under the window on his morning rounds, whistling. That was Nora's signal to sneak out and hurry home. Ti rolled over and went back to sleep. Sometimes he dreamed of her. Sometimes during poker games he pictured Nora undressing instead of picturing the cards that hadn't been dealt yet, which was no good at all, so he married her. They put on their Sunday best and strolled arm in arm to the office of the justice of the peace, who closed the ceremony by exclaiming, "You may now kiss the loveliest bride I have seen in all my years," which was what Ti had tipped him fifty dollars to say. The happy couple emerged onto Main Street as Mr. and Mrs. Alvin Thomas. As Ti remembered it, the squabbles started right then. Nora's wedding ring seemed to have cut off the supply of blood to her brain, causing her to think her husband might suddenly stop playing crooked games with crooked men and become a grocer or a druggist. Or a bank teller—he was good with money, and didn't he know a banker in town?

"I have a job," he said.

"What job?"

"Delivering peanuts. Today I delivered one over the bank."

The walnut-thrower had switched to peanuts, one of which he had pegged onto the roof of the Joplin National Bank to the consternation of a couple of locals who tried to match him only to see their own peanuts fall short of the whole bank. They told themselves they should have known better. Hadn't Beanie Benson and Hickory McCullough warned them not to bet with the Derby Kid?

Titanic was itching to get out of town. His Joplin profits were peanuts compared to the action in Kansas City, where checkers king Lock Renfro dared any man to play him for ten thousand dollars. Ti hadn't played checkers since his days as a Rogers schoolboy, but he took up the challenge. He went to Kansas City and sat down across a checkerboard from Renfro, who thought the young man seemed nervous. With a small crowd peering over his shoulder, Titanic dithered over every move, but to the champion's surprise every move he made was the right one. Ti won so easily that the endgame was obvious half-a-dozen moves in advance, yet still he waffled—teasing him, Renfro thought, dragging things out to embarrass him. Renfro stalked out of the room while Ti hesitated before making his final, clinching move. The crowd applauded as Ti took a bow and said he owed it all to the man upstairs. That was a lie. He owed only half his winnings to the man upstairs—Harry Lieberman, the U.S. chess champion he had brought from Detroit to watch the game through a peephole Ti had drilled in the ceiling. Lieberman sat by a wire called a "thumper" that ran from his perch over the checkerboard to the basement, then up through a hole in the floor near Ti's shoe and up his pantleg. The thumper's business end was taped to Ti's leg. When Titanic lifted a checker and hovered it over another square, Lieberman pressed a button that sent a spark through the thumper if he disliked the move. If he approved, he held his fire. Thus Ti's hesitance as he tested one checker, then another. That night he gave Lieberman a train ticket home to Detroit and five thousand dollars, his end of an even split of Renfro's ten thousand.

Titanic stayed in Kansas City, a town so crooked even the local police called it the Midwest's "playground of criminals." He heard that a poker hustler named Smoke Wilson wanted a shot at him. Wilson was a big talker who would drink a fifth of bourbon and chase it with another fifth. "He marked cards and thought he was clever. Of course I could read his marks as good as he could," Ti said. "I made sure I dealt when we played, and when I saw from the mark on his card that Smoke had an ace, and I peeked and saw the next card coming was another ace, I dealt him the second card down instead—so fast he couldn't see it. So now Smoke, who thinks *he's* hustling *me*, gets a five. '*Where's my ace?*' he hollers and reaches out his big log arms and pulls in a pot over eight hundred dollars. Like he thought I'd let him do it. That's when I drew my German Luger and aimed it at his nose."

Wilson wasn't ready to relinquish the pot. He pulled the chips closer. Titanic said, "Smoke, you got eight hundred dollars there. How would you like to make forty thousand? I'll put forty thousand against that eight hundred, but you've got to earn it. Go buy a gun. We'll meet outside in five minutes, and the man that lives keeps all the money."

Wilson thought about that for a good minute before he stood up. He backed toward the door, leaving the chips on the table, saying it wouldn't be a fair fight. "I'm too drunk to shoot," he said, "and you're too skinny of a target."

A hundred miles due south, Nora Thomas waited up. Her home-making skills were lost on her husband, who never said a word about her cooking, cleaning, and making their bed with knife-edge creases. He spent most of his time on the road, and when he was in town he stayed out until after the milkman whistled past the porch. He said gambling was an all-night game—once you got to winning it was bad business to stop. When Nora offered to go out gambling with him, he laughed. That world was no place for a girl, much less a wife. Did she want to get ogled by men like Smoke, who thought it was funny to put his hand on a girl's behind?

"Would you really have shot him?"

"Of course." Ti always said he figured big Jim Johnson had pretty much killed himself by being so rotten and unable to swim. But he knew he could kill any man who needed killing. He knew it from the way he had felt when he was aiming at Smoke Wilson, squeezing the trigger just enough to feel it budge, the way you can squeeze a grape without quite bursting it. "A calm feeling came over me," he remembered, "the way it always does when there's big trouble or big stakes."

Nora told Ti their marriage was about to go bust. What wife could tolerate a husband who stayed out all night when he was in town and spent weeks on the road without so much as a telephone call or telegram? Then he'd turn up unannounced and want to jump into bed. Which she did because that smile of his was hard to resist and because he was a thoroughbred in bed, worthy of his nickname. In some ways he was the ideal husband. Didn't drink, didn't smoke, wouldn't dream of lifting his hand to her. He was funny in his country way and easy with his money. One day when he was gone, she picked a pair of panties from her underwear drawer and found a hundred-dollar bill inside. He had put one in every pair in the drawer.

What hurt was that he didn't need her. She might as well have married the holstered gun he hung on a bedroom chair because if there was anything softer to him, he didn't reveal it. The one secret she learned in six months of marriage was that he hated thunderstorms. Lightning frightened him. They were in bed one night when a storm rattled the windows. A lightning bolt split an eighty-foot oak up the street into halves that fell like twin soldiers. Her Alvin, sitting up in bed, rocked back and forth with his arms around his knees. "I'll wait it out," he mumbled. Eighteen-year-old Nora pulled her twenty-two-year-old husband under the covers and curled up with him until they fell asleep. In the morning he was gone. She wouldn't see him again for weeks.

Nora heard gossip that he was sleeping with other girls on the road. It was true. Ti always said God gave every man enough blood to operate his brain or his private parts, but not both at the same time. He figured he wasn't cheating on Nora as long as he was faithful when he was in Joplin. She figured differently, and divorced him.

Titanic shrugged when he heard the news. He was on his way to Pittsburgh, his first trip east.

THE STEEL CAPITAL was like no town he had ever seen. If Rogers was a fencepost, Joplin a three-story bank, Hot Springs a hotel porch, and St. Louis a bustling wharf, Pittsburgh was what one visitor described as "hell with the lid off." The city's population had grown from 46,000 in 1850 to more than 300,000 in 1901, the year Andrew Carnegie met J. P. Morgan at St. Andrews Golf Club in Yonkers, New York—the first American golf club—and agreed to sell United States Steel to Morgan for $480 million. By the time Titanic arrived in 1917, Pittsburgh's population had nearly doubled again. Foundries rumbled day and night, producing more than half the country's steel. Smoke from the steel mills darkened the skies; the city's streetlights were lit at noon. "Here was a scene so dreadfully hideous, so intolerably bleak," wrote H. L. Mencken, "that it reduced the whole aspiration of men to a macabre and depressing joke."

But Ti liked Pittsburgh. Sidewalks teemed with businessmen wiping soot off their pocket watches, steelworkers arguing in English and German, shopgirls, fruit vendors. The tall young hustler fresh off the train gawked at pedestrians streaming like soda bubbles around a streetcar that rang its bells and blew its whistle at them. He was striding down Smithfield Street when he felt a light-fingered touch in his left-hand pants pocket, where he kept his bankroll. He snatched the thief's wrist and met Pittsburgh's best-looking pickpocket.

3 ALICE AND THE SERGEANT

HE TURNED AND SAW A BLACK-HAIRED, BUTTON-NOSED beauty, spitting mad. Dressed like a schoolgirl in a pleated skirt and white blouse, she kicked at him but missed, then slapped him hard enough to knock his hat off. Still he kept his hand clamped around her wrist. "Settle down or I'll take you to my friend over there," he said, nodding toward a policeman.

She settled. Titanic retrieved his hat and reached into his pocket for his bankroll.

"This what you're after?" A stack of bills folded in half, thicker than a pack of cigarettes. He leafed the edges with his thumb to show that the bills were all hundreds. She was looking at ten thousand dollars in a time when workingmen earned five hundred a year and most of the wallets she filched held less than twenty.

He pocketed the money and started walking. She had to follow; he hadn't let go of her arm. "I'm Alvin," he said as they passed the cop. He said he made his living playing cards and other games of chance. He had traveled a good part of the country but he swore he'd never seen a place like Pittsburgh, where people walked right down the middle of the street and the pickpockets were pretty as a picture.

Was he making fun of her? She couldn't tell. But when he released her wrist, she didn't run. She linked arms with him. "I'm Alice," she said, and they were on their way.

Alice Kane was a free spirit. Seventeen years old, she spent her weekdays shoplifting and picking pockets. The money she stole went for movies and perfume and restaurant meals and ten-dollar bribes to the truant officer. Ti was curious: Where were her parents? What did they think about her stealing? She said her parents thought she was in school all day, and she kept her money hidden. They never saw it. "It's not near as much as you've got in your pocket."

"Do you like ice cream, Alice Kane? I might just buy you an ice cream."

"I'll buy," she said, handing him a wallet she had stolen while they passed through the crowds on Smithfield Street.

Ti liked that. He picked out a dollar and dropped the wallet on the sidewalk—a little good fortune for whoever found it. He gave the dollar to a street vendor, who spooned two dollops of vanilla ice cream into what the vendor called pastry horns. Ti and Alice walked uphill eating their ice-cream cones, a novelty item invented at the 1904 St. Louis World's Fair. He let her lead him to a slump-shouldered row of brownstones a mile from the crowds below. "Don't you tell my parents I don't go to school," she warned.

The Kanes' cramped flat overlooked a trash-strewn alley. The curtains and wallpaper near the open windows were gray from exposure to Pittsburgh's sooty air, but Alice's mother kept the rest of the place spotless. She and Alice's father weren't much bigger than their petite daughter. They were graying with age, not just their hair but their skin too, like the wallpaper. Ti introduced himself as Alvin Thomas and said he was a traveling salesman. It wasn't quite a lie. He told Mrs. Kane she kept a nice house, and he meant it. He said she and Mr. Kane had raised a fine girl they ought to be proud of. With that, he tipped his hat and thanked Alice for letting a lonesome traveler walk her home. On his way out he noted the number on their door; that evening he paid a florist to deliver a large bouquet to Mrs. Kane.

The next day Titanic left his room at the William Penn Hotel a little after his usual waking hour of noon. He was passing through the lobby when Alice stopped him. "You're a late sleeper, Mister Alvin," she said.

"How'd you find me?"

Easy, she said. She knew he'd be staying at "the grandest hotel in town."

They had lunch at a diner. She ate her meal and some of his. Then they went to the movies at the Cameraphone Theatre on Pittsburgh's Penn Avenue. Ti bought a five-cent bag of popcorn from a vendor on the street. Inside, the film clattered audibly through the projector while a phonograph record played music synched to the pictures—the new technology that gave the Cameraphone its name. The system worked fine till the film jammed; by the time the projectionist wrestled it back on track, image and sound were hopelessly mismatched, the strains of a harp playing over a train crash. Ti and Alice, two truants kissing in the dark, ignored the crash.

Thinking back on it decades later, Ti couldn't remember which picture they saw that day. It might have been a Tom Mix film. *Hearts and Saddles*, maybe, or *Durand of the Bad Lands*. The silent cowboy in the twenty-gallon hat was one of Ti's favorites, along with the slapstick Keystone Kops and Ham & Bud comedies and Charlie Chaplin. Ti loved the Little Tramp and carried a torch for Theda Bara, whose title role in *Cleopatra* was the sensation of 1917. Born Theodosia Goodman in Cincinnati, Bara was, like Ti, a striver whose name was as fake as her ambition was titanic. He remembered thinking Alice looked a little like a younger Theda Bara, with a grin instead of the vamp's pout.

He spent almost a month courting Alice, taking her on long drives in his boxy open-cockpit Packard, to restaurants and movie houses, and up to his hotel room. He loved her long, shiny black hair, spilling over her shoulders onto the pillow. He called her his "candy Kane" and bragged about her to other gamblers, calling her "one fine pickpocket and a good driver to boot." At a time when few women drove, Alice piloted the Packard while he rode shotgun, keeping an eye out for hijackers. She knew her firearms too. One night she pulled the Luger out of his shoulder holster. She made a face, calling it "a kraut gun." So he bought a Colt .45 and stowed the Luger in the Packard's glove box.

Each week's Pathé newsreel showed the ink stain of war spreading over a map of Europe. Titanic had learned of the war's beginnings while sitting in the Princess Theater in Hot Springs three years earlier, the pit orchestra playing a dirge under images of the funeral of Austria's Archduke Franz Ferdinand. That newsreel proved that human history can make the craziest long con look sensible. A would-be assassin's bomb had bounced off the archduke's car and blown up the car behind it. The bomber ate a cyanide suicide pill, which only made him vomit, so he jumped into the Miljacka River, but it was only four inches deep. An angry mob beat him senseless while the archduke rode on to Sarajevo's town hall, where he read a speech off bloodstained notes before climbing back into his car, which happened to roll past the delicatessen where another conspirator, Gavrilo Princip, cursing his comrade's failure, sat eating a sandwich. Seeing the royal motorcade, Princip ran out and shot the archduke in the neck. Within a month the war was on.

Ti had followed the bloodshed on newsreels in little bandbox theaters in Quincy, Illinois, and Henryetta, Oklahoma. He had sat in a St. Louis movie palace watching French soldiers huddle in trenches after the Germans released chlorine gas. The gas melted their lungs, and the stricken soldiers suffocated in open air. In 1916, ten thousand British soldiers had died in the first hour of the Battle of the Somme. Fifty times that many would die trying to break the German lines there, enough dead to empty Pittsburgh. A year later, while Ti was courting his pickpocket, America joined the fight. Ti and Alice watched the Pathé newsreel of April 6, 1917: senators in black suits waving their fists, soldiers marching while the Cameraphone Theater's phonograph played "The Battle Hymn of the Republic." People said there was sure to be a draft unless enough boys volunteered.

Ti wasn't the volunteering type, and hearing that single men would be the first draftees may have kindled his ardor for Alice. Later that month, Alvin Clarence Thomas, twenty-five, married Alice Kane, seventeen. He bought her a diamond ring the size of a tooth, and a house half a mile from her parents' apartment. The house was white with a wide porch that reminded him of the Arlington Hotel in Hot Springs. There was a woolen hammock on the porch. Inside was a big upstairs bedroom with a double-king bed that filled almost half the room, and a guest bedroom where Alice's parents sometimes stayed to escape their dowdy sixteen-dollar-a-month flat. The guest room was far enough from the upstairs bedroom—down a staircase and around a corner—to be out of earshot. Unlike Nora, Alice never learned to keep quiet in bed.

She did learn not to disturb her husband's sleep, which he prized like money. "Let this sleeping dog lay or he bites," he told her. He would roll out of bed around noon and come to the kitchen table expecting breakfast. Alice, who was no cook, learned to make biscuits. After breakfast she'd watch him practice stiff-armed dice rolls or deal off the bottom of a deck. He called dealing cards "peddling the papers" and liked to make a game of it.

"Watch me peddle 'em," he said, "and say when I deal one off the bottom." She never could. He was too quick. He dared her to spot when he was "dealing seconds," peddling the second card down, or "cold decking"—exchanging the deck with another deck in his pocket so quickly she couldn't see it until he told her to keep her eye on his right hand. "Nothing but my right hand." Then he showed her the gaff in slow motion: He would cough and cover his mouth with his left hand to misdirect other players' attention while his right hand ducked the deck into his pocket and exchanged it with one that was prearranged to favor the dealer.

"Of course you've got to know beforehand how many players are in the game, or it won't work. You set up the cold deck so the pigeon, the fellow you're here to beat, gets a swell hand," he said. "The second-best hand."

"Teach me." Alice learned to shuffle a deck one-handed. After a week's practice she could deal seconds better than most card mechanics. "I'll go with you on the road," she said.

He told her that was for men only, but he'd let her take him duckpin bowling.

Duckpins is a northeastern cousin of bowling that features thin, widely separated pins and a two-and-a-half-pound ball no bigger than a softball. Players get three throws per frame; still the game is so difficult that 150 is a solid score for a professional duckpin bowler. Ti bent his long frame forward as he released the little ball left-handed, planting his right foot while his left leg kicked up behind him "like a ballerina's," Alice noted. Not that he bowled like one. After a week of practice he was averaging 150. When they bowled together he never let up, never once let her beat him. Ti never went easy on anyone he wasn't cheating. Alice felt the cold in him, but there was generosity in him too. He often paid five-dollar restaurant tabs with twenty-dollar bills. After he bowled he'd go to the pinboy—a youngster of twelve or thirteen, usually, with bruises up and down his arms—and hand him a ten-dollar tip that sent the boy running to show the others what you get when you set pins for Mr. Thomas.

By summer he was the city's unofficial duckpin kingpin. He and

Alice were the most colorful couple in town. Everyone wanted to know who they were. Ti liked being talked about but knew it was bad for his prospects in Pittsburgh. As he won hundreds and then thousands of dollars shooting dice in riverfront warehouses, shooting pool in billiard parlors all over town, playing poker in the card rooms in back of the pool parlors, he began hearing whispers: "That's Titanic Thomas"—his cue to move on to virgin turf. And if he were to tell his wife the truth, which he didn't, he might have admitted that there was more than his business sense urging him to move on. Half a year into his second marriage—the same six months his first marriage lasted—he was getting antsy. Walking the same streets every day, seeing and hearing the same gamblers do the same things (one clucks his teeth no matter what cards he gets, trying to put Ti off the scent, but narrows his eyes without knowing it when he likes his hand; another breathes slower when he's bluffing) made him itchy for the road. He told Alice he needed a change. "Change the air, change the chair." That was one of his corny lines Alice didn't like. And no, he said, she couldn't go along. The road was full of bad men; he couldn't watch over her and play his propositions at the same time.

"Won't you worry about me here all alone?" she said.

He was honest. "No."

He thought she might cry or make a scene. Instead Alice looked him in the eye and said she'd be all right. "I won't try to change you," she said.

FOR A WHILE, TITANIC SAW their arrangement as the perfect marriage. He separated gamblers from their bankrolls through-out the Midwest and Southeast while she stayed home, taking her mother to tea on Sundays at the William Penn Hotel. Alice might pick an occasional pocket to keep her skills sharp, but after lifting a man's billfold she would tap him on the elbow and give it back—

"Sir, did you drop this?"—because she had promised not to get arrested while Ti was on the road.

He drove west to Indiana and from there to Knoxville and Savannah and back, padding his bankroll, always leaving town before anyone knew him too well. More at home in hotels than in his own house in Pittsburgh, which he thought of as Alice's house, he would mosey around downtowns in his tailored suits and shiny shoes, looking for a game. Between games he made proposition bets. "Ti got to be a regular whiz with those big hotel-room keys they had in those days," said gambler "Fast Larry" Guninger. "The keys were heavy, maybe three inches long, like skeleton keys. The slots they went into were so large you could peek through key-holes and see couples doing their thing in bed. Well, Ti would bet he could stand across the hall and toss his room key right into the slot. It looked impossible. Then he underhands that key and it sticks right in the lock. He won thousands with that trick." Skeptics have long claimed the trick *was* impossible, but poker legend Doyle "Texas Dolly" Brunson backed Guninger's account. "I saw it—Ti tossed a key right into that keyhole," Brunson said.

Titanic won free nights in hotels by betting clerks and managers that he could toss his key over the front desk into a particular mail slot behind the counter—an easier trick than the keyhole toss. Such stunts wouldn't have remained one man's secret in an age of cell phones and email, but Ti used them for decades. In his day each town was an island. A proposition could be stale in St. Louis but brand new to Memphis or Louisville. With rare exceptions, local news traveled by word of mouth. Telegrams were for special occasions. It often took an hour or more to connect a telephone call on a long-distance trunk line to a town ten miles away. There were no lights on the roads between towns until the Thirties. Gamblers weren't rolling through the dark to tell other gamblers in neighboring cities and states their business, and the same went for policemen. The FBI had been born as the Bureau of Investigation in

1908, but J. Edgar Hoover's G-men wouldn't launch their federal "war on crime" until a quarter-century later. The lack of a national communications grid allowed Ti to sail between towns like a pirate, skinning the locals and hitting the road again before they felt the breeze of his passing. Just before leaving a town he usually arranged a getaway score, one big bet to fatten his bankroll for the road ahead, preferably at the expense of an arrogant swell who could afford to lose and who, in Ti's eyes, deserved to.

Early in 1918 he spent a week in the Hoosier resort town of French Lick. One of his fellow guests at the French Lick Springs Hotel was a prizefighter, a vain young buck who moved through the lobby like he owned it, handing clerks and bellhops ten-dollar bills without bothering to look at them. Until Titanic blocked his path. "You're not so tough," he said.

The boxer laughed. Who did this stringbean think he was?

"My name's Alvin Thomas. I got a thousand dollars says you couldn't knock me down if we were standing on the same newspaper."

As with all of Titanic's propositions, the idea was to make the mark believe he couldn't lose, when the truth was the opposite: It was Ti who couldn't lose.

The fighter looked around the lobby, smiling. "You're on, mister." Titanic rustled up some side bets, getting five- and ten-to-one for twenty dollars and up from members of the boxer's entourage, and when the bets were down he took a copy of the *Springs Valley Herald* from the front desk. Spreading the newspaper over the threshold of the dining-room door, he invited the boxer to stand on one page. Now he and the proud pug were almost nose to nose. Then Ti took a step back, shut the door between them, and stepped onto the paper again.

An hour later and a couple thousand dollars richer, he was whistling a blues tune, feeling the wind in his hair, driving on a blacktop road that split cornfields north of Floyds Knobs, Indiana. He sped through the night, the moon and his headlamps the only lights in sight, until another pair of headlights filled his rearview mirror. Before he knew it he was overtaken by a gleaming Pierce-Arrow, a yacht on wheels that sold for three times the cost of his $2,200 Packard. As the Pierce-Arrow whooshed past, he felt the same envy he had felt spying the Fancy Dan's rod and reel at that Benton County fishing hole twenty years before. He wanted one.

He was looking forward to the action ahead. The way he'd beaten the boxer in French Lick, like he beat almost everyone else, confirmed Ti's belief that he was one of a kind. He wasn't unbeatable—his propositions often left his marks a sliver of a chance. But unless the odds were nine-to-one his way or better, he didn't bet.

During a lucrative swing through Kentucky and Tennessee he took in a Tom Mix movie at the Bijou, a Knoxville palace with a cavernous arched ceiling and a twelve-piece orchestra that played Beethoven while Mix shot it out with a pack of Indians. The Bijou was a rarity, an integrated movie house, though black patrons were restricted to a balcony with a separate side entrance. Ti thought it was funny how the Negroes cheered for the Indians shooting arrows at Tom Mix.

He circled back to Pittsburgh in time for his first wedding anniversary, but the timing was coincidence. He didn't buy Alice a gift, not because he forgot but because he didn't care for holidays— he never observed birthdays or Christmas, which some gamblers wasted in church or with their families. A day was good if he played and won, bad if he didn't. There was no other kind of day. When Alice mentioned that the traditional first-anniversary gift is paper, he gave her a hundred-dollar bill.

A week later he was drafted. Private Alvin C. Thomas reported to Camp Zachary Taylor in Kentucky, an hour's drive from the site of his newspaper proposition in southern Indiana, for basic training. After two weeks of boot camp he rode a troop train to Fort McClellan in Anniston, Alabama. On his first day there, looking spic-and-span for inspection, he caught an officer's attention. "Private Thomas," the lieutenant said, "are you an idiot?"

"No sir."

"Do you think you could take these other men out and teach them the field manual?"

"Yes sir."

"Good. I'm making you a sergeant."

Rank had privileges that Ti soon monetized: After drilling his squad by day, he taught the boys to play craps and five-card stud.

Seldom played today, five-card stud is one of the simplest forms of poker. The first card is dealt face-down, the other four face-up for all to see. Sergeant Thomas spent hours dealing demonstration stud hands, providing a running commentary on each hand, training his men to calculate the odds of an opponent's having an ace or king or deuce in the hole, telling them when to bet harder and when to fold their tents, so they could beat all the poor dumb soldiers who trusted to luck. He was passing down a tradition almost as old as Christianity. Gamblers were playing cards within a century of the invention of paper around 100 CE. Fourteenth-century crusaders brought premodern cards from Persia to Italy, where artists hand-painted decks of fifty-two cards honoring royals and courtiers, with face cards showing a king, a knight, and a soldier. Around 1500 the French introduced a deck with four suits, two black and two red, adding a queen between the king and the knight and banishing the infantryman. The queen was supposedly inspired by Joan of Arc, who led French armies to victory over the English in 1429.

The modern deck with four kings, four queens, and four knights, whom the English called knaves, was set by 1700. All cardplayers know their faces, but few know that they are not generic medievals but stylized figures out of history and myth. The king of hearts is Charlemagne; the king of diamonds, Julius Caesar; the king of clubs, Alexander the Great; and the king of spades, King David of

Israel. The clubs' knight is said to be Lancelot du Lac, who stole Guinevere from King Arthur and was the only member of that trio to make the face-card pantheon.

The French peddled their fifty-two papers in a bluffing game called *poque*. French soldiers brought *poque* to New Orleans, America's first gambling mecca, during the War of 1812. Americans pronounced it "poke-uh," which became "poker." Louisiana gamblers liked to keep their cards close to their silk vests, fanning them just enough to see the numbers or letters on their corners. The *K* for king and *Kn* for knave looked too similar, so the knave became Jack, his American nickname. Soon there was a rule that said players could open the first round of betting only if they had a pair of jacks or better, and had to build the pot if they did—the source of the term *jackpot*. Early American cardmakers left the backs of playing cards plain white, which led to a custom that survives today. A caller who rang at a prominent person's home and found the person absent was handed a playing card. He wrote his name on its blank back—a practice that led to calling cards and business cards. Playing cards evolved further because those blank backs were easy to mark. By Ti's time, the backs of playing cards featured convoluted patterns that foiled all but the best cheaters.

The Civil War helped make poker America's card game. Gambling historian David Schwartz tells of the aftermath of 1862's bloody Battle of Shiloh, with its twenty-three thousand casualties. Following the battle, the story goes, Yank and Rebel fighters settled into lines a few hundred yards apart. According to Schwartz, "after shooting at each other, more for sport than to advance any military strategy, the opposing sides started swapping newspapers, coffee and tobacco. Relations became so cordial that a Yankee corporal soon sauntered over to the Confederate post, sat down, and produced a deck of cards." There were Johnny Reb decks with Jefferson Davis and Robert E. Lee as kings, but this was a traditional array featuring Caesar, Charlemagne, and Lancelot. The rebels were ahead when a Union party led by General Ulysses S. Grant rode up. The Union men hustled back to their posts, leaving Grant peering down at the enemy cardplayers. He asked a Confederate soldier who was winning.

"We are," the man said. "These chumps you've brought down here can't play poker. But General, they can fight."

"Have to, sometimes," Grant said, spurring his horse back to Union lines.

Soldiers on both sides took poker home with them. During postwar Reconstruction, the game got a new wrinkle: Players were allowed to throw away up to three cards and draw three new ones. Draw poker made a five-card contest with bluffs and do-or-die raises more American than ever: Every hand promised a new beginning.

Titanic taught his Fort McClellan conscripts draw poker and five-card stud—games whose rules were settled less than thirty years before his birth. At the fort, every other Friday was payday. That made every other Friday night casino night in the barracks overseen by Sergeant Thomas. And after giving his men gambling lessons that would keep them ahead of the world's countless suckers for the rest of their lives, Titanic exacted his fee:

"I busted them shooting dice, playing blackjack and poker."

But he didn't bust everyone. There were a couple of country boys in his unit who waited for payday and then folded their dollars into envelopes they sent to backwoods addresses ending with the letters *RFD*—Rural Free Delivery. He made sure those boys came out a little ahead on casino night. The rest he fleeced without a second thought. "Most Army fellows are as greedy as anyone else," he told Alice.

The one who irked him most was the regiment's overbearing pistol-shooting champion. So Ti set a trap. He shot well but not too well in target practice—hiding his light under a bushel, as his uncles would have put it—and passed the word that he would challenge the champion for the right stakes at the right odds. The marksman smelled easy money. They settled on three-to-one odds for a thousand dollars, and soldiers jogged to the pistol range to watch the contest. Almost all except Titanic's men were betting on the champion, who warmed up with a few bull's-eyes from fifty yards while Ti complimented his steady hand and smooth breathing, admitting that he himself was nervous as a cat. "And here I'm just thinking about my own thousand while you've got all these fellows betting on you—money they haven't got, some of 'em. But you're steady as a rock." The shooter knew the cornpone sergeant was trying to unnerve him, but couldn't help listening. He missed his first shot by a fraction of an inch, his next by more. There were hoots from some of the soldiers. The marksman pretended not to hear, but Ti saw him blink. After that the champion had no chance.

THE GREAT WAR ENDED before Titanic was shipped overseas. Preparing to leave Fort McClellan after seven months, he packed up his gambling profits and sergeant's pay, totaling more than fifty-five thousand dollars. He stuffed the money into a pair of shoeboxes, tied the boxes shut with bootlaces, and stowed them in a duffel bag he tossed onto a troop train to Louisville. Alice was waiting in Pittsburgh, but Ti wanted to spend some time on the road. He wanted to drive his car, stay in hotels, get a barbershop shave. So he drove south and west from Louisville instead of north and east. One chilly afternoon he walked into the First National Bank in Monett, Missouri. "I'd like to make a deposit," he told the teller. "Fifty thousand dollars."

The teller looked at Ti's stack of cash and excused himself. Moments later the bank president, a round man in a black suit, came out to shake depositor Alvin Thomas's hand. He thanked Ti for his business and asked a favor: Could he give them a day's notice if he planned to make a large withdrawal? "We don't normally keep so much cash on hand," the man said before adding, under his breath, "Bank robbers, you know." Ti got a kick out of that: He had more money than the bank.

From Monett he drove south to Rogers, Arkansas. He hadn't called ahead or sent word. It was ten years since he had set out with fifty cents in his pocket.

The farmhouse looked smaller now. Sarah Thomas was heavier and grayer. Her breath caught in her throat when she saw the tall, clear-eyed man at the door. He wore a suit that must have cost twenty dollars or more. He smelled of talcum powder and pomade. "Mother," he said.

They sat at the kitchen table by the old tin washtub. Sarah made a pot of tea. She said her second husband had left her as suddenly as the first, but not on purpose. He'd had a heart attack. She said she had no plans to marry again.

Ti's step-uncles and cousins came around, all except one who had died in the war. They shook his hand, patted him on the back, and thumbed the thread of his suit. Ti told them about St. Louis and Pittsburgh. He said he had been married twice himself. His first wife was a Joplin girl who divorced him for being a money-hungry gambler, which was true enough, and a pistol-packing lowlife—"she was right about that too"—as well as a lousy, stinking lowlife, which he most certainly was not. "I smell pretty good!" He said he had heard that Nora went on to marry "a more settled fellow. A bank robber." His uncles and cousins laughed. A couple of the men whistled when he passed around a photograph of his second wife, Alice, who Ti said was in the dry-cleaning business in Pittsburgh, specializing in men's suits. He said he was headed back there, but first he had some business near here. He wanted to buy a house up in Monett. For his mother, if she wanted. She had family up there, didn't she?

"Would you be willing to leave here, Mother?" he asked.

Sarah looked around at the soot over the fireplace, the rust on

the washtub, the old sink with its hand pump. The floor was clean
but marred by years of grease and tobacco stains. She said, "Son, I
have hated this place since the day I set foot here."

Ti gave the First National Bank two days' notice and paid cash for
a white two-story house on a quiet street in Monett. Sarah invited
one of her stepsons and his family to live with her, rent free, to look
after her and keep her company. Ti gave them all careful instructions for using a potentially dangerous appliance he installed in
the kitchen, one of the first electric toasters in Barry County. They
had barely finished their first batch of toast when he got up to
leave. He renewed his vow not to smoke or drink and again he was
gone, not walking this time but driving a 1916 Packard, picking up
speed when he reached the main road to St. Louis, imagining his
mother's surprise when she found the thousand dollars he left in
the sugar bowl.

He didn't go on to Pittsburgh. Not yet. After Rogers and Monett,
Pittsburgh seemed to offer more ties that bound while the open
road beckoned. He bought presents for Alice—jewelry, candy,
lingerie—stuck them in the trunk, and kept going.

On the way to St. Louis he hired a bodyguard. There were good
reasons to do so. Hijackers looking to loot a game could get the
drop on a lone gambler no matter how quick he was; two men had
a better chance to slip an ambush. There was also a certain pres-
tige to traveling with a hired man. Top road gamblers like million-
dollar man "Nick the Greek" Dandolos had hirelings open doors
for them and make sure any heisters busting through those doors
got a bullet for hello. Titanic's bodyguard was Wes Billinger, a rawboned young Army veteran from Missouri. "He drove my car and
watched my back in exchange for 10 percent of my winnings, which
were considerable," Ti recalled. Billinger drove Titanic to a crum-
bling stretch of St. Louis riverfront while Ti wrapped the stock of
his Colt .45 with adhesive tape for a better grip. They stopped by a

gray cement wall. Behind the wall was a tailor shop with red letters on the window: *Dalton's*.

"Don't look like much," Ti said.

Through the window they saw men standing and kneeling in a circle. One was rolling dice. "The shooter's George Dalton," Billinger said. "The others are bail bondsmen, loan sharks, a fellow who runs a numbers game." Billinger had telephoned ahead, so they were expected. When they entered, Dalton stopped the game. Billinger introduced his boss as Alvin Thomas from down in Monett. Dalton said there was no call for false modesty. "Everybody here knows about the great Titanic Thomas."

Ti joined the craps game. He didn't think much of Dalton, who cussed and drank from a bourbon bottle the other men passed around, and bet more aggressively the drunker he got. Dalton lost more than five thousand dollars that night and almost as much the next night. This went on for two weeks, with Dalton's losses mounting until he owed Ti forty thousand.

"That's when he offered to steer me to a payday game—a bunch of boys betting their two-week paychecks on a Friday night, just like in the Army," Titanic recalled. "He said he'd cash the checks I won in exchange for half my action and pay what he owed me out of his end. I knew he was setting me up." Still Ti went along with the plan. He won a rumpled stack of dockworkers' paychecks and took them back to Dalton. "Billinger and I went to a room in back of the tailor shop where some of Dalton's crew was drinking beer with a couple of girls. We sat around telling jokes, and pretty soon Dalton brings me my forty thousand. So I'm fixing to leave. It's dark by now, and this sorry little fellow who works there flips a switch that turns a light on outside. 'Oops,' he says, and turns it back off. That's a signal if ever I saw one. So I stop at the door and say, very loud, 'Hey girls, I got another joke for you.' I start telling the joke, and the girls are already laughing because I tell it so funny." Titanic edged closer to the door, his voice loud enough to be heard outside. He pulled the .45 with the taped handle. "I kicked the door open and saw two men with handkerchiefs over their faces and guns in their hands." The gunmen had relaxed when they heard him telling his joke. "They looked surprised. I shot them both dead."

Billinger ran out to look at the bodies. "We'd better get out of here," he said.

These were Ti's first intentional killings. He felt nothing but calm. "Call the police," he said. "Tell them what happened." He intended to shoot Dalton too, for setting him up, but Dalton begged for his life long enough for the cops to roll up outside. Ti rode with them to the police station, where he waited on a long wooden bench until the chief came out.

"Alvin Clarence Thomas," the police chief said, reading off a clipboard.

Ti stood up. "Yes, sir."

"Thomas, do you have a permit to carry that six-shooter you used tonight?"

"No, but I carry a lot of money and I'm going to kill any hijacker who's out to rob me. That's pure self-defense."

The chief said they could argue about that, but he was sure of one thing. "You did our city a favor tonight." The men Ti had shot were two of the most-wanted criminals in the country. "They're wanted for murder and armed robbery in Pittsburgh, your city of residence. They kidnapped a baby and killed it. We're real glad you got those birds." Ti left the station with a permit to carry a pistol in St. Louis.

He gave Billinger four thousand dollars, the bodyguard's 10 percent, and drove alone through Illinois, Indiana, and Ohio to Pennsylvania. A day and a night later he parked in front of a white house on a leafy block in Pittsburgh. Alice looked out the picture window and saw him coming up the porch steps with an electric toaster under his arm.

4 CAPONE, HOUDINI, AND A COUPLE OF CORPSES

IT WASN'T LONG BEFORE PITTSBURGH GAMBLERS HEARD that Titanic was back. Within a month of his return he was leaving a dice game in a riverfront warehouse, a few thousand to the good, when Alice drove up in the Packard. This was how they had planned it: a quick exit. She scooted over to the passenger seat while Ti took the wheel. He was pulling away when two men stepped out from opposite sides of the street with pistols raised. As Ti drove between them, they opened fire. Bullets pocked the Packard. He yanked the Colt from his shoulder holster and tried to drive and shoot while Alice grabbed the gun in the glove box—his old Luger. She leaned out the window and fired back.

"Girl, get back in here!"

Instead she squeezed off another shot. "They'll never hit us," she said. "If they could shoot, they'd have got us by now!"

They wheeled around corners while Alice emptied the Luger, Ti fired his .45, and pedestrians ran for cover. When they lost their pursuers, he parked behind a warehouse on the outskirts of town.

"Where'd you learn to shoot like that?" Still flushed from the chase, Alice said, "I can do lots of things." She had gone hunting with her father "a hundred times," bagging raccoons, birds, possums, and squirrels. This was the first time she had fired at a man. She wondered how it would feel to shoot one who was looking you in the eye.

No different from an animal, Ti said. You draw a bead and squeeze the trigger. Shooting those men at the tailor shop in St. Louis, he said, he had aimed for a spot between the armpits. The chest is a better target than the head "because the head can move faster. It's the same as shooting a bird. You aim for the center of gravity. The middle."

She still wanted to know how it felt to kill a person. Ti wasn't sure he understood the question. By his reckoning any man aiming a gun at him was making a losing wager, betting he could outshoot or intimidate him. "How'd it feel when I shot those men? It felt like good shooting."

They celebrated Alice's marksmanship by trading in the Packard for a 1920 Pierce-Arrow Touring Car with white-sidewall tires and front-mounted headlamps. At $6,750 the Pierce-Arrow was a luxury unimaginable to most Americans. More than half the cars sold in the world that year were three-hundred-dollar Model T Fords that started with a hand crank, topped out at forty-five miles an hour, and came in all the colors allowed by Henry Ford, who said customers could have a car in any color "as long as it is black." Ti's pale turquoise Pierce-Arrow started with the flick of an electric switch. It had a seventy-horsepower engine, more than three times the horses in the Ford, and a top speed of eighty, fast enough to compete in the Indianapolis 500. He could have bought more than twenty Model Ts for the same price. The salesman said that the president, Woodrow Wilson, had a car just like it, but Vice President Marshall with his twelve-thousand-dollar salary couldn't afford one. Titanic called his first Pierce-Arrow a business expense. "I need a faster car than any heister's got."

Alice drove it home. Ti said she might be the first woman in

Pittsburgh to pilot such a car, but he figured there would be more and more woman drivers with the passage of the Nineteenth Amendment. He and Alice were on opposite sides of the suffrage issue, though he never thought politics was worth arguing about. He laughed when she read him an editorial by a suffragette who claimed men should *lose* the vote because they were too emotional, as proved by their behavior at baseball games: "Men's place is in the Army, and they would lose their charm if they stepped out of their natural sphere into matters other than arms, uniforms and drums." Alice told him she was his equal now that women had the vote. He said she was better than equal in most ways, "especially looking."

In the third decade of the still-new century, prosperity spread outward from the cities, shrinking the frontier, worrying rural folk who saw urban streets as the devil's playground. The U.S. population reached 100 million in 1920, and for the first time most Americans lived in cities. Air mail, radio, Maybelline eye shadow, and rubber condoms were all new. In Boston, greedy financier Charles Ponzi bilked investors out of fifteen million dollars. In Chicago, the national pastime unraveled as eight "Black Sox" players went on trial for throwing the previous year's World Series. A wave of bombings blamed on Communists triggered a nationwide "Red Scare." White supremacists lynched black men and boys from the Deep South to Duluth, Minnesota, where a mob hanged three accused rapists while thousands cheered. In the first presidential campaign to be reported on radio, Republican candidate Warren Harding promised a "Return to Normalcy," a vow that proved as empty as the nation's shuttered taverns.

Nothing embodied the collision of urban and rural, old and new, like Prohibition. At midnight on January 16, 1920, the Volstead Act banned the manufacture, import, export, transport, or sale of alcoholic beverages—the nineteenth century's last strike against the twentieth. At a tent revival in Virginia, evangelist Billy Sunday presided over a mock funeral for John Barleycorn. Titanic, who considered a good tent revival even better entertainment than a movie, particularly liked the rabble-rousing preacher whose temperance crusade had helped get the Volstead Act passed.

William Ashley Sunday—his real name—was Ti's favorite tub-thumper. Once the fastest man in major-league baseball, Sunday had stolen seventy-one bases for the 1888 Pittsburgh Pirates and set a record by racing around the bases in fourteen seconds. Three years later, after hearing a call to "join a higher league," he rejected a three-thousand-dollar offer from the Pirates to work as a minister for eighty-three dollars a month, railing against devil rum and demon wine. "Whiskey and beer are all right in their place, but their place is in hell!" bellowed Sunday, who spoke to crowds of ten thousand and more with no amplification, not even a megaphone. Prohibition was a battle won for the heavenly host led by the Holy Ghost, he said. But the war went on because many men were breaking the law, drinking bathtub gin, moonshine, and smuggled liquor. The night Titanic saw him, Sunday strode a raised platform in a revival tent in Roanoke, Virginia, a two-acre expanse of white canvas lit up like a paper lantern by banks of electric lights. The air inside was flecked with sawdust, redolent of the sweat of men and women clapping, singing, and waving their hands.

Titanic had left Alice in Pittsburgh with plenty of money and a new pistol, a lady-like Derringer that fired bullets so slow you could see them in flight. She had said he could go if he wanted—she'd fend for herself till he came back.

"Get on the water wagon!" Sunday shouted. His listeners answered, "Amen." The preacher wore an all-white suit. He was fifty-seven years old, his sweaty pate gleaming with reflected light. He ran across the stage and slid into an imaginary home plate, scoring a run for righteousness. Prohibition was only a first step, Sunday said, declaring that "seventy-five percent of our idiots" come from drunken parents, "and eighty percent of the paupers." Even with alcohol illegal, "eighty-two percent of crime is committed by men under the influence of liquor." Ti liked the way the preacher used numbers. Sunday cast the annual toll of illegal drink as "a funeral procession three thousand miles long, with six hundred thousand hearses in the procession." He said it cost twenty cents to make a gallon of bootleg whiskey that sold for five dollars, making a profit of 2,500 percent for Beelzebub. Ti saw numbers the same way, as shifting likelihoods, measures of strength, intangible but vivid as the shadows on the tent's canvas walls. He wasn't so sure about Sunday's religion. Cards, dice, coins, billiard balls, and other arithmetical forms often did unlikely things, but he had seen no miracles in gambling, and he suspected that the miracles in Bible stories and the speaking in tongues at revivals were no more or less than wishful thinking. The faithful who saw God's plan in the fall of a sparrow were like the poker player who thanks Lady Luck for filling an inside straight—an attitude that guarantees he'll go bust in the long run.

"Get on the water wagon!"

The crowd took up the chant. Ti slipped out of the tent and brushed off his polished shoes. It wouldn't do for the great Titanic to take the locals' money with sawdust on his shoes.

ALONG WITH PROHIBITION AND women's suffrage, the Twenties brought the first golden age of American sport. As the decade began, "sporting" was slang for having sex. Now came a time of great public entertainments as athletes took their place in the American pantheon beside war heroes and movie stars. Babe Ruth revolutionized baseball with a home-run swing that made him the most famous man in the world. (Asked why he got paid more than the president, the Babe said, "I had a better year.") "Big Bill" Tilden won Wimbledon and the U.S. tennis title in 1920, the year Man o' War took the Preakness and Belmont Stakes. Golfer Bobby Jones, who qualified for his first U.S. Open in 1920, would close the decade by winning the Grand Slam in 1930. Sport's golden Twenties were actually born prematurely on the Fourth of July, 1919, in Toledo, Ohio, where heavyweight champion Jess Willard fought a younger, smaller challenger from Manassa, Colorado.

The bout was billed as David versus Goliath: the six-foot six-inch, 245-pound Willard against twenty-four-year-old Jack Dempsey, who stood six feet one inch and weighed in at 187. Yet to the astonishment of bettors—including Titanic, who had several thousand on the champion—Dempsey gave the bigger man the beating of his life. He knocked Willard down seven times in the first round. He broke Willard's jaw, his cheekbone, and two ribs and knocked out six of his teeth. Only later did word filter out that Dempsey's trainer had wrapped his hands with plaster of Paris before lacing his gloves; the young "Manassa Mauler" may as well have been swinging bricks. Later in this golden age Ruth became famous for whoring and guzzling illegal booze as well as hitting homers; Tilden hid his homosexuality; Jones sponsored "battles royale" in which blindfolded black men beat each other senseless; and even Man o' War was said to be "hopped up" on a then-legal stimulant, cocaine. In Billy Sunday's words, the modern world was wrongside-up.

That suited Titanic just fine. In the wake of the Dempsey-Willard fight, which made Toledo a destination for gamblers, Ti played poker in a Toledo nightclub run by Johnny "Get Rich Quick" Ryan, rubbing elbows with cigar-chewing gangsters out of Chicago. Ti was twenty-seven, but the crooks all talked down to him. One night, taking a break to go to the bathroom in the cellar, grumbling to himself, he was startled by a rat. He bumped a crate that fell and pinned the rat to the floor. Watching the animal struggle, he thought there had to be a play in this.

He rejoined the card game, and soon enough another player got up to go to the toilet. "Watch your step down there," Ti said. "That cellar's crawling with rats. I swear I could go down there and kill one inside a minute."

That got a laugh from the loudest gangster. "This kid thinks he's the Pied Piper!" He asked Ti if he'd like to put his money where his mouth was. Ti bet every dollar he had and headed for the stairs.

"No tricks, kid," the gangster said. "That rat better be warm. I ain't paying off on some dead pelt you got in your pocket. And I'm timing you. You got sixty seconds."

Titanic returned to the cellar. A few seconds later the poker players heard a gunshot. Ti came upstairs and dropped the still-warm rat in the loud man's lap. They stopped calling him "kid" after that.

The money Ti took home that night, or any night, meant little to him except as a means of keeping score. He would have agreed with W. Somerset Maugham, who wrote in 1915's *Of Human Bondage* that for gamblers, money is not so much a goal as a catalyst, "like a sixth sense without which you cannot make complete use of the other five." For Ti, the width of his bankroll measured his victories not over the odds—there was no beating the odds—but over other men, starting with his father. His goal, his compulsion, was to prove he could beat any man at anything.

"I'll show you a white blackbird!" he'd say. He meant he could make you think you had seen a miracle. More often than not he was right.

He heard of a horseshoe pitcher, Frank Jackson, who challenged anyone to play for any sum. Titanic didn't play horseshoes, but how hard could it be? The shoe weighed about the same as a duckpin bowling ball. The underhand motion was similar. He drove to Des Moines, Iowa, Jackson's town, and built a horseshoe court in an alley behind his hotel, where he practiced with his usual focus, tossing the shoe thousands of times until it spun a perfect three-quarters of a turn in flight and clanked around the ten-inch stake at the far end of the alley, time after time. When schoolboys stopped by to watch, the lanky stranger said he reckoned he could beat any man alive.

"Not Frank Jackson, mister. He'll ring eight out of ten," a boy said. "He's the world's champion."

"Frank who?"

Before long Jackson came around. A muscular man whose right forearm was thicker than his left, he watched Ti, throwing lefty, ring one and miss one. Jackson shook his head no when Ti offered to play for ten dollars.

"I only throw for real money," he said.

"Twenty dollars then."

Jackson turned to go. One of the boys piped up: "He plays for thousands. Millions!" Which was all Ti wanted to hear. In a loud voice, he offered to play for ten thousand dollars. "Every cent I've got in the world. Right here, right now. Unless Mister Jackson's scared."

The local hero asked to see Ti's money. Ti produced a roll of hundreds that drew gasps from the boys.

Did the champion suspect he was stepping into a trap? If so his ego kept him from showing it. He rubbed dirt on his hands and told the stranger to fire when ready.

"After you, sir," Ti said, offering the first throw as a courtesy.

Jackson leaned back, stepped forward, and lobbed a shoe that traced a lazy, ten-foot-high arc, turning 270 degrees in flight. And plopping into the sand a foot short of the stake. The same thing happened to his next two tosses while Ti, who had played a little possum when the boys watched him, ringed three in a row. Jackson couldn't understand why he was so weak today. He shook his head all the way to the Des Moines Bank at Third and Walnut streets, where he withdrew a hundred $100 bills and handed them to a man he would never see again. After that, Jackson avoided the back-alley court where the schoolboys flung horseshoes, and apparently never learned that Ti had put the stakes forty-one feet apart, a foot more than the regulation forty.

THE PIERCE-ARROW SAILED through an Oklahoma heat wave, fending off tumbleweeds on the road between Tulsa and a mining town called Picher. Titanic pulled over at a lemonade stand. He watched a fellow hitting golf balls down into a field that had little signs with numbers on them. It was the first driving range Ti ever saw. He said, "Hey there, let me hit one." The other man owned the little range and had a single left-handed driver in a barrel of hickory-shafted clubs near the lemonade stand. That was lucky for Ti, who took a couple practice swings and then larruped a ball that carried and rolled downhill more than three hundred yards. "The fellow says, 'Good Lord, where'd you learn to play golf?' " Ti recalled years later. "I said, 'Right here. That's the first ball I ever hit.' "

He went on to Picher, where the gamblers loitered in a pool parlor, and spent the evening playing one-pocket billiards, losing several hundred dollars. Ti kept saying pool was a difficult game but golf was easy. It had to be or how could he, a beginner, drive a ball three hundred yards? This attracted the attention of a few golfers who were willing to bet he could do no such thing. The golfers' friends wanted in too, and the next morning the Pierce-Arrow led a caravan of Model Ts to the driving range, where the proposition man teed up a ball with more than a dozen witnesses gathered around him. One, the town's best pool player, had on a suit and tie. The others wore overalls and straw hats. They pooled their money, including a single silver dollar from a farmhand who had happened by. Three thousand and one dollars. Titanic matched that total out of his pocket, though without any bills smaller than a hundred he had to put up thirty-one hundred dollars. He handed his jacket to the spiffy pool shark and took a pinch of sand from a little box beside the barrel of clubs. The peg-shaped wooden tee, a recent invention, had yet to arrive in this corner of Oklahoma, so like most golfers of the early Twenties he teed up his ball on a mound of moist sand. He pulled the left-handed driver from the barrel. He spat on his hands.

"One swing," said the pool player.

Ti cracked his knuckles. He was stretching the moment, enjoying himself. "One's all it takes," he said.

He smashed a drive down the hill. The ball bounced and stopped. He knew he had caught it flush, but nobody whistled, clapped, or cursed. In fact, Ti would tell Alice later that there wasn't a sound in the whole state of Oklahoma.

"That's no more than two-eighty," someone said.

The grass was wet. It had rained the night before. No ball would roll far enough for him to win the bet. So Ti paid the Oklahomans, shaking some of their hands, giving the farm boy a hundred dollars for his silver dollar. He always said he learned a lesson at that little range outside Picher: In poker, pool, and dice you've got to worry about your game and the other man's. In golf there's also the weather.

"I went purely crazy over golf," he said. No sooner had he checked into the St. Charles Hotel, a brick shoebox in sweltering St. Joseph, Missouri, than he found a sporting-goods shop and bought a set of clubs. They were right-handed, so he practiced that way. He used his niblick, a club with the loft of a modern nine-iron, to chip balls off the rug in his hotel room until he could chip nine out of ten into a water glass. Here was another way to turn a profit on a lazy afternoon—a wrinkle on his cards-in-a-hat routine: He would chip a few balls at a tumbler he'd placed on the floor in a hotel lobby. He would miss, curse his luck, draw a small crowd, and finally bet he'd make the next one. His chipping trick became a consistent moneymaker once he discovered that an inch of water in the glass kept the ball from bouncing out.

In St. Joseph, he agreed to sit in on a regular game of five-card stud in an upstairs room at a shuttered saloon. "It was a tough bunch around there," he remembered, "with quite a few hijackers." The game got hijacked so often the proprietor had installed a crude alarm, a bell that rang if anybody came up the back stairs. Ti hired bodyguard Dick Wade to keep an eye on the door while Ti watched the other players' eyes. He knew that the upper eyelids tighten, revealing more of the iris, when a person feels fear—like when he's bluffing. Ti also watched noses for a subtle sign of excitement: the slight flare of nostrils that suggests a newly dealt card matches the player's hole card. Even the most poker-faced professional's nostrils widen almost imperceptibly at the sight of a good card. Ti had trained himself to erase that tell from his own poker face. He would inhale just before a new card was turned, and exhale when the dealer turned it, so his breathing never varied. As he told Wade, he had a poker nose on his poker face.

"We'd barely started that night when that alarm bell rang and every man dove for cover," Titanic recalled. "Me and Wade turned the poker table over and got down behind it. Two hijackers slammed through the door, guns blazing." A bullet chipped a corner off the table inches from Ti's ear. "Wade and me fired back and down they went." One man fell backward through the doorway. The other staggered forward, his blood streaming down the table. Both were dead. Titanic checked their wallets. He and Wade had killed Skeet Young of Tulsa and Arch Lupee of Minot, North Dakota. "I didn't know if I'd shot one of them or both or neither one, since Wade and me were both blasting away. I figured I got one at least." One would bring his body count to four including Jim Johnson on the riverboat *Rambler*. Again he called the police and claimed self-defense. Again he got a pat on the back for doing the community a favor.

Young and Lupee were wanted criminals. Their killers walked out of the police station to the Western Union office, where Titanic dictated telegrams to the dead men's wives, telling them it was nothing personal.

"Then I went up to Chicago. I'd heard about Nick the Greek gambling high up there." By 1921 Titanic had beaten small-timers all over the Midwest, Texas and Oklahoma, the Southeast and as far north as Pittsburgh. He was ready to move up in class.

NICHOLAS ANDREAS DANDOLOS, the most famous gambler of his time, was known for the cut of his tailored suits, the glint of his gold-and-diamond cuff links, and the fortunes he won and lost at racetracks and gaming tables from Monte Carlo to Hong Kong. Dandolos, thirty-eight, came from a wealthy family in Crete with interests in shipping, tobacco, and figs. After studying poetry and philosophy at the Greek Evangelical College of Smyrna, in Turkey, he settled in Chicago, where the bang-bang pace of life matched the speed with which "Nick the Greek" did the only thing he ever wanted to do. "The next-best thing to gambling and winning," he liked to say, "is gambling and losing." He would play poker, a game he called "the art of civilized bushwhacking," for three or four days without sleep. He had the guts of a burglar, and when sheer guts failed him, his father and uncles back home would wire him another two hundred thousand dollars. He let more than ten million slip through his hands before he turned thirty. "Luck is a lady, and she is the love of my life," said the poetical Dandolos. Damon Runyon would remember that line and attribute it to another, better player.

There are several accounts of how Titanic and Nick the Greek met: between trains at Chicago's Union Station; between bullets during a South Side shootout; at a Palmer House poker table where hundred-dollar bills were stacked two feet high. "The one I heard goes like this," said Doyle Brunson. "They're in the Chicago train station. Titanic introduces himself and says, 'Nick, I hear you've got a lot of gamble in you.' Nick says, 'Yes, I do,' and throws down his bankroll. Fifteen thousand. So they flip a coin for it. Ti flips and Nick calls heads, whereupon Ti grabs his two-headed coin out of the air and says, 'Damn, you *are* a gambler!' He claps Nick around the shoulder and off they go."

Nick the Greek was the highest-money gambler since Diamond Jim Brady, who once cut a deck for five hundred thousand dollars. No glutton like Diamond Jim, a New Yorker celebrated in the Gilded Age of the late 1800s for gorging on three dozen oysters, six crabs, a bowl of turtle soup, two whole ducks, six or seven lobsters, and a sirloin steak at a typical meal, the trim, cultured Dandolos preferred a few bites of filet mignon, a flute of champagne, and a Cuban cigar. He may have winced a bit at Ti's widebrim fedora and garish green suit, but Nick liked the gamble in this newcomer. Rather than compete, they teamed up, with Dandolos providing entrée to millionaires' games in which an oilman might see a racketeer's twenty-five thousand dollars and raise fifty thousand—enough money at that time to buy Ti's weight, 160 pounds, in gold. Dandolos noticed that the stakes never affected Titanic's play or even his breathing. Ti was the coolest cucumber the Greek had met.

"Nick and I played partners. We'd look at our hands and signal each other," Ti recalled. A blink might mean Ti had queens, a sniff might mean kings. The signals varied and a meta-signal could change them, the way a catcher shifts to a new set of signs if there's a curious runner on second base. "If the Greek had a better hand, I'd get out of the road." But before folding, Ti might bet another five or ten thousand, building the pot for his partner, and Dandolos would do the same for him. In time they worked up a simple system cheaters still employ: If Partner 1 bets rather than folding, partner 2 raises; if partner 1 raises again, partner 2 raises more.

After the game they split their winnings, and Titanic made more in a few months in Chicago than in his three years on the road after the war.

He spent his afternoons walking, exploring a town full of music, muscle, and hustle. The Great Migration of black workers from the South had helped double Chicago's population since the turn of the century. Now a riotous city of three million, Chicago had replaced New Orleans as America's jazz capital. On the South Side, King Oliver and his Dixie Syncopators dazzled Lincoln Gardens with twenty-four-year-old Louis Armstrong on second cornet. On Michigan Avenue the neo-Gothic Tribune Tower and the Wrigley Building, both new, faced each other beside a drawbridge that stopped traffic while cruise ships on the Chicago River paraded upstream to Lake Michigan. In one of the first feats of twentieth-century engineering, the river's course had been reversed in 1900. During the 1800s the river wound east through Illinois, carrying sewage to the lake, Chicago's source of drinking water. Epidemics of typhoid and cholera killed one in twenty Chicagoans until the city's engineers built locks and canals that sent the water flowing back the other way, west to the Mississippi. Now green-and-yellow El trains rumbled over the river, kicking sparks, carrying workers to the granite buildings going up all over town. At every construction site, builders paid a percentage in tribute to gangsters armed with Thompson submachine guns, tribute that worked its way up the chain of command to Al Capone.

Prohibition brought profits by the boatload and truckload to the "Paris of the Prairie," the Midwest's entry point for liquor smuggled from Canada. There were an estimated ten thousand speakeasies in 1920s Chicago, including several in the backs of funeral homes. Dozens of street gangs shot it out over the boodle generated by bootlegging and other crimes until Capone, a recent arrival from Brooklyn, consolidated the gangs into a citywide organization he called "The Outfit."

Many of Chicago's mobsters and gamblers also played golf. Capone set the tone by dressing in knickers and monogrammed silk shirts and playing for thousands of dollars. To get in on that action, Titanic adapted his propositions to the links. During a lull in a country-club card game he announced that he could drive a ball more than five hundred yards. While booking a handful of five-figure bets at favorable odds, he added, "I'm not saying when—I've got to *feel* it first—but I'll do it." For short-term action he led a few well-heeled golfers from the clubhouse to a tee beside a pond where he put up one thousand dollars that he could knock a ball into the water, wade in, and retrieve the ball. To prove it was the same one, he marked his ball with an *X*. This time Ti was his own water spaniel: He leaped in, splashed around, and emerged with one of the dozens of marked balls he had hit the day before. Sopping wet, he collected.

One day Nick, who seemed to know everyone, took Titanic to the Palace Music Hall. "I want you to meet another miracle worker," he said. "You've heard of him. Harry Houdini." Born Ehrich Weiss, the son of a rabbi in Budapest, Hungary, Houdini had launched his career at the Chicago World's Fair of 1893 and spent the next thirty years slipping out of handcuffs, chains, and straitjackets while hanging upside down from cables, submerged in water tanks, or squeezed into three-foot milk cans. What Ti liked about Houdini was that he never claimed his act was magic. In fact he exposed phony psychics and debunked Twenties fads for séances and Ouija boards. Houdini wrote books telling how he sucked air into his lungs while being chained to give him room to move after, or swallowed handcuff keys and regurgitated them later. Like Ti he was a proposition artist who promised the seemingly impossible and then delivered it. No longer the dashing young daredevil who had piloted his canvas-winged biplane over Australia in 1910, the five-foot five-inch Houdini was pushing fifty now. He had the same blue-gray eyes and bone-crushing handshake as in his youth, but his pomaded hair, parted straight down the middle, was going gray. Comparing card tricks with Ti, he was amused to find that they knew many of the same ones. Titanic liked his answer to the only question Ti had time to ask: What's the key to your tricks?

"Practice," Houdini said.

Ti took in that day's sold-out show at the Palace. He applauded without joining in the crowd's gasps. Were the paying customers really amazed that the great Houdini could pull off the feats pictured on the poster outside the theater? Ti admired Houdini's technique but was never entirely sure what the fuss was about. "I like the fellow, but he's no miracle man," he told Nick the Greek. "It's all preparation—good set-ups."

Houdini was only passing through Chicago while Capone was as much a fixture as the gargoyles on the Tribune Tower. Still only twenty-five, not yet ravaged by the syphilis that would kill him, Alphonse Capone was a round-faced, balding, pig-eyed man with thick Cupid lips and three jagged scars on his left cheek. He was always daubing his sweaty forehead with a handkerchief. A former bodyguard and strong-arm goon, the Brooklyn-born Capone ruled Chicago's bootlegging, prostitution, and gambling rackets. At least half the Chicago Police Department was on his payroll. More famous than the mayor or the local big-league baseball stars, he rode through Chicago and Cicero, a nearby town he practically owned (a badge in his wallet identified him as Cicero's sheriff), in an armored car outfitted with a police siren, bulletproof glass, and portholes for his soldiers' machine guns. His driver would pull up at the Bella Napoli restaurant in Chicago's Little Italy, where the boss dined on gold-plated dishes stacked with enough food to sate Diamond Jim Brady. "Mountains of pasta and Niagaras of chianti had deposited layers of fat" on his frame, wrote one biographer, "but the muscle beneath the fat was rock-hard." The young boss was all appetite—for food, drink, money, sex, power and attention.

When he went to a Cubs or White Sox game, he sat in a front-row box and waved to the crowd. Players asked for his autograph.

Capone's dirty mouth offended Titanic. The boss used the foulest profanity in mixed company, which Ti never did, and he was vain too—using makeup to hide the scars on his cheek. Ti told Nick they should "steer clear of this fellow," but the Greek said they needed Capone's blessing if they wanted to play high-money cards in Chicago without getting robbed. As it turned out they got more than his blessing. Capone did most of his betting on horses and baseball, but he saw that Titanic and Nick the Greek were bamboozling the best local poker talent, and he wanted in. He arranged for them to play against the richest gamblers in the Midwest. Even with Capone taking 25 percent for his trouble, Titanic's take was more than a hundred grand. In a single hand of stud, Ti beat a Milwaukee gambler out of a restaurant, the Golden Pheasant, by winning six side bets in a row.

Titanic and Capone were playing five-card stud in a windowless cellar on the South Side one night when a thug named Izzy Lazar delayed the action. The bet was five hundred dollars to Lazar, but his chin was on his chest. It was late; he was drunk. Izzy would rouse himself long enough to bet or fold, then put his head on the table beside his dwindling stack of chips. Ti thought Capone might shoot him.

Ti nudged Lazar. "Izzy, wake up." No response.

So Ti pointed to the light switch. Capone understood. The boss of the Outfit, Chicago's most feared criminal organization, tiptoed to the switch and doused the lights. The room went dark. Ti kicked Lazar. "Izzy, it's to you. Is you in or is you out?"

Lazar, waking to a pitch-black world, rubbed his eyes. Capone said, "Come on, we're all waiting. In or out?" Lazar jumped and yelled, "Jesus, I'm blind, stone blind!"

Ti and Capone laughed all the way to the street. They'd had a good night. Ti could have left it that way; instead he pressed his luck. He knew that men who crossed "Scarface" Al had short life expectancies, but he couldn't keep himself from conning Capone at least once. He wanted to beat the boss. "He *had* to," said a gambler who knew Ti's hustles. "Because that's the game. If there's a top guy in town, you have to deflower that guy. If he's too big to beat, you do it like a mosquito—so quick and slick he don't even know he's beat."

The morning after he and Capone scared Izzy Lazar must have struck Ti as the time to make his move. As they strolled toward Capone's car, Ti stopped at a fruit stand and bought a lemon. He said he had a hell of an arm, probably better than any big-league pitcher. "In fact," he said, "I'd bet five hundred dollars I can fling this lemon to the roof of that hotel."

Capone looked up. The hotel across the street was five stories high. "You got a bet," he said. "But wait a second."

He bought a lemon of his own. Smiling, Capone squeezed it dry and handed it to Ti. The squashed yellow fruit was sticky, lopsided.

"Fling this one."

Ti hadn't counted on this. The lemon he had bought was filled with buckshot—he'd planted it with the fruit vendor the day before. Capone had outfoxed him. There was only one thing to do. Ti reared back, coattails flying. He took a hop, skip and jump, and let fly.

The two of them watched the lemon clear the edge of the roof across the street. Capone whistled through his Cupid lips. "You're a versatile son of a bitch," he said.

5 HIS FIRST MILLION

AFTER FOLDING CAPONE'S FIVE HUNDRED DOLLARS INTO his bankroll, Titanic backed off. He resisted the temptation to hustle Capone again. If the mercurial boss ever found out that Ti had palmed the squeezed-out lemon during his elaborate windup and tossed the weighted one—a bit of misdirection Houdini would have spotted in an instant—Ti might have wound up as full of buckshot as the lemon. He had pricked the arrogant Capone; that was enough, at least for now.

Settling for a five-hundred-dollar score against a man who ate off golden plates suggests a discretion Titanic hadn't shown before. Maybe he was wising up. He spent the rest of the year in Capone's orbit but never hustled Scarface Al at golf. It must have been hard for him to watch Capone at Chicago's Burnham Woods Golf Course, decked out in his knickers and silk shirt, with flunkies teeing up his ball and applauding his bouncing drives. Capone's remoras had funny names: Jack "Machine Gun" McGurn, Jake "Greasy Thumb" Guzik, a bodyguard known only as "Banjo Eyes." McGurn, a scratch golfer who would help plan the St. Valentine's Day Massacre of 1929, was the worst. When comedian Joe E. Lewis refused to perform exclusively at the Green Mill, a cocktail lounge backed by Capone, McGurn pistol-whipped him, cut off the end of his tongue, and slit his throat. Lewis survived. Doctors used tweezers to pull bits of McGurn's gun butt from his brain, and he spent more than a year learning to speak again.

Titanic gave Capone and his men a wide berth until the winter of 1923–24, when he was ready to leave town. Then he pulled the trigger on a proposition that drew in many of Chicago's big-money golfers.

One winter night, sitting in his usual spot at a South Side poker table, he folded his hand. There was snow on the window behind him, icicles on tree limbs outside. "I feel it," Ti said. Cashing in his chips, he announced he was ready to launch the impossible drive, the five-hundred-yarder he had promised to hit when he first came to town.

He gave the other gamblers a day to pass the word, and booked a slew of new bets. Various accounts put the total between twenty and fifty thousand dollars. Ti wrote every bettor's initials and the stakes of each bet in a notebook he carried in his jacket pocket. There was no *A.C.* in the notebook but some of the money was likely Capone's, placed by an underling. Capone didn't like being left out of any action in his domain.

The next day, Titanic led a parade of bettors and hangers-on to Jackson Park Golf Club, a nine-hole links on the shore of Lake Michigan. The white frozen lake stretched out behind him. The course had been closed for two months. Ti shoved a cone-shaped Reddy Tee—the newly invented improvement on a dollop of sand—into the frigid ground. He peered down the frosty fairway toward the green, a snowed-over spot in the distance with no flag in it, and took a practice swing. Then he walked around to the other side of the ball. Now he was facing the lake. He leaned into his slow backswing and smacked a drive that flew two hundred yards before it bounced on the ice, the ball picking up speed as it bounded toward Michigan. By the time it stopped rolling, Titanic was collecting. Nobody dared complain—the gamblers' code held that a man pays up when he's beaten, even by trickery. Ti had done what he said he would do. And he could always enforce the code with the Colt in his shoulder holster.

He told Nick the Greek he was ready to move on. Nick said they ought to try California. The weather was perfect and he knew some fellows out there. Leaving frozen Chicago behind, Ti and the Greek rode the Southern Pacific's Overland Limited out of Union Station. They played cards in the club car throughout the fifty-eight-hour trip, which paused after fifty-seven hours when the rails ran out at the edge of California's Suisun Bay. There was no bridge there, so the train was disassembled, each car ferried across the bay and then reattached to the others for the slow final roll into San Francisco.

THE POWELL STREET CABLE CAR moved invisibly through fog, ringing its bell. The Greek led Titanic to a corniced building at 216 Powell, near Union Square. A neon sign over the door: *The Kingston Club*. Inside, chandeliers glinted over rows of velvet-covered card tables. Waiters carried trays of hors d'oeuvres, crystal decanters of bootleg brandy, and flutes of champagne to dark-suited gamblers. Pale girls with bobbed hair and short skirts—flappers—reached out to intercept some of the champagne. Ti called it "the kind of place where you feel like a gentleman." He sat in a leather chair beside a man who owned a gold mine. Nick pointed out other men he said were bankers, lawyers, and politicians, as well as a few wealthy bootleggers who made a sideline of buying the lawyers and politicians. Ti would never have gotten through the door if not for Nick, who commandeered a seat beside a window as if he owned the place, trimming the tip of a ten-dollar Cuban cigar and signaling for a waiter to light it. Ti was eager to play, but Nick said there was no hurry. They were going to make plenty of money after he finished his El Rey del Mundo.

There were usually several games going in the club, but the main event was lowball, in which the lowest hand wins. The game was $80 ante, $160 to open, with raises of $320 and $640. The action grew so quickly that a fifteen-minute cold streak could cost a player $20,000. Playing partners with Nick, Ti got hot. Over the course of several months he won more than $250,000 at the Kingston Club, a sum equal to about $3 million today. His haul included a Cadillac wagered by a player who ran out of chips and bet the car on one last hand.

Ti admired Nick's card-playing stamina but didn't share it. Marathon poker in shadowy rooms made him feel like a mole. He longed for a chance to stretch his muscles in the sunshine and found it on the golf course.

In the Twenties, golf still belonged mostly to country-club swells and strongmen like Capone. Titanic had enjoyed his occasional long-driving stunts but never gave the game much thought until he got to San Francisco, where he found a public course in Golden Gate Park. "For the next twenty years I had a club in my hands nearly every day," he recalled. The game may as well have been invented to suit his talents. It rewarded Ti's penchant for incessant practice and offered more bets per game than any other sport. Golfers bet on their total scores, their nine-hole scores, and their scores minus their handicaps. They bet on long drives, putts, sand shots, and countless permutations. Best of all, they overestimated their skills. Ti liked to say golf was like sex: "Most men think they're better at it than they really are."

He bought a set of left-handed clubs to go with his right-handed set so he could practice from both sides. Like many artists, actors, and other unconventional people he was left-handed, but his persistence and natural gifts made him nearly as good right-handed as lefty. He evened up the gap by spending more practice time swinging right-handed. From both sides he held the club with a modified baseball grip, wrapping three fingers of one hand around the thumb and index finger of the other, a grip that kept his hands hinged. He paid teaching pros at the public course double the usual rate for lessons, and hit hundreds of balls between lessons, learning to make near-perfect contact. That meant striking the ball with the pencil-point sweet spot on the face of a hickory-shafted club that was practically a cudgel compared to the graphite-and-titanium clubs of the twenty-first century.

Golf clubs had been made of wood since Scottish shepherds began using their crooks to knock stones at rabbit holes more than five hundred years ago. By the nineteenth century the wood of choice was whippy ash, which is still used to make baseball bats. Stronger, stiffer hickory replaced ash in the mid-1800s. The best hickory came from hillsides in Tennessee—not hilltops, which yielded brittle wood, or lowlands, where soft "swamp hickory" grew, but reddish wood from middle altitudes, which had a steely suppleness the Scottish golf patriarch Old Tom Morris called "fine music." Still, wooden shafts made golf about as easy to play as bagpipes. Wood tends to torque unpredictably when whipped through the air. Bobby Jones, the last great hickory player, spoke of "the twisting stresses against which the player always has to be on guard." Even with the finest hickory, controlling the position of the sweet spot at the center of the fast-descending clubface at the far end of the shaft called for last-instant corrections by the wrists and hands. But that was something Titanic, with his preternatural dexterity, was born to do. Tall Ti would pull the club back, rotating his front shoulder under his chin. After a short backswing, he whipped the club back through the same arc to the ball. Great golfers like Jones, Harry Vardon, and Walter Hagen generated power by shifting their weight toward the target on the downswing, as

Jack Nicklaus would do half a century later, but Ti did something different. Twisting away from the ball on the backswing, he built power by rotating his torso, and released it by untwisting during the downswing. In that way he resembled Tiger Woods more than Jones, Vardon or Nicklaus. The golf pros he worked with called it a quirk, and Ti, who kept his secrets to himself, never taught anyone his peculiarly modern swing. He delivered the clubface squarely to the ball, which took off with a *crack* like a small-bore rifle shot, a sound that recalled his days with the Bogardus medicine show.

Determined to keep a low profile around the course, he did most of his practicing behind a line of oaks that blocked the view from the clubhouse and driving range. Knowing that golf pros were tanned, he wore long-sleeved shirts and stayed in the shade "so I'd look pale like a beginner." And he spent 90 percent of his practice time chipping and putting. Ti estimated that nine of ten bets were won or lost around the greens, "so I'd chip and putt, chip and putt. In a few weeks I could hole that ball in two from a hundred yards a lot of the time, and never more than three. But I still didn't play anyone. Didn't play a full round of golf till I'd practiced for a year."

Buddy Brainer was a golf pro from another San Francisco course. He gave lessons to several Kingston Club gamblers. Brainer liked to drink at the club and watch the poker games. The cardplayers said he was the best golfer they knew, the best stick in town.

One night Titanic looked up from his cards and disparaged Brainer's line of work. "I hear golf's for girls," he said. "There's nothing much to it."

"Maybe you'd like to put your money where your mouth is," Brainer said.

"For how much?"

"Ten dollars a hole."

They met at the tee the next day. Brainer striped his first drive down the middle and went on to shoot par while Ti did nothing right. His first drive sliced into the woods. He shanked a chip shot and missed putts long and short. He lost every hole, resembling a real golfer only in the way he made excuses. Peeling bills off his bankroll in the clubhouse, he griped about the fog, his sore back, and his bum luck, drawling, "My first ball bounced so far into the woods I thought I'd get et by a bear."

That evening, Ti stepped off the elevator at the Kingston Club to a chorus of snickers. Brainer had told the cardplayers about the match and Ti's many excuses. They ribbed him until Ti said, "That son of a biscuit-eater's a hell of a golfer, I'll admit it, but I believe I can beat him." Turning to Brainer, he offered "a real bet." A thousand dollars a hole over eighteen holes. "But you're so good you've got to give me three shots a hole."

Brainer laughed. "Not three. One stroke a hole."

Ti had already won the most crucial part of any golf match, the pre-round barter of strokes and stakes. He said, "Buddy, you got a bet."

There was dew on the first fairway when they teed up the next morning. The golfers were trailed by a shuffling bunch of woozy Kingston Club gamblers unaccustomed to being upright before noon. The gamblers sipped black coffee from paper cups. They had more than a hundred thousand dollars in bets and side bets on the match, most of it on the young professional. Brainer himself was on the hook for fifty-six thousand, ten times what he made in a year, almost all of it fronted by gamblers who advanced him the money. If Brainer won, he could quit teaching lessons and spend a year or two working on his game, maybe qualify for the U.S. Open.

Titanic cracked a 270-yard drive that bisected the first fairway. Over the next three hours Brainer's grin faded as Ti matched him almost shot for shot. The young pro won as many holes as he lost, but Ti's stroke-a-hole handicap put him one ahead as they played the eighteenth, where he lofted a niblick shot to the green and lagged a putt to the edge of the cup, ensuring a par that closed out the match. Brainer offered a limp handshake and trudged off the course. He wasn't seen around the Kingston Club after that.

Later, Ti heard that Buddy Brainer worked for two years to repay the backers who had put up the money he lost that day. When Alice asked if he ever felt sorry for luring Brainer into a trap, Ti swore he didn't. He said golf gamblers were no different from heisters who came at him with guns. They were all after his money. "Nobody ever got hustled who didn't ask for it one way or another."

He also swore that he never regretted losing a bet. Many if not most of his losses came at racetracks. He and Nick the Greek were alike that way. They never outsmarted the so-called sport of kings and never quit trying. For Ti, that was the allure of the sport—it was the only game he couldn't beat. He left hundreds of thousands of dollars at tracks from coast to coast and still claimed he enjoyed every minute he spent within sniffing distance of the ponies.

Another of his losses came in a San Francisco golf match against the Greek. Titanic was a far better golfer, so they started out playing for nothing—for fun. Ti knew that wouldn't last long. He liked to say that without betting, golf is nothing more than a long walk with three other liars.

At the first par-three hole, the Greek made an offer. "Five thousand says I can make five on this little hole."

"Nicky, that's a bet."

The Greek whanged his ball off several trees. Moments later, lying five, he marched back to the tee shouting, "Double or nothing!" Again he butchered the hole. Now Nick Dandolos hated the game of golf, this little par-three hole, the grass under his ball, and the whole world under the grass. He was muttering curses while he walked up behind Ti.

"Quiet," Ti said. "I'm trying to sink this birdie putt."

Nick was in no mood to wait. "Come on. That's practically a gimme."

"Oh, really?" The putt was about ten feet, sidehill. "You're down ten thousand. Want to try this 'gimme' for another ten?"

"No," said the Greek, "but I'll make it for twenty."

Nick studied the twenty-thousand-dollar putt. It was about eight feet longer than any putt he had made that day. "I calculated he had a one-in-ten chance at best," Ti recalled. "Putting wasn't Nick's strong suit as a golfer. In fact, he didn't have any." At last Nick yanked his putter back and shoved the ball toward the hole. As it dived in, Titanic swooned. He clutched his chest. "You got me!"

The tale of Nick's twenty-thousand-dollar putt became one of Ti's favorite stories. He said it proved something important. There may be no such thing as luck, but some guys are just lucky.

THE ACTION AT THE Kingston Club ebbed and flowed with the gamblers' fortunes. During one lull Titanic drove down the coast to Los Angeles. A couple weeks later he moved there.

Golf gamblers in LA were spreading money around like grass seed. One Hollywood golfer, a young millionaire newly arrived from Texas, would become Ti's particular quarry. But a man couldn't just blow into town and tee it up with Howard Hughes. First Ti would have to worm his way into the right foursomes, and he began with a bootlegger named Ed Marsh, who had a mansion in Beverly Hills and a sideline in real estate. Titanic spent weeks playing daily rounds with the left-handed Marsh. He shot in the nineties using his right-handed clubs, winning a few hundred dollars a round. "We were eating dinner when I lit into him," Ti recalled. "I said, 'Marsh, how come you think you can play golf? You can't play a lick.' He says, 'You don't beat me by much.' I said he was so bad I could beat him with his own left-handed clubs. I said we'd play for a thousand dollars. That's when he got greedy. 'Ten thousand,' he says. Of course I beat him by a stroke." It could have been twenty strokes, but Ti liked to keep things close. "If a man shot eighty-nine, I'd shoot eighty-eight. If he shot sixty-eight, I'd shoot sixty-seven. I wanted them to want to try me again."

Instead of trying Titanic again, Marsh sold him a house at a favorable price and Ti wrote off the debt. Now the Ozarks boy owned a hacienda in Beverly Hills. He phoned his wife in Pittsburgh, as he did from time to time. Alice's voice on the long-distance trunk line reminded him that he was a married man who didn't act like one. He hadn't seen her for almost a year. She must have known he wasn't faithful when he was on the road—he didn't have a week of celibacy in him, much less a year. Still she waited, trying to be the wife he wanted, the one who accepted him for the charming cheat he was.

"Sell the house and get out here," he said. Alice said hooray and jumped to it. She sold the Pittsburgh house, gave her parents a shoebox full of cash, and hopped the California Limited to Los Angeles, where the sun shone 350 days a year and a palm tree shaded Alvin and Alice Thomas's front porch. In the blacktop drive sat a 1926 Pierce-Arrow, a Series 33 Phaeton as shiny as a diamond, with a top speed of 115. This one was hers.

Alice was never happier. Ti bought her a new Derringer for the Phaeton's glove box. "Bought her some diamonds too," he remembered, "and we loaded up on stylish clothes." She got her hair done in a Marcel wave, the hairdresser using electric curling irons to make Alice look like Mary Pickford. She and Ti dressed up and went to movie premieres at Sid Grauman's gaudy Egyptian Theatre, which had opened in 1922, five years before Grauman's Chinese. The Egyptian's massive doors swung open to a courtyard studded with imperial palms. Grauman had taken advantage of the region's weather by building a topless entrance hall, open to the sky. Inside the theater, columns adorned with hieroglyphs rose into the darkness. At premieres, Alvin the Arkansas penny-pitcher and

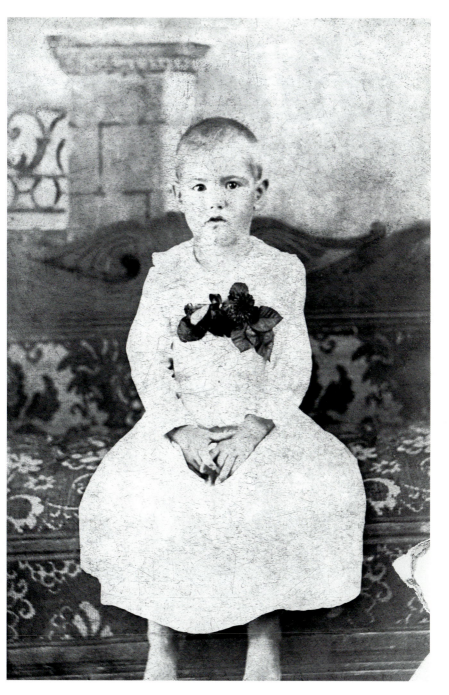

Alvin Clarence Thomas, about two years old, 1895.
(Family photo)

Rogers, Arkansas, around 1909, the year sixteen-year-old
Alvin Thomas left town with fifty cents in his pocket.
(Courtesy of University of Arkansas Libraries, Fayetteville)

Captain A. H.
Bogardus (*center, with
his sons*), the world-
champion shootist
who gave young
Alvin a job in his
Miracle Medicine
Show.

(Courtesy of Richard Hamilton)

The young Titanic on a visit to Arkansas around 1915.

(Family photo)

Arnold Rothstein, the New York crime boss known as "the Brain." He fixed the 1919 World Series but lost a fateful card game fixed by Titanic.

(Courtesy of David Pietrusza)

Eddie Cicotte, the Chicago White Sox ace corrupted and finally ruined by the "Black Sox" scandal.

(Courtesy of Library of Congress)

Damon Runyon in 1944, two years before his death.

(Time & Life Pictures / Getty Images)

Titanic's last name became "Thompson" during the Rothstein murder trial, when newspapers got his correct name, "Thomas," wrong.

(Courtesy of David Pietrusza)

George "Hump" McManus, charged with Rothstein's murder, couldn't suppress a grin while conferring with his lawyer.

(*Courtesy of David Pietrusza*)

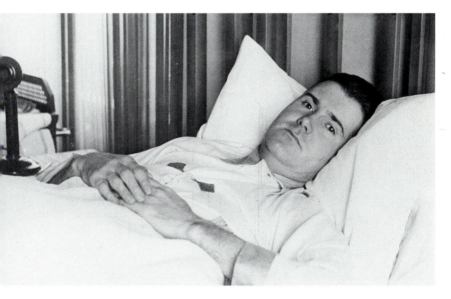

Star witness Titanic delayed the Rothstein murder trial—he was in a Milwaukee hospital, suffering from a convenient case of pleurisy.

(© *Bettmann/Corbis*)

Titanic Thompson on his way to the Criminal Courts Building in New York City in November 1929, to testify in the Rothstein murder trial.

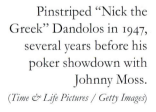

Pinstriped "Nick the Greek" Dandolos in 1947, several years before his poker showdown with Johnny Moss.

Alice the Pittsburgh pickpocket breathed the same air as Pickford and her husband, Douglas Fairbanks, as well as Chaplin, Valentino, Tom Mix, Gloria Swanson, and other film stars. Ti thought they all looked surprisingly short. Apparently none of the film people were on the water wagon.

They employed private bootleggers and lived in gilded, giddy opulence. Valentino's castle, Falcon Lair, featured a bedroom of black marble and black leather. Swanson, who spent $150,000 a year stocking her closets with furs, French lingerie, and jeweled, peacock-feathered gowns, was said to bathe in champagne in a golden bathtub. Dusty cowboy Tom Mix had a rainbow-hued fountain in his dining room. The most exclusive address of all was 1143 Summit Drive: the green-gabled mansion called Pickfair, where Pickford and Fairbanks outdid other film-colony nobles by playing host to intellectual royalty. At Pickfair dinner parties, Chaplin and other silent-film stars rubbed elbows with Noël Coward, George Bernard Shaw, Sir Arthur Conan Doyle, and Albert Einstein. Titanic and Alice got nowhere near that guest list, but Ti heard a bit of Pickfair gossip that got his attention. Fairbanks had taken up golf.

Ti bought his way into the Hollywood Country Club, where money counted more than social standing. He was heading from the course to his car one afternoon when two men stuck pistols in his face. The thieves took his gun and stole his bankroll, a little over ten thousand dollars. Ti, thinking of the eight thousand hidden in his back pocket, broke loose and took off running, only to stumble over an out-of-bounds marker. While golfers played the eighteenth hole a few yards away, the heisters caught him and trundled him into a waiting car and drove into the hills. "I thought I was a dead man." He gave them the eight thousand and they tossed him out of the car. "I rolled down a hill, expecting to feel bullets in my back any second." Instead he dusted himself off and walked home. Several days later a policeman caught his attackers and recovered the cash they had stolen. Titanic thought he'd get his money back.

Instead the cop, whose salary was less than two hundred dollars a month, disappeared. Ti said that being robbed twice in one robbery taught him "Hollywood's as full of thieves as anyplace, if not more so."

George Von Elm was Hollywood's golfing golden boy. The dapper, blond Von Elm, playing in white knickers and argyle socks, came in second to Bobby Jones in the 1924 U.S. Amateur Championship. Two years later he tied Walter Hagen, the world's top professional, for third behind Jones in the British Open. Three months after that, the twenty-five-year-old Von Elm finally won the U.S. Amateur, edging the great Jones in a match that brought hurrahs from a gallery of thousands. "The monarch of golf was toppled from his amateur throne by flaxen-haired George Von Elm in one of the most stunning upsets of links history," wrote an Associated Press reporter. Von Elm returned in triumph to the El Rancho Country Club in Los Angeles, which Titanic had joined in hopes of doing some hustling. When club members took up a collection to buy Von Elm a car to celebrate his victory over Jones, Ti was the biggest contributor.

Perhaps he was expecting a thank you the day Von Elm turned up at the practice range where Ti was chipping balls. Instead Von Elm said, "Look here, fellow. I hear you think you're a player, but you never enter tournaments. Are you afraid?"

Titanic chipped another ball. "Nope."

"You and I should play, then. I'll spot you nine holes. The stakes will be a hundred dollars a hole." Von Elm stuck out his hand. They shook on it.

A hundred a hole was pocket money, but there was more at stake for Titanic. Von Elm was friendly with another El Rancho golfer, Howard Hughes. The twenty-year-old oil millionaire, who hoped to make a name for himself in the film business, was a serious golfer who played with one of the first sets of steel-shafted clubs.

For Ti, the play was obvious: He'd lose a few hundred to Von Elm, moan about bad luck and bad bounces, then demand a rematch and lose thousands. At that point, he figured, Von Elm would bring the golf-mad Hughes into the picture.

A dozen club members gathered to follow the match between their amateur champion and the lanky left-hander. Von Elm laced long drives with a smooth, languorous swing. Titanic, with his shorter, more percussive move, hooked a ball into the rough on the first hole, as he had planned. His recovery shot found a greenside bunker. By now he had noticed that his opponent wasn't watching. Von Elm gazed into the distance, looking bored, as if Ti were delaying the match. His imperious manner irked Ti as they split the first few holes. Titanic liked to think he could get along with anyone, but it wasn't true. The more golf he played, the more well-to-do golfers he met who were amateurs in name only. They considered themselves pure because their tournaments didn't offer prize money, but they played private matches for more money than professionals like Buddy Brainer ever saw. "It must be distracting to swing with a silver spoon in your mouth," he used to say. Now the smug look on Von Elm's tanned face changed his plans. He outdrove Von Elm on the next hole, punched an iron shot at the flagstick, and made the putt. The rout was on. After nine holes, Titanic had matched the U.S. Amateur champion shot for shot, hole for hole. They were dead even. That meant that Von Elm, who had rashly spotted Ti nine holes, would have to sweep the back nine just to tie.

Von Elm fired a mid-iron shot to the edge of the tenth green. Titanic hit a low approach that bit the green and stopped a yard from the flag. Von Elm, looking stunned, spent a long time looking over the thirty-foot putt he needed to sink to stave off defeat. Then he threw down his putter and stalked off the course, swearing he'd get back at the "dirty cheat" who had hustled him. So much for stalking Howard Hughes, at least for now.

A week later a new mark appeared at El Rancho, a knickers-clad hacker who passed cash around the club for days, talking big without once breaking eighty. He said he was from Omaha, where he was "county champion." Ti picked up the scent and struck up a conversation. They played a round for a hundred dollars a hole. Neither broke ninety. Suddenly the Omaha man offered to play for fifteen grand straight up—no strokes given either way.

Ti blinked. He realized this was a hustle. *His own hustle.* This fellow from Omaha, or wherever he was really from, had set a trap, waiting for the moment when there was real money at stake so he could drop the pretense and play for all he was worth. Ti should have laughed and walked away, but his ego wouldn't let him. Hadn't he just beaten the U.S. Amateur champion? There was room for exactly one top hustler in any town Titanic visited, and he was it. He said, "Omaha, you got a bet."

On the day of their match he was surprised to see a crowd of spectators at the first tee. Then he understood why: George Von Elm, smiling, stood at the head of the crowd.

Titanic opened with a long, arrow-straight drive. Omaha smoked a rocket that outdistanced Ti's ball by thirty yards. The man's second shot homed in on the flag. He birdied the first hole.

Ti had his work cut out for him. Champion golfers, from Jones and Von Elm to Nicklaus and Woods, try their best at all times, but golf hustlers face a different and sometimes trickier task. A hustler spends days topping drives and chunking chips and then, when the time is right, strikes a 280-yard drive followed by a lofted iron shot over water to a green behind a tree. Ti had a knack for that sort of gear-shifting—shooting a hundred as convincingly as seventy—but his opponent had transformed from a nineties-shooter into Bobby Jones. He birdied the second hole to go two-up on Titanic. Fully snookered, Ti had no choice but to tee a ball up and give it a wallop. The way he saw it, "There's times when you just have to put your head down and play."

The course record at El Rancho was sixty-four. Von Elm's ringer from Omaha shot sixty-six. Titanic sank a curling putt on the eighteenth green for a sixty-five. Von Elm turned his back in disgust as Ti and the ringer walked off the green together, Omaha clapping Ti on the back, calling it a hell of day.

6 THE WRONG KIND OF HERO

In the years of his early manhood, no one knew of Titanic except gamblers, a few rich suckers, a few golf pros and, by rumor, the police of the Middle West and California. If Titanic had taken from the rich and given to the poor, as Robin Hood and Jesse James are said to have done, the legend-makers of the gambling world would want no part of him. He would be the wrong kind of hero. But he has always taken very frankly to give to himself, or to split with the people who stake him. He has seldom made a bet he wasn't sure of winning.

—JOHN LARDNER

JOHN LARDNER, THE SPORTSWRITER SON OF FAMED columnist Ring Lardner, was drawn to sports' shady side. He saw Titanic as heavyweight champion of the hustle and wrote up some of his exploits in *True: The Man's Magazine*. Still Ti kept Lardner at arm's length. The last thing he wanted was fame. What Ti wanted, as he built his bankroll in the middle and late Twenties, was a place at the table with the richest men in America. After his victory over George Von Elm's ringer at El Rancho, he returned to San Francisco, but the action there had cooled. Ti and Nick the Greek spent a few nights winning poker pots of one or two hundred dollars, then Nick said they should go to New York, where the action never stopped.

Ti let Nick go first.

The Greek's half of their Kingston Club loot had been burning a hole in his pocket since he heard about a new round of high-money action in Manhattan. By the time he reached Grand Central Station on the 20th Century Limited, after three days and nights in a first-class sleeping car, Nick's pockets felt hotter than the million-plus bulbs that lit Times Square.

He could have walked the four blocks from Grand Central to Broadway, where one night a hundred or so fans waiting for Al Jolson to emerge from the Winter Garden were scattered by Babe Ruth swerving around a corner in his Stutz Bearcat. Nick could have tapped a shadowed door on Forty-seventh Street and slipped into the El Fay Club, a speakeasy where newsman Damon Runyon admired the "many beautiful young dolls who dance around with no more clothes on them than will make a pad for a crutch." But Nick the Greek never walked if someone could drive him, and he wasn't in town to see the sights. He hailed a taxi and told the driver to take him to Lindy's.

Crime boss Arnold Rothstein had his own table at Lindy's, a glorified deli at Fiftieth and Broadway. Rothstein, known to his underlings as "the Brain," was a racketeer, bookmaker, and gambler. The *New York Times* called him "America's kingpin gambler" and "Broadway's greatest chance-taker." Forty-five years old, jowly and balding, he had the pallor of a lifelong indoorsman. He sat in his booth at Lindy's taking telephone calls, giving orders, sipping coffee. Harpo Marx, another Lindy's regular, used to complain that he couldn't hear himself think with all the "cardplayers, horseplayers, bookies, song pluggers, agents and actors" jostling with "Jolson and his mob of fans, and Arnold Rothstein with his mob of runners and flunkies." *Time* magazine described Lindy's as the hub of Broadway nightlife: "All around the little restaurant is a forest of 'broadminded' hotels where a man can keep a girl or a case of liquor or organize a fairly professional gambling game."

Nick found Rothstein at his usual table near the cashier, using a fork to pick at the cheesecake beside his coffee cup.

"I'm looking for some action," Nick said.

Rothstein spoke without looking up. He said, "I might have something."

NEW YORK'S VICE KING had sprung from a virtuous home on the Upper East Side. His father, Abraham, was so revered by his fellow fabric merchants in the Garment District that they dubbed him "Abe the Just." Abraham Rothstein never understood his second son. When the boy was three, he caught him holding a knife to his brother's throat while the older boy slept, saying, "I hate Harry." Ten years later, while Harry studied to be a rabbi, Arnold hocked their father's watch to support a growing gambling habit. "Let Harry be a Jew," he said. "I'll be an American."

As a teenager Arnold gravitated from the respectable Upper East Side to the lawless Lower East, where young goons ganged up on law-abiding shop owners, tenement dwellers, and each other. One thug dispatched enemies by bending them over his knee and snapping their spines. Another handed potential clients a price list: *Shot in leg, $1 to $25; Throwing a bomb, $5 to $50; Murder, $10 to $100.* Arnold, who so abhorred all things physical that he put on his pajamas in the dark each night to avoid seeing his naked flesh, paid other young men to soil their hands on his behalf. He built a small fortune by loaning money at 25 percent interest, fencing stolen goods, and arranging craps games in exchange for a cut of the action. He kept the police out of his hair by buying them off. According to Rothstein biographer David Pietrusza, the going rate for police protection was three hundred dollars a month. Payoffs to New York City police totaled an estimated three million dollars a year. The head of the Police Glee Club shoveled thousands of dollars into his own pockets—in one year he set a record of sorts, selling fifty thousand tickets to a Glee Club show in a hall that seated two hundred.

Rothstein was the slipperiest of them all. During a late-night power outage at Lindy's, "the room momentarily went black, but when the lights returned, A.R. no longer sat where he'd been," Pietrusza wrote. "He had bolted from his chair, maneuvered silently through total darkness and serenely ensconced himself at another table." Rothstein even got away with shooting policemen. When a squad of vice cops pounded on the door during one of his poker games, A.R. fired three shots through the door, felling three cops in their tracks. When the bluecoats burst in to round up the gamblers, his chair was empty. Only later, after an ambulance and a paddy wagon sped into the night, did a bystander point to the fire escape, where Rothstein crouched in the shadows. He was charged with assault, but the charge was dropped after the accused made generous donations to the cops' families and his political friends in Tammany Hall. Walking down the courthouse steps a free man, Rothstein said he might take in a ballgame.

For baseball fans, that was like hearing John Wilkes Booth say he was going to the theater. Baseball betting was the illicit national pastime, and the Brain was its commissioner. John "Muggsy" McGraw, the brawling manager whose New York Giants won the first World Series in 1903, openly bet hundreds of dollars a game on his team. Rothstein was his bookie. Countless fans wagered a dollar or two in weekly baseball pools, with an outfit called the Keystone Pool selling more than 160,000 betting tickets a week.

The money riding on each ballgame dwarfed the players' meager salaries—a gap Rothstein was about to exploit.

The Chicago White Sox, baseball's dominant club, loathed their skinflint owner. Charles Comiskey paid his best players six thousand dollars a year, a third of what other teams' stars earned, and made the Sox pay for their own beer while he treated the sportswriters who covered them to lobster-and-champagne dinners. There was no escape from Comiskey's clutches, since ballplayers were employed in a kind of indentured servitude. They could change teams only if their owners traded or sold them. And so in the summer of 1919, Sox first baseman Chick Gandil hatched a plan to throw the World Series for one hundred thousand dollars. The question was, Who could put up so much cash? Gandil sent an emissary to the one man everyone knew had a hundred grand in his desk drawer if not his pocket.

"Forget it," said Rothstein. The players were unreliable, he said. "They're a bunch of loose lips. I heard you were coming before you got here. Everybody in the country thinks the fix is in." But as the Series between the Sox and the overmatched Cincinnati Reds approached, with the sports pages full of conspiracy theories, with sportswriters and fans wondering if this or that gambler or syndicate was financing the fix, the Brain began to think that all those loose lips could float his boat. As Rothstein put it, "If a girl goes to bed with nine guys, who's going to believe her when she says the tenth one's the father?" He sent Gandil forty thousand dollars as a down payment. Gap-toothed knuckleballer Eddie Cicotte, the best pitcher in the game, sewed his ten thousand into the lining of his sport coat to keep it safe. In the first inning of Game One he dutifully plunked the Reds' leadoff hitter, as A.R. had demanded—a sign that the Sox ace was pitching for Rothstein. Catcher Ray Schalk, who wasn't in on the plot but knew of it, yanked off his mask and fired a new ball to the mound at bullet speed. Schalk's message was clear: *Get an out.* But the pitcher had his orders. After winning twenty-nine games and losing only seven that year, with a 1.82 earned run average, Cicotte grooved slow fastballs and knucklers that didn't knuckle, allowing six runs before manager "Kid" Gleason came out to take the ball. As Cicotte left the mound, catcher Schalk spat at him.

Rothstein was following the game from a packed ballroom in New York's Ansonia Hotel, the city's first air-conditioned building, where a teletype operator handed dispatches from Cincinnati to an announcer who called out the play-by-play. Another man used a six-foot pole to move runners from base to base on a diamond-shaped board that covered one wall. Rothstein had spread $270,000 in bets on the underdog Reds among bookies all over the country. In the first inning, hearing "Cicotte hits Rath with the pitch!" he knew he was calling the shots in this Series. Chicago fans would boo the "Black Sox" during their home games—even "Shoeless" Joe Jackson, the jug-eared slugger from South Carolina who'd had second thoughts after joining the plot and finished the Series with a batting average of .375. Still the fix held. The Sox lost; Rothstein won.

Six months later a Chicago grand jury brought conspiracy charges against the players. "Say it ain't so, Joe!" a boy cried as Jackson walked to the courthouse. Sportswriters said baseball was finished as a major sport. But after Rothstein rode a carpeted, chandeliered railroad car to Chicago and lied under oath, the eight Black Sox defendants were acquitted. Judge Hugo Friend smiled at the "not guilty" verdict. Bailiffs applauded and whistled while Jackson, Cicotte, and the other Sox lifted jury members onto their shoulders as if the jury had won the World Series. Later, when the ballplayers and jurors wound up in the same Italian restaurant, they shoved their tables together and celebrated as one big team. The scandal ended well for Rothstein and for several jurors who made subsequent trips to New York, where A.R. treated them to dinners and ballgames, as well as for Babe Ruth, who erased the stain of

1919 with a 1920 home-run barrage that remade the game. With help from a new, harder, livelier baseball, Ruth swatted fifty-four home runs in 1920, his first season with the Yankees, outhomering McGraw's entire Giants roster. Major-league attendance surged from 2.8 million in 1918 to more than 9 million in 1920. But the show went on without the eight not-guilty Sox. Baseball's new commissioner, a flinty federal judge named Kenesaw Mountain Landis, hired by the owners to clean house, banned the acquitted defendants for life. With that, the Black Sox began their long fade into sepia. Jackson, the best of them, petitioned for reinstatement again and again, citing his .375 average in the Series and the fact that he hadn't taken a penny of the payoffs, but Landis cut him dead. Jackson was reduced to playing semipro ball and running a liquor store in Greenville, South Carolina, where Ty Cobb came in one day for a bottle of whiskey. According to Cobb, "Shoeless" Joe rang up the sale without a word.

Cobb said, "Joe, don't you know me?"

Jackson nodded. "Sure I do, Ty. I just didn't think anyone I knew would want to know me."

Rothstein's role in the Black Sox scandal was his worst-kept secret. The national pastime was tainted forever, some thought, and Rothstein was the one who had tainted it. He was the crook who stole America's innocence. In *The Great Gatsby*, published in 1925, F. Scott Fitzgerald caricatured him as Jay Gatsby's backer Meyer Wolfsheim, "a small, flat-nosed Jew" whose cuff links are made of human teeth. As Gatsby boasts to the book's narrator,

He's the man who fixed the World Series back in 1919.

"Fixed the World Series?" I repeated.

The idea staggered me. I remembered, of course, that the World Series had been fixed in 1919, but if I had thought of it at all I would have thought of it as a thing that merely happened, the end

of some inevitable chain. It never occurred to me that one man could start to play with the faith of fifty million people—with the single-mindedness of a burglar blowing a safe. . . .

"Why isn't he in jail?"

"They can't get him, old sport. He's a smart man."

Rothstein bought an estate in Saratoga Springs, summer play-ground of wealthy New Yorkers. The Brook, a working farm with a thoroughbred stable and water supplied by local springs churned by windmills, would soon become the most exclusive and profit-able casino in America. Men in tuxedoes played craps, roulette, and baccarat, all of it illegal, at velvet tables manned by croupiers culled from Rothstein's stable of up-and-coming thugs, the "hard boys" he sent north from the city. The boss's favorite was Maier Suchowljansky, who shortened his name to "Meyer Lansky." Sens-ing a kindred spirit in feral little Lansky, Rothstein recruited the five-foot five-inch teenager at a bar mitzvah and schooled him in schemes that called for more than the shivs and muscle that passed for criminal enterprise on the Lower East Side. Lansky, a future CEO of Murder, Inc., brought other young hoods into the fold: Ben "Bugsy" Siegel, Charles "Lucky" Luciano, Dutch Schultz, Carlo Gambino, and Frank Costello. Under Rothstein, American crime was getting organized.

Croupiers Lansky and Luciano wielded the rake at the Brook for millionaires like Joshua Cosden, Oklahoma's so-called Prince of Petroleum. Cosden lost three hundred thousand dollars one night and two hundred thousand the next day. On his third day he won twenty thousand dollars and went home to Tulsa boasting about his winnings. He proved Damon Runyon's line, "A man will invariably lose more when he is losing than he will win when he is winning." Runyon's Law favors the house, and at the Brook that meant Roth-stein, who made millions selling his customers casino chips and almost as much selling them drinks.

After the passage of the Volstead Act, Rothstein, who drank nothing stronger than coffee, summoned Lansky. "There's going to be a growing demand for whiskey," he said. "Not the rotgut rubbish your Italian friends are busy making in their chamber pots on the Lower East Side. Good whiskey." One of their early ventures was 100-proof Rothstein: He used a front man in Glasgow to buy twenty thousand cases of Scotch that sloshed across the Atlantic on a rented freighter that dropped anchor off the tip of Long Island. Speedboats met the ship and shuttled the hooch to shore, where it was loaded onto trucks that rumbled west toward the Brooklyn Bridge. This overland part of the operation was run by Jack "Legs" Diamond, a glimmer-eyed twenty-three-year-old psychopath who had gotten his nickname by outrunning the police. Diamond didn't see the point of killing a man without torturing him first. He taught one handcuffed, hog-tied snitch not to snitch by burning off one of his eyelids. Legs saved his victim the trouble of trying to sleep with one eye open by burying him alive in a Long Island pumpkin patch.

Diamond led Rothstein's whiskey trucks to Manhattan, where Lansky directed them to delivery points around town. Other caravans brought booze smuggled from Britain, Canada, Mexico, and the Caribbean. Beer was another moneymaker: A barrel that cost five dollars to brew and transport brought thirty-five dollars at the back door of a speakeasy. With teetotaler Rothstein collecting a generous cut and plowing the proceeds into numbers, prostitution, and narcotics rackets, Prohibition profits built the foundations of twentieth-century organized crime.

ARNOLD ROTHSTEIN WAS SITTING PRETTY the night Nick the Greek turned up at Lindy's in the winter of 1927–28, fresh off the train from California. Rothstein took a bite of cheesecake. He ate with fussy precision to spare his false teeth, which didn't fit right.

His lower teeth were still his own but his false upper plate, unnaturally white, gave him the wolfish aspect Fitzgerald turned into a Semitic cartoon in *The Great Gatsby*.

Rothstein might have smiled up at Nick Dandolos; he was certainly happy to see him. He had heard about the Greek's San Francisco bonanza, and over the next few weeks he lightened Nick's million by two hundred thousand in a series of craps games. Nick demanded a chance to get even at poker. A magazine writer recorded the result: "He dropped $797,000 to Arnold Rothstein in the biggest stud-poker pot ever recorded, Nick's kings losing to Rothstein's diamond flush." That tale may be apocryphal, but there is no doubt that Rothstein and Lansky beat the Greek like a bongo. All winter the name "Nick the Greek" served as a punch line for vaudeville comedians who cracked, "It's the first time the Jews knew Santa Claus was Greek!"

Back in Beverly Hills, Titanic heard about the Greek's tragedy and figured he could give it a happy ending. He knew the men who had broken Nick would think they could break him too. In the spring of 1928 he gassed up the Pierce-Arrow and told Alice, "I'll send for you."

He drove east for a week, stopping here and there to play a little poker. He bought new clothes in Chicago and honked his horn on his way through small towns in Indiana, Ohio, and Pennsylvania, tossing dollar bills at children who came running after his pearl-blue nickel-plated roadster with its leaded windows and wooden-spoked wheels. In easternmost New Jersey he paid a fifty-cent toll and drove into the brand-new Holland Tunnel, a mile-and-a-half concrete tube under the Hudson River. The tunnel smelled of fresh paint. Titanic drove under the river and up into Manhattan with his bowling ball, horseshoes, and golf clubs in the trunk. A satchel in the backseat held his Kingston Club booty: $960,000 in cash.

He couldn't have rolled into New York at a headier time. Paul Robeson was bringing down the house every night at the Ziegfeld Theater, singing "Ol' Man River" in *Show Boat*. Fanny Brice, who had been a galumphing Yiddish vaudevillian billed as "Sadie Salome" when Florenz Ziegfeld discovered her, dueled for the title of Queen of Broadway with her rival Mae West, who had served eight days in jail for corrupting public morals with a Broadway show titled *Sex*. Producer Ziegfeld kept his mistress Lillian Lorraine in a love nest above the thirteen-room suite he shared with his wife at the Ansonia, where Enrico Caruso had a suite down the hall and another tenant, Babe Ruth, rolled baseballs down the stairs. The Tammany Hall puppet Jimmy Walker, a.k.a. Beau James, the Jazz-Age Mayor, danced with Ziegfeld showgirls in a black-glass room at the posh Central Park Casino—"Jimmy Walker's Versailles"—sipping Black Velvets made with Guinness stout and champagne smuggled into town by Rothstein's men. Mayor Walker was nothing if not progressive: He wanted to put a giant lighted wristwatch on the Statue of Liberty.

Titanic passed Times Square on his way north from the tunnel. Perhaps he parked and got out to stretch his legs. A six-foot-two blade of a man in a gabardine suit, he might have bought an ice-cream cone and tipped his hat back to watch the lights blinking firefly patterns up and down the towers on both sides of Broadway.

He rented a suite facing Central Park at the Mayflower Hotel, one of the first in town to offer hot- and cold-running water right from the tap. The next day he tracked down a former Columbia University math professor, Patrick McAlley. Titanic told McAlley that he wanted a crash course in gambling odds, "and I'll pay top dollar." Starting that day they spent long afternoons in the professor's apartment discussing poker, craps, and the odds of various propositions. Ti was most interested in counterintuitive bets. He nodded when McAlley said the odds of getting dealt a pair in a five-card poker hand were not eight-to-five against, as most gamblers believed, but closer to fifty-fifty. Ti had intuited as much while dealing hand after hand on his bed back in Rogers. Now he tallied the results while McAlley dealt five hundred hands. "Turns out it's 103-to-100 against getting a pair," he said years later, "so if anybody lays you eight-to-five or even eleven-to-ten, you get the best of it." Never satisfied with the game on the table, Titanic would put his knowledge to use on side bets: "I'll bet I pair up, and I'll bet *he* pairs up too." The odds were relentless: For every hundred $10 bets he made at six-to-five, he came out $350 to $450 ahead.

McAlley showed Ti that in five-card draw, the chance of turning a dealt pair into two pair or better on the draw is one in three. The odds say *raise*.

The chance of improving two pair on the draw is only one in eleven, since you only get one card. Most players think their odds are far better. Picturing full houses, they raise too much and lose to anyone hiding three of a kind.

The odds against filling an inside straight are 11.8-to-1.

The odds against filling an open-ended straight are twice as good: 5.9-to-1, or 17 percent.

In dice, the odds of rolling doubles are six-to-one. The odds of rolling doubles twice in a row are thus thirty-six-to-one. But the odds of rolling *particular* doubles twice in a row are the square of thirty-six, or 1,296-to-1. Bet a guy that he can't roll boxcars twice in a row in half an hour and you'll win all day long.

There was more: Suppose you flip two coins—it's even money that you'll get a head and a tail. But what are the odds of throwing four coins at once and calling them all? Most people would say four-to-one, but if you call two heads and two tails it's only five-to-three. Flip six coins, call three tails and three heads, and you'll be right almost a third of the time. That one is an eleven-to-five proposition, but Titanic found he could get longer odds from bettors who didn't know the percentages.

He took notes during his math tutorials. His notes were columns of numbers. Still functionally illiterate, he could sign his name and spell simple words but could not read a newspaper. Unable to write the text of a telegram on a Western Union form, he had to tell the clerk what to write. At restaurants, he'd put the menu aside and ask the waitress what was good. But he didn't need words to remember what *1,296–1* meant, any more than he needed names to go with the telephone numbers in his notebook. His mind was numeric; he could scan a row of thirty phone numbers and recognize McAlley's or Nick the Greek's at a glance.

Some New York gamblers carried what was called an East Side bankroll, a wad of singles with a hundred-dollar bill on the outside. Not Ti. When he was ready to challenge the locals, he folded an inch-thick stack of hundreds into his pocket, with a couple thousand-dollar bills on the outside. He combed a dab of Brilliantine through his hair, poked a diamond stickpin through his lapel, tucked his .45 into its shoulder holster, and sauntered south from the Mayflower to Lindy's, where placards in the window advertised FAMOUS CHEESECAKE AND GIFT AND STEAMER BASKETS. He found Arnold Rothstein at the same table where Nick had found him six months earlier. "He always sits facing the door," Runyon wrote of Rothstein, "so nobody can pop in on him without him seeing them."

Ti studied the criminal genius he planned to outsmart. He offered his hand. "Howdy. I'm Alvin, but they call me Titanic." Rothstein, averse to touch, made no move to shake Ti's hand. But that *Howdy* might have gotten a smile out of him. This Titanic character was laying it on a little thick, even for a road hustler.

He invited Ti to sit. They shot the breeze about baseball and the weather. Later, Rothstein told Damon Runyon he had never heard anyone talk like this crossroader who called shrimp "crawdads" and bragged that his car could go from zero to sixty as "fast as a minnow swims a dipper." It was Runyon who noted that for all their differences, Arnold "the Brain" Rothstein and Alvin "Titanic" Thomas had much in common. Neither man smoked or drank. Both were health-conscious to the point of neurosis. Ti never touched fried food—one reason he stayed thin all his life—and spent his first night in any town scouting for a diner that served boiled ham, beans, and potatoes. (Never mind boiled squirrel; nobody had it.) Rothstein had heard figs were healthy, so he nibbled them constantly, keeping a jacket pocket full of figs and replenishing his stash at an all-night fruit stand on Broadway. Ti followed him out there on the night they met. Picking a peanut from the vendor's stand, he bet Rothstein ten dollars he could throw it across Times Square. The vendor reached into his apron and put up a dollar of his own. Ti wound up like Lefty Grove and pegged the peanut over four trolley tracks and five lanes of traffic—the same trick he had pulled in Hot Springs and a score of other towns, palming the real nut and throwing a buckshot-weighted peanut instead. Rothstein laughed and said it was worth ten bucks to see such a stunt.

Runyon took notes that night. Small and nattily dressed, with watery blue eyes behind wire-rim glasses, the famed newspaperman was a Broadway character himself. Runyon shadowed Rothstein night after night, staying awake by drinking forty cups of coffee a day, smoking a cigarette with every cup. His color-coordinated suits matched his socks and his tiny, size-5½ shoes. Runyon was the best writer in the world if you went by his word rate: His sports column in William Randolph Hearst's *New York American* paid him five hundred dollars a week, which was less than the Yanks paid Babe Ruth but more than they paid Lou Gehrig. Still he was usually broke—a steady loser on the baseball bets he made with Rothstein. Already famous, he was about to start the second act of his career: writing fiction loosely based on the gamblers, thugs, and showgirls he knew, sentimental tales in cynical threads that readers came to know as "Runyonesque." But not even Runyon was fully Runyonesque in 1928. At age forty-eight he was just starting work on his first Broadway story, and meeting his unlikeliest hero.

Not until Bill Clinton at the far end of the century would an Arkansan charm the big-city folk the way Titanic did with his quaint talk and clever wagers. He was "tickled" by a joke, riled by a "low-down polecat." Who else would bet he could throw his shoe to the top floor of the fifty-seven-story Woolworth Building, and win the bet? (After making a show of warming up his arm, he walked into the lobby, flipped his loafer to his accomplice, the elevator operator, and said, "Top floor.") Who else could slice a flower off its stem without going near it? To do that Titanic, sitting at Rothstein's table at Lindy's, pointed to a daffodil in a pot. "I'll cut it down from ten paces," he said. He stepped off ten paces, took a few bets, then stepped back five more paces and got some more action. When he was halfway across the restaurant, he pulled out a deck of cards and tossed them one after another. "He scaled cards so skillfully that each sharp edge left its mark," sportswriter Shirley Povich recalled, "until the thirty-fifth card snapped the stem of the flower clean."

One night Titanic stood outside Lindy's with Rothstein and Runyon. No member of this trio could take ten breaths without making a bet. Ti pointed at a passing car and asked the others if they had noticed that license plate numbers could be poker hands too. "I'll bet a thousand dollars the next New Jersey plate we see beats the next New York plate."

Rothstein said, "You got a bet."

A New York plate with a pair of nines looked like a winner until Titanic took off his hat—a signal to a driver he had flagged down hours ago. The driver pulled into traffic and paraded past the three men at five miles an hour, giving them a clear look at the *333* on his New Jersey plates.

Another time Ti bet the Brain could stop thirty strangers and two of them would have the same birthday. Rothstein smelled a rat but couldn't resist 365-to-30 odds. To prevent any cheating he led Ti and Runyon around corners until they faced an oncoming throng in Times Square. Feeling smug, Rothstein popped a fig into his mouth while Titanic stopped passersby and wrote their birthdays in his notebook, with Runyon checking his notes to keep him honest. The twenty-fourth and twenty-fifth failed to correspond with any others. He was running out of chances. But the twenty-sixth was a match, and there was no trick to it. Ti had learned from McAlley that the odds shift in favor of a match with the twenty-third person and improve from there until, by the thirtieth, the wager is a sucker bet.

"I'll explain the math, Arnold, after you pay me."

The counterintuitive math, now studied as "the birthday paradox" in collegiate statistics classes, has to do with increasing likelihoods of an unlikely event. Two people seldom share a birthday, but the chances rise faster than you'd think in groups of ten or more. As the group grows, each new person has an increasing chance of matching birthdays with one of the others. The equation is $p(n) = 1 - p(n)$, where p is probability and n is the number of people. The odds of a match reach 50.7 percent in a group of twenty-three. In a room that holds fifty-seven people, the odds that two of them have the same birthday is 99 percent. Titanic didn't know the equations, but with McAlley's help he understood the odds.

Dice were even simpler: Two dice with six sides each made for thirty-six possible results. For Ti that meant fewer than thirty-six likely results. Rothstein's "floating" craps games, held in shady spots up and down Broadway to escape detection by vice cops, were perfect for Ti and his stiff-wristed dice roll. "The good Lord made the lilies of the field, manna from heaven and lots of fellows who think they can shoot dice," he told Alice, who came to New York to share his rooms at the Mayflower in the summer of 1928. She told him to forget about gambling for once and show her the city. She wanted to dress up, link arms with her husband, and go walking through the crowds up and down the wide avenues. What a wonderful place this would be, she said, for picking pockets.

After a noon breakfast they'd go to the pictures. Ti liked Buster Keaton and the cartoon shorts *Krazy Kat* and *Steamboat Willie*.

Alice loved the new talkie, *The Jazz Singer*, still playing at the War-
ners' Theatre, and Ti told her some gossip about its star, Al Jolson. According to Runyon, Jolson got so jumpy en route to his live
shows at the Winter Garden that his manager had to hire a hooker
off the street to fellate him in the limousine. Jolson often turned
up in the crowd at the El Fay Club, where Titanic and Alice were
welcomed as acquaintances of Rothstein. Owner Larry Fay had
festooned the place with swastikas, his favorite good-luck charm—
Fay also had a fleet of taxis adorned with them—but the club's
real symbol was hostess Mary Louise "Texas" Guinan, a blonde,
buxom former sharpshooter in Wild West shows who perched on
a stool at the door. The critic and writer Edmund Wilson described
Texas Guinan as a "formidable woman, with her pearls, her pro-
digious gleaming bosom, her abundant yellow coiffure, her bear-
trap of shining white teeth." She greeted customers with a hearty
"Hello, sucker!" and waved her favorites to tables near the spotlit
stage where they basked in cool air provided by a bank of electric
fans blowing across hundred-pound blocks of ice. Weekend crowds
included Irving Berlin and Mae West as well as Gloria Swanson,
then starring in the film scandal *Sadie Thompson* and acting offscreen
as mistress to Rothstein's bootlegging rival Joseph Kennedy. One
night George Gershwin jumped onstage to play the house piano.
He was working on a new composition called "An American in
Paris." At the El Fay, celebrities and swells rubbed elbows with
crooks and molls, clinking tumblers of Rothstein's whiskey and
stem glasses of champagne at the starry center of the world. As
Texas Guinan liked to say, "Better a square foot of New York than
all the rest of the world in a lump."

Titanic and Alice drank soda and ginger ale, respectively. Ti paid
for every drink and tipped double. He didn't want to owe Arnold
Rothstein a dime. "Rothstein's a swindler and a gangster and a very
smug fellow," he told Alice, who knew how her husband relished
cutting arrogant men down to size. Some days Ti slipped out of bed

early to join Rothstein, Runyon, Nick the Greek, and other horse-players in a Long Island Rail Road smoking car bound for Aqueduct Racetrack or Belmont Park. "At Aqueduct," the Greek said, "a girl could walk naked ten minutes before post time and be safer than if she was in jail with two eunuchs." They all loved the races—haggling with bookmakers who worked the crowds, keeping an eye out for vice cops since horse-race betting was illegal. Ti dropped around a hundred thousand dollars at Aqueduct and Belmont that year. Nick, more compulsive, lost at least twice as much. Rothstein came out ahead despite getting banished from Aqueduct for fixing a Fourth of July card there, slipping an equine ringer named Sidereal into a minor race. "He's not allowed there anymore," Ti told Alice, "but he goes anyway and nobody stops him."

As the commuter train neared the racetrack, city streets gave way to pastures where cattle and horses grazed. One morning the gamblers were all guessing how many white horses the train would pass that day. They tossed a thousand dollars into a hat, winner take all. Rothstein's "guess" triggered Ti's hoodwink detector. "His estimate was surprisingly high," John Lardner reported in the *Herald Tribune*. "Titanic studied the tycoon thoughtfully before he made his own guess, just one horse above Rothstein's." Sure enough there were fifteen white horses grazing near the next station and a dozen more at the one after that. "The first batch had been planted by Titanic," Lardner wrote, "the second by Rothstein. 'That will teach you not to be close with your money,' said Titanic to Rothstein as he pocketed the money. 'For thirty bucks, you could have had a whole livery stable.' "

The Brain was having his first losing year. He had blown $130,000 at Aqueduct that Memorial Day, dropping $2,000 on the first race and chasing his losses like a sucker, trying to get even until he had lost all six races. Nicky Arnstein said he'd never seen his friend so manic. Arnstein had stayed loyal to A.R. despite being betrayed after they stole five million dollars in Liberty Bonds. (When the district attorney went after the "criminal mastermind" behind the heist, Rothstein let Nicky take the fall. Reporters ran to Arnstein's wife, Fanny Brice, for her reaction. "Mastermind?" she said. "My Nicky couldn't mastermind an electric light bulb into a socket.") After three years in Leavenworth Penitentiary, Arnstein was free again, joining his old confederate at the track and asking why he was betting so madly. Rothstein snapped, "Why do you eat?"

For all the millions he controlled, A.R. was spread thin in 1928. His narcotics trade had grown tenfold in two years, but paying smugglers, distributors, and still more cops every week tied up too much of his cash. A real-estate buy on Long Island went sour. Heavy bets on the upcoming elections—he had Herbert Hoover for president and Franklin Roosevelt for governor of New York—stood to net him more than $550,000 but left him short until November. And while his troubles didn't keep him from betting on cards, craps, horse races, and ballgames, they slowed his paying. When one creditor phoned Lindy's demanding five hundred dollars, Rothstein barked, "I can't hear you." The operator broke in to say, "He wants five hundred dollars."

"If you heard him," said Rothstein, "*you* send him the money!"

According to a *New York World* reporter, Rothstein "loved, almost viciously, to collect, and he hated, almost viciously, to pay." In poker and dice games the son of Abe the Just collected his winnings in cash and left markers—IOUs—to cover his debts.

"I don't have any kind of respect for that man," Titanic told Alice.

He had watched A.R. play cards and dice and knew that the Brain preferred dice. Rothstein was better tuned to the shifting odds of craps than to poker's interpersonal subtleties. Raising, bluffing, checking like a possum when you've got what gamblers call "the nuts"—the unbeatable hand—takes patience, and that was never Rothstein's long suit. So the trap would be a poker game. But first Ti had to make a long-distance call to San Francisco.

• • •

SEPTEMBER 8, 1928: The usual crew sat around Rothstein's table at Lindy's on a Saturday night. Titanic sipped soda water. Rothstein nursed a glass of milk. Runyon lit a Lucky Strike off the butt of another and pinned a fresh red carnation to his lapel. Finally a phone call came for Mr. Rothstein, who listened, nodded, hung up. He reached for his coat. "It's on."

Knowing how Rothstein hated to be touched, Ti clapped him on the back. "Arnold, let's go play some cards."

What the *Times* would call "the biggest stud poker game ever held" began just before midnight that Saturday night. The two gamblers walked five blocks from Lindy's to the Congress Apartments at Fifty-fourth Street and Seventh Avenue, where a Rothstein flunky named Jimmy Meehan met them. Meehan had stocked his apartment with booze, coffee, and a quart of milk for A.R. The host and venue made it a home game for the Brain. Still he stopped Titanic at the elevator. "I'll go up on one condition," Rothstein said. "We play as partners."

For the first and last time, Ti shook Rothstein's hand. "Partners it is."

The game had been arranged by George "Hump" McManus, a lantern-jawed bookie with a smirk that suggested he was thinking of a dirty joke. Hump was a well-connected Irishman with one brother who was a New York City detective and another who was a priest. He led Ti and A.R. into Meehan's apartment, where five professional gamblers sat around the dining-room table: Joe Bernstein, Martin "Red" Bowe, Abe Silverman, and the Solomon brothers, Meyer and Sam, a stubby pair of Beantown sharps the others called Meyer and Sam "Boston." The game was five-card stud, hundred-dollar antes. No poker chips, just cash. In its first hours Titanic and Rothstein, signaling each other when to raise and build the pot, when to fold and limit their losses, were up fifteen grand. Then, just before dawn, one of Titanic's Kingston Club cronies came through the door.

Nathan Raymond was as Jewish as Jolson, but his frizzy hair and rumored sexual taste for black women had earned him a nickname he loathed. Other gamblers called him "Nigger Nate." Titanic knew him as one of the country's top card cheaters and baseball bettors—he had been barred from all Pacific Coast League parks for fixing games—as well as its highest-flying bridegroom. Raymond had married silent-film starlet Claire Omley on an airplane over Mexico, with heavyweight champ Jack Dempsey serving as best man.

"Sorry I'm late, boys," Nate told the others, "but not *too* sorry. I just won eight Gs shooting dice!"

Rothstein instantly offered to high-card him for the eight thousand dollars.

Titanic and Nate Raymond traded glances. This was the moment they had discussed on the phone. Titanic nodded, signaling that he would cover the eight thousand dollars if Nate lost. "I knew right then we'd do some big business," he said later. What Titanic didn't know was that by choosing to double-cross the criminal king of New York, he was changing the course of his life. His signal to Nate Raymond would be a turning point for all of them.

Nate got the high card. Rothstein was out eight grand. The game within the game was on. "I got Rothstein off to the side," Ti recalled years later, "and I said, 'I'm twelve thousand up on the night, so here's your six. We're not partners anymore.' Rothstein got worried. I told him, 'I can't partner a guy betting on high cards. That's an even break I want no part of.' The fact was, Nate and I were going to beat him out of his money."

The next step was enlisting the others. "I slipped everybody money and told 'em to bet like Nate did." Everybody except Hump McManus. Hump would join Rothstein in the loss column that weekend but would lose far less than A.R., who made one-thousand- and five-thousand-dollar side bets on top of the poker hands he played, betting he'd get the next ace or the high spade in the hole. Cheating Rothstein was child's play for Ti and Nate, who marked the cards and traded the usual signals—holding their cards with the top edges flat or at an angle, for instance, or touching their noses or chests, or mentioning a code word ("Need me a *pretty* hand") to tell each other when to fold and when to stay in. Again and again Rothstein got the poisonous second-best hand. The side bets went the same way, his jacks falling to the others' kings and bullets.

The cards flew from Saturday night into Sunday morning. The players heard the bells of St. Patrick's Cathedral in the distance. Meehan dozed on the couch, rising now and then to go out for more food and booze. The action picked up speed on Sunday night, by which time the players could all have used a shower and a shave. As the game entered its thirtieth hour, just before dawn on Monday, Rothstein began betting tens of thousands per hand in a frantic attempt to catch up. Paying with markers, yanking money off the table when he won, he stood beside his chair, eyes bloodshot, his Sulka tie damp with sweat. "I bet ten thousand Nate beats you," he told Titanic, "and five thousand Sol beats you, and twenty thousand *that* guy beats you and twenty thousand *I* beat you!" He lost again and smelled six rats.

Rothstein offered Nate Raymond one last high-card cut of the deck for forty thousand dollars. The others crowded around as Nate held the deck in his palm like a guy offering his girl a diamond ring. Rothstein cut the cards. A deuce.

"It don't appear to be your night, Mister Rothstein," Nate said, cutting a higher card.

"I think some of you play cards with more skill than honesty. I think I've been playing with a pack of crooks," Rothstein said. He grabbed his hat and left.

He had won $51,000 from McManus but lost far more to the others: $319,000 to Nate Raymond; $69,000 to Bernstein; a little less to Bowe, Silverman, and the Solomons; and $30,000 to Titanic, who had played possum, angling for half the others' winnings in exchange for staking them. As Ti tallied it, Rothstein had lost more than half a million dollars, "and half's mine." But all they had to show for their winnings was a stack of IOUs.

Nate said, "Christ, all we got is his word he'll pay."

"Don't sweat. He's good for it," said McManus, whose duties as the game's organizer included making sure any markers were made good. "He'll call you in a couple days."

But Rothstein didn't call. He didn't hide either. Nicky Arnstein found him sitting at Lindy's, grousing about "Nigger Nate" and the rigged game.

"Rigged or not, you have to pay," Arnstein said. "There's no point advertising you were a sucker."

Six weeks passed. Ruth and the Yankees swept St. Louis in the 1928 World Series. The Dow Jones, driven by speculators' bets and consumers' growing appetite for credit, soared toward 300. Both of these outcomes were predictable and potentially profitable for Rothstein, but he made little more than cab fare on the Yanks and the Dow. With half a million riding on Hoover and Roosevelt, he was stalling for time until November 6. When Runyon told him there was talk that Arnold Rothstein was turning into a Welshman, Rothstein swore he wasn't welshing. "I'm just making them sweat a little."

His creditors did more than sweat. Someone phoned Lindy's with a message: "Rothstein, pay your debts." Someone hired a pair of kidnappers who abducted the wrong man, an unlucky haberdasher whose thinning hair and swell suit resembled Rothstein's. An hour later they dumped the panicked fellow in Central Park.

The kidnapping hardened the real A.R.'s resolve. "I'm not giving them a cent, not yet—the gamblers or their gorillas," he said. "If they're looking for me, I can be found any night at Lindy's."

Runyon sat in his customary catbird's seat at Rothstein's table, watching the rain blur the twenty-five-watt bulbs that spelled *Lindy's* on the other side of the window. It was a Sunday in November, eight weeks after the poker game and twenty-six hours till Election Day. Runyon never tired of sitting at the cheesecake-clotted heart of Manhattan, but he had another reason to be at Lindy's that night. He was falling behind in his baseball betting. As Runyon biographer Jimmy Breslin noted, the writer "sat with Rothstein because Sunday night was 'wash night,' when Rothstein and his bookmakers met and straightened out the previous week's sins, of which the only one recognized on Broadway was losing." As usual, Runyon was behind on his bets.

Runyon envied Titanic, who was always ahead of the game. If a guy buying into a poker game asked what the limit was, Ti said, "Sky's the limit." Runyon remembered that line when he wrote "The Idyll of Miss Sarah Brown," his most famous Broadway story, and named his gambler hero "Sky Masterson." Sky's last name was a nod to William Barclay "Bat" Masterson, who had stepped smoothly from life as a Wild West buffalo hunter, cardplayer, and gunfighter to a desk job as sports columnist for the *New York Morning Telegraph*. By 1921 the aging, mustachioed Masterson spent his days getting drunk and his evenings knocking out his column for the rag, a staple of what wags called "the whore's breakfast," consisting of a cigarette and the *Telegraph*. One evening he had a heart attack and died face-down on his typewriter. His final column, unfinished in the machine, read,

> *There are those who argue that everything breaks even in this old dump of a world of ours. I suppose these ginks who argue that way hold that because the rich man gets ice in the summer and the poor man gets it in the winter things are breaking even for both.*

Masterson's hardbitten style influenced Runyon, who described a sermon as "nothing but the phonus balonus" and a scheming showgirl's hair as "black as the inside of a wolf." But Bat Masterson was never a proposition gambler, dice-roller, or country moralist. It was Titanic who ruled Broadway's floating craps games and who, like Sky, first amazed the city boys by chucking a peanut faster and farther than other men could throw a baseball. Ti was the man Runyon had in mind when he introduced *Guys and Dolls* gambler Sky Masterson. As Abe Burrows, who co-wrote the musical, told a reporter, "Runyon had a model for Sky. There was a great gambler and proposition man in those days called Titanic Thompson."

"Of all the high players this country ever sees," Runyon wrote, "there is no doubt but that the guy they call The Sky is the highest. In fact, the reason he is called The Sky is because he goes so high when it comes to betting on any proposition whatever."

Sky Masterson also had a code of honor that set him apart from Runyon's favorite crime boss: "It is well-known to one and all that he is very honest in every respect, and that he hates and despises cheaters. . . . He will never take the inside of any situation, as many gamblers love to do, such as owning a gambling house and having the percentage run for him instead of against him, for always The Sky is strictly a player."

At ten o'clock on November 4, 1928, Hump McManus, seven blocks away in a fourteen-dollar-a-night room at the Park Central Hotel, dialed Central 3317, the phone at Lindy's. Abe Scher, the night cashier, answered.

Scher carried the phone around the cash register to Mr. Rothstein's table. Rothstein, resplendent in a crisp blue suit with white pinstripes, listened. He grunted yes, hung up, and motioned to Jimmy Meehan, who was sitting alone near the kitchen.

"McManus wants me over at the Park Central," Rothstein said. "This won't take long."

Runyon watched Meehan follow A.R. outside. They stood in

shadows, but Runyon saw Rothstein pull a pistol from his coat pocket and hand it to Meehan.

No guns, McManus had said on the phone. No dramatics. That was fine by A.R. He knew it was Hump's job to make sure Nate Raymond and the others got paid, but Hump had held them off for two months already. He could hold them off for two more days. Hoover and Roosevelt looked golden—Rothstein's Election Day winnings would easily cover his debt. And the Brain might get off lighter than Raymond, Titanic, and the others expected. He might offer them fifty cents on the dollar and dare them to go to the cops if they didn't like it.

Hump McManus was registered as "George Richards" at the Park Central Hotel, a pair of brick towers on Seventh Avenue with a courtyard between. There was nothing dramatic about his alias; just a bookie keeping his head down. Rothstein rode a south-wing elevator to the third floor. He tapped on the door of room 349. McManus answered and ushered him into a room that stank of smoke and sweat. There were three other men inside: two tall, thick-chested lugs and Hyman "Gillie" Biller, McManus's bag man, a bantamweight pug who collected on the debts Broadway gamblers owed Hump. Rothstein saw newspapers and empty liquor bottles strewn around the room, and ashtrays overflowing with cigarette butts. A few of the cigarettes bore traces of lipstick, but there were no women in sight.

"Mister Rothstein," McManus said, "I'm getting a lot of static from the boys you owe."

Rothstein took a seat in an armchair near an open window. "They cheated me," he said, "but I'm not going to cheat them, as much as they deserve it. It's just that I couldn't pay now if I wanted to. Tell them to keep their shirts on till Election Day." He was telling the truth, or at least today's truth. Hadn't he stalled the Black Sox when they balked in the middle of the World Series? Stalling worked then and would work now because, as he patiently explained to the drunken Hump, the dubs had two choices: They could wait two days and get paid, or they could annoy him and get nothing.

McManus leaned closer than he would have dared if he were sober. "Mister Rothstein, I got nothing against you, but I am *telling* you to make those markers good." He pulled a revolver. As if on cue, the other three did the same. They stared down at Rothstein, who stared back. Then A.R. started to rise from his seat. He was going to walk out on them. "Goodnight, Hump," he said.

The next sound was a gunshot.

AL BENDER WAS SITTING in his taxi across the street from the Park Central when something shiny hopped the curb and skidded across Seventh Avenue. Bender retrieved it—a snub-nosed .38 Special. Its two-inch barrel was warm.

Mrs. Marian Putnam of Asheville, North Carolina—"an attractive looking woman," according to the next day's newspapers—was waiting for the elevator on the hotel's third floor when a balding man in a gray suit bumped past her. Mrs. Putnam was offended to see that the man was touching his groin.

Two minutes later, at 11:07 p.m., Arnold Rothstein staggered out of the Park Central's ground-floor service entrance, his hands pressed to the wound between his legs, leaving a trail of spotted blood on the sidewalk. To no one in particular he said, "I'm shot."

7 TRIAL AND ERROR

SHOT THROUGH THE GROIN AND BLADDER, ROTHSTEIN slumped against a wall. A crowd gathered. Two policemen hustled up the sidewalk and knelt beside the fixer.

"Who shot you?" they asked.

Rothstein honored the code that said no honorable crook ever yaps to the cops. "With the pain of his wound biting at his vitals and the peering eyes of the cops close to his white countenance, he reverted to type," Runyon reported. "He was no longer the money king with property scattered all over the Greater City, a big apartment house on fashionable Park Avenue, a Rolls-Royce at his beck and call, and secretaries and servants bowing to him. He was a man of the underworld. 'I won't tell.'"

An ambulance sped Rothstein to Polyclinic Hospital, where he got two transfusions and a double dose of morphine. He drifted in and out of consciousness. A detective tried to interrogate him but the patient only smiled and put his finger to his lips. *Shhh.*

The next day brought an unexpected visitor. Rothstein's father, Abraham, had long since declared his son dead to the family, but now the stooped, white-bearded Abe the Just moved through a gaggle of reporters outside the hospital. "He's still my son," the old man said. He spent the day upstairs, holding Arnold's hand. The next day Arnold Rothstein died at age forty-six. The papers called his killing the "Crime of the Century." It was now Election Day, 1928. Had he lived another day he would have won more than half a million dollars for his bets on Hoover and Roosevelt, and the subsequent history of organized crime might have been utterly different.

Three days later a rosy-cheeked Rothstein was placed in a twenty-five-thousand-dollar bronze-and-mahogany coffin with a glass lid. He was buried at Union Field Cemetery in Queens, a short drive from Aqueduct. Twelve policeman were dispatched to the service "to preserve order," the *New York Times* reported. "The crowd, however, was small and the services of the police were not required."

Detectives questioned cabdriver Al Bender, who had retrieved the snub-nosed pistol he saw skidding across Seventh Avenue. They told him he shouldn't have touched the gun. He had tampered with evidence—the only clear fingerprints on it were his. Bender said, "I never thought about fingerprints. I am a hackie, not Sherlock Holmes."

Federal agents searching Rothstein's files discovered records of his payments to Cicotte, Gandil, and other members of the Black Sox. (The fix was his legacy. Forty-five years later, in *The Godfather Part II*, Hyman Roth would tell Michael Corleone, "I've loved baseball ever since Arnold Rothstein fixed the World Series.") Cops at Grand Central Station opened two trunks meant for Rothstein and found two million dollars' worth of opium, cocaine, heroin, and morphine. Fortunately for Mayor Walker and police chief Grover Whalen, who were under pressure to strike back against "lawlessness," the case had the makings of a quick trial and conviction. In his haste to leave room 349, prime suspect McManus had left his velvet-collared overcoat behind. Police found a handkerchief monogrammed *GM* in one pocket and the name *George McManus* embroidered in the coat's lining. McManus was arrested for murder.

By then Titanic had made himself scarce. Initially held as a material witness, he put up his own hundred-thousand-dollar bail and was next seen at Grassy Sprain Golf Club in Bronxville, just north of the city. He promptly won a car in a golf bet with Walter Chrysler, whose art-deco Chrysler Building, then jutting up half-finished from midtown Manhattan, would be the world's tallest when it opened the following year. A gambler of Rothstein's acquaintance had arranged for Ti to play Grassy Sprain club pro George McLean, whose friends put up thirteen thousand dollars and spotted the gangly left-hander eight strokes. Ti, who hadn't played golf on his New York sojourn, used up every stroke. He and McLean stood all square with one hole to play—a commanding position for the pro, whose backers were eager to add a few side bets. After booking their bets, Ti blooped a low niblick shot that hopped to the green and stopped a couple of feet from the hole. A lucky bounce, McLean called it. Titanic, the soul of fair play, agreed. He offered to forget that lucky shot and try again for double the stakes. McLean and his backers couldn't agree fast enough. Now Ti struck a high, postcard-pretty niblick shot that bit the green beyond the flag and sucked back even closer than the first ball. His birdie beat the pro's par. Somebody took his picture and tacked it to the wall in the locker room—not to celebrate the winner but to warn Grassy Sprain golfers not to play the damned hustler in the photo.

Titanic and Alice drove west from Bronxville to Capone's Chicago, then north along the lake to Wisconsin. He wanted to visit a restaurant he had won in a card game. The Golden Pheasant, one of Milwaukee's better speakeasies, offered coffee and sandwiches in a small dining area upfront and gambling in a spacious back room. He and Alice rented a hotel suite nearby and settled into a pattern of late breakfasts in bed and late nights at the Golden Pheasant while the Rothstein case boiled in New York. It was a pleasant enough routine, but if Ti could really see around corners he would have been looking for a more remote corner of the world.

People v. McManus was scheduled for the second week of November 1929, three weeks after the stock market crashed. The trial was delayed for a week because one of the star witnesses was too ill to testify. Titanic lay in a steel bed in Milwaukee's Misericordia Hospital, suffering from a convenient case of pleurisy. "I don't know why they'd want me as a witness," he told reporters, looking pale in his red silk pajamas. "We played cards. McManus lost a lot of money. That's all I know." In fact he also knew that the district attorney misunderstood the case. The prosecution erroneously saw Hump McManus as a vengeful loser rather than as a game operator whose duty it was to make Rothstein pay his debts.

Defendant McManus flashed an odd smile as Judge Charles Nott rapped his gavel in Manhattan's dusty red-brick Criminal Courts Building. Hump turned in his seat and waved to detectives who hoped to send him to the electric chair (where, in the newspaperese of the day, he could "grease the griddle"). In the coming weeks *People v. McManus* would push the stock-market crash and Commander Richard Byrd's South Pole expedition to the bottom of New York's front pages. The state's exhibits included documents proving Rothstein's wealth and the reach of his tentacles, as well as McManus's overcoat, the snub-nosed .38 Special cabbie Bender retrieved, and Rothstein's white silk shirt, stained with sweat and blood.

Early witnesses identified the players in the card game at Jimmy Meehan's apartment. They told of the stakes and the postgame tension between McManus and Rothstein. Detectives recounted finding four whiskey glasses in room 349 at the Park Central Hotel, where Rothstein was shot. A Park Central chambermaid, called to describe the clutter she found in what the *Times* referred to as the death room, made the most of her day in court, dressing in an emerald gown, silver stockings, and golden-heeled shoes. Then came the city's imperious coroner, Charles Norris, who testified that it would be "rather annoying" to be shot in the groin. Later, when the judge called a recess, newsmen charged to a bank of telephones in the hall outside the courtroom. They had nothing to report, but it was almost post time at Aqueduct. They were calling their bookies.

Many witnesses were what the papers called undesirables: crooks, bookies, hustlers. Jimmy Meehan testified that Rothstein carried a snub-nosed revolver to room 349—a lie. Nate Raymond denied pressuring A.R. to make good on his markers. He too was lying. The gamblers agreed on one point: Defendant George McManus was a good sport who wouldn't dream of taking revenge on a welsher.

McManus's bag man, Gillie Biller, the squat five-foot four-inch collector with a scar across his forehead, went unnoticed during the trial. Biller had been a suspect at first, one of America's most-wanted fugitives after he fled to Havana following the shooting. He had been in the room when Rothstein was shot. While detectives examined the death room hours later, the phone rang. It was Biller, asking for "Mister McManus." Was he checking up on his boss? Or trying to incriminate him? The New York police sent a detective to Havana to track down Biller, and twenty-five members of the Cuban secret police helped the detective comb the city, but the bag man got away and prosecutors focused on McManus.

Flashbulbs popped when Titanic entered the courtroom. His picture would be in all the papers. He looked sharp and youthful, according to the *Times*, which put his age at twenty-six, though he was a week shy of his thirty-seventh birthday. In his first public appearance since his days as a medicine-show sharpshooter, Alvin Thomas placed his left hand on the bailiff's Bible and swore to tell nothing but the truth. "Thomas was quite the most sartorial picture among the witnesses," the *Times* reported. "There was not a sag or a wrinkle in his close-fitting suit of light brown. A silk handkerchief, edged with matching brown, drooped from his breast pocket. His tan shoes were twin mirrors of high polish and his plentiful hair was slicked to the last hair. He is a big man, probably on the six-foot mark, and of powerful physique. His eyes are sunk deep in his face—rather boyish, by the way, and his eyebrows, heavy and jet black, added to the cavernous effect of his eyes." Titanic was appearing as a prosecution witness in exchange for reduced bail, but prosecutor Ferdinand Pecora still treated him as a suspicious character. Pecora—a bespectacled crusader who would go on to lead a federal probe of the Wall Street crash and help found the Securities and Exchange Commission—began by asking the witness what he did for a living.

"I play a little golf for money."

The prosecutor feigned surprise. "Isn't it right that you are, in fact, a man who makes large sums of money by gambling at golf, and that you bet on the horses, and that you have played in a number of high-stakes poker games?"

Titanic admitted betting on horses but swore he had a hard time recalling specifics. "You see, I just don't remember things," said the man who knew betting odds down to the decimal point. "If I bet on a horse today and won ten grand, I wouldn't recall the horse's name tomorrow."

Pecora tried again. "Is poker a game of chance?"

Ti told the truth. "Not the way I play it."

Despite laughter from the gallery, Pecora pressed on, asking Titanic to admit that the fateful poker game was rigged. He suggested that Ti and Rothstein had teamed up to fleece McManus, who shot A.R. to get revenge. Titanic said Pecora was wrong, and that too was the truth—the prosecutor still didn't understand that after organizing the game, Hump McManus had been duty-bound to make Rothstein pay the winners. With a glance at the defendant, Ti said Hump McManus wouldn't kill Rothstein to avenge his own losses. McManus, he said, was "a swell loser."

Damon Runyon, sitting in the press gallery, wrote a word in his notebook: *Slim*. Runyon had recently hit on a way to spin what he witnessed on Broadway into colorful fiction. It didn't take much embroidering. His first short story, published in *Cosmopolitan* that year, introduced Dave the Dude, a thug based on New York mobster Frank Costello. (Costello spoke in a throaty rasp that would be the model for Marlon Brando's voice in *The Godfather*.) Another of Runyon's *Cosmo* tales featured "Armand Rosenthal," a Jewish crime boss known as "the Brain." One night Runyon was sitting at Lindy's when a small-time crook offered to take him along on a job. Butch the safecracker brought a neighbor's baby too, because who suspects a man carrying a baby? They slipped into the basement of a coal company, where Butch set the baby on a towel beside a safe. He reached into the child's diaper bag for a fuse and a bottle of nitroglycerine. At this point Runyon took a walk. He was fifty yards away when an explosion shook the sidewalk under his two-tone shoes. Butch ran past with the baby bawling in his arms. When a policeman stopped him, Butch said he was looking for medicine for his kid, and the cop gave him directions to a drugstore. When Runyon published "Butch Minds the Baby" in *Collier's* magazine, the story became one of his most popular pieces of fiction, despite being true right down to the safecracker's name.

Slim. In his reporting on the Rothstein murder trial, Runyon referred to witness Alvin C. Thomas as "Titanic Slim." Three years later, when he turned the gambler on the witness stand into fictional gambler Sky Masterson, he wrote, "As far as The Sky is concerned, money is just something to play with and dollars may as well be doughnuts."

When other reporters altered Titanic's name by accident, calling him "Thompson," not Thomas, press-shy Ti let them perpetuate the new moniker with its tommy-gun echoes. What he didn't like was seeing his picture in the papers. A month before, the only photograph he had to worry about was hanging in the locker room at

Grassy Sprain Golf Club. Now, with the AP and UP news services wiring photos of "Titanic Thompson" to papers all over the country, his picture may as well have hung in every golf club, card room, and dice den in the country.

There was another detail he chose not to correct. As he told his wife and a few others—but not police or prosecutors—he knew who shot Rothstein, and it wasn't McManus.

IN DECEMBER 1929, JUDGE NOTT directed the jury to acquit Hump McManus. Too many witnesses had been "drawn from the most undesirable elements of the population and feel no obligation whatever on taking an oath," the judge declared. The government had failed to prove that defendant McManus had sufficient motive to kill Rothstein or had fired the murder weapon. The government hadn't proved McManus was in room 349 when Rothstein was shot—or even that *Rothstein* was in the room. The trial had collapsed into farce. McManus left the courthouse wearing the monogrammed overcoat that had spent almost a year as police evidence. He rode a limousine from the courthouse to his mother's apartment in the Bronx, where he gave reporters a handwritten note. *"I was innocent of shooting Arnold Rothstein,"* it read. *"This is all I have to say, outside of wishing everybody a merry Christmas."*

More than eighty years later, the Rothstein murder is still officially unsolved. Only the gamblers knew what happened and they didn't talk, at least publicly. On the day McManus went free, Titanic was back on the road. He would not set foot in New York again.

Another hustler might have played it better. Another man might have stuck with Rothstein to the end of the poker marathon at Jimmy Meehan's place, even if it meant carrying him, letting him think he could play cards with the big boys. A less predatory character might have settled for a place in Rothstein's circle, where there was plenty of money for everyone. But Titanic couldn't do that. He had to double-cross Rothstein because Rothstein thought he was smarter than everyone else, Ti included.

As for the murder, Titanic always said he wasn't to blame, not even indirectly. He had rigged the game that led to the shooting, but Rothstein got himself shot by welshing on his markers. The funny thing was that McManus—the low-life gambler everyone from Mayor Walker to a million tabloid readers *knew* was guilty—wasn't. Ti told a few intimates something that has never been reported before: He said bag man Gillie Biller was the one who shot Rothstein. According to Titanic it was Biller, not his boss McManus, who got away with murder.

TITANIC KNEW HE HAD misplayed his hand in New York. "Ti was a hard-headed son of a bitch, and a genius in some ways, but there was a flaw in his act," said Jack Binion. "The flaw was that word gets around. His cons wouldn't work twice on the same suckers, so he'd break people and leave town. And there are only so many towns."

Titanic's frontiers weren't closed, but they were shrinking. He had tipped his hand as a hustler in San Francisco and Los Angeles. He had made fools of the mobster-golfers in Chicago, gotten himself banned at Grassy Sprain and a score of other golf clubs, and now he had burned his bridges and tunnels to Manhattan. Looking back on the double cross that put him in the headlines, he said, "I famoused myself out of a good situation."

He sent Alice home to Pittsburgh while he drove west. He promised to phone her soon. Communications were improving, which was a mixed blessing for Ti, who became the subject of a telegram from Oklahoma City police to the NYPD: *Alvin (Titanic) Thompson, figure in Rothstein murder case, in Okla City, claims to be diamond salesman.* Ti fled to Arkansas, where he hustled a little cold-weather golf. He was in Little Rock on December 31, the last day of the Twenties.

That morning's *New York Times* headline read, ROTHSTEIN ESTATE GETS $12,700 JUDGMENT—*Default Judgment Against "Titanic Thompson."* Rothstein's lawyers, chasing down the remnants of an estate valued at three million dollars, had called in an old marker of Ti's as well as a $1,173 IOU from Fanny Brice. On the same day, as if to prove Lady Luck was as fickle as Runyon claimed, Ti was arrested in Little Rock. The city's publicity-hound police chief told reporters that the notorious Titanic Thompson was "in our fair city hiding from New York underworld figures." So Ti spent New Year's Day of 1930 in a Little Rock jail cell on a charge of illegal gambling—or, as the chief quipped, "making golf too expensive for members of our local country club." Jailed overnight for the first time in his life, Titanic pitched pennies with the guards and said hello to citizens who came to gawk at him. He was sitting in his cell when the word came from Pittsburgh: Alice was dead.

She had gone for a walk. Not far from the spot where seventeen-year-old Alice tried to pick Titanic's pocket a dozen years before, she stepped off the curb. A speeding car sent Alice flying. She died before the ambulance arrived.

The Little Rock police chief let Titanic out of jail on his promise not to hustle golf in Little Rock, at least while the chief was still chief. Ti reclaimed his .45, his bankroll, and his diamond rings from a sergeant who had kept them in a lockbox. The sergeant offered to drive him to his hotel, but Ti chose to walk.

He wasn't the brooding type. Brooding wouldn't bring Alice back. Regret made no more sense than wishful thinking. Nor did love, as far as he could tell. He had always had a farm boy's skepticism about romantic love, suspecting it was some poet or preacher's idea to gussy up the barnyard realities of sex. Maybe love was just sex with a ring on your finger. Still he suspected he had lost something irreplaceable when his second wife died. Titanic would marry three more times, but long after Alice's death his last wife would say, "Alice was the one he really loved."

8 THE WIDOWER'S AMBUSH

TITANIC WAS A GHOST IN HIS OWN HOUSE, RATTLING around his empty mansion in Beverly Hills. Alice's clothes still hung in the closets, scented with her perfume. He thought about selling the house but decided to stay long enough to attend to some unfinished business. He still wanted to hustle Howard Hughes.

The film mogul stood six feet three and generated power with a frame even leaner than Ti's. Hughes entertained Hollywood friends in a Spanish-style villa wrapped in bougainvillea beside the eighth hole at the Wilshire Country Club. With a handicap of two he dreamed of being, in his words, "the best golfer in the world." Hughes apparently didn't know that the gulf between two-handicappers and the best golfers in the world was as wide as the muscle gap between Mickey Mouse and Jack Dempsey. He fancied himself a bit of a hustler, betting tens of thousands of dollars per round and distracting opponents by having naked girls appear on the balcony when the golfers passed his villa. He also liked to double or triple the stakes on the eighteenth hole. As Hughes told his tutor, George Von Elm, "Golfers wilt when there's real money at stake."

Ti's old nemesis Von Elm came within a whisker of immortality at the 1931 U.S. Open. Tied with Billy Burke after four rounds, he battled Burke through a thirty-six-hole playoff at the Inverness Club in Toledo, Ohio, and tied him again. Out they went the next day for another thirty-six holes in 105-degree heat. Their two-man playoff would last as long as the tournament that led up to it. Finally, on the 144th hole, Burke lit the last of the thirty-two cigars he smoked during the Open. Later he said the smoke from that cigar helped him gauge the wind. He beat Von Elm by holing a final putt in what is still the longest playoff in U.S. Open history. For the tournament, Burke took 589 strokes to Von Elm's 590.

Von Elm warned Hughes about Titanic, who prowled around El Rancho and the Wilshire Country Club looking for a game. When Ti asked the starter if Mr. Hughes had a tee time today, the answer was always no. He was told Mr. Hughes was on a movie set. Or perhaps he was "auditioning" an actress. (Hughes's favorites received gifts of mink-lined lingerie.) Maybe he was playing another course, or flying a plane of his own design. Or both: Running late for a golf date with Katharine Hepburn one day, Hughes crash-landed on the eighth fairway at Bel-Air Country Club. He climbed out of the wreckage, pulled his golf bag from the cockpit, and joined Hepburn at the ninth tee.

While stalking Hughes, Ti infiltrated the movie colony. His new friends drank champagne while he stuck to soda water, known as "two cents plain" for its price at newly popular soda fountains like Schwab's on Sunset Boulevard, where Charlie Chaplin liked to jump behind the counter to mix milkshakes. Actresses and would-be actresses were attracted to the tall gambler with the slight drawl, and losing Alice hadn't erased Ti's libido. "He was magnetic," said one of his golf partners. "He'd look at a girl and she'd go weak in the knees." If they wound up in bed he didn't disappoint. According to a woman who slept with him years later, Titanic was a sexual athlete whose nickname suited his private dimensions. "Most men were nowhere near him," she said.

Ti claimed Myrna Loy was his first great Hollywood flame. As he told it, the button-nosed beauty was with him the day he crashed one of his Pierce-Arrows. She escaped unscratched while he banged his head on the windshield, emerging with a gash that left a scar on his scalp, a thin bare spot where no hair grew back. He told later lovers that after his fling with Myrna Loy he bedded Loy's costar in *Libeled Lady*, Jean Harlow. The platinum-blonde sex symbol was bubbly company, he said, and beautiful—as lean and fit as he was. "But scratchy," he said. "Her skin was rough to the touch."

Still hoping to corner Hughes, he left word at El Rancho, Wilshire, and Bel-Air, offering a friendly round. Titanic thought he'd struck paydirt when another golfer told him Mr. Hughes had agreed to play him at dawn the next day. Late-sleeper Ti stayed up all night. At 6:00 a.m. he dropped his golf bag in dewy grass at the first tee. He waited an hour. A foursome teed off and moved down the fairway into morning mist. Then another. Hughes never showed, and Ti thought he knew why: Von Elm had sent the other golfer to lie about Hughes's plans, leaving him waiting around like a sap. A match between Titanic Thompson and Howard Hughes would have been a showstopper—they were almost mirror images, tall, thin, and beady-eyed, both with powerful upright swings, Ti from the left side and Hughes from the right. Ti would have made sure they reached the last hole all square, with something like a million dollars on the line. But to his lasting regret, Hughes eluded him. They played the same courses and some of the same golfers in 1931 but never played each other. In the end, Hughes would quit the game when he realized he lacked the talent to be a world-class golfer. He threw his clubs away—by then he was afraid they carried syphilis germs—and never played again.

With Von Elm warning golfers to avoid him, Titanic had

famoused his way out of another gambling opportunity. In Los Angeles, New York, Chicago, and many other towns he was now, in the words of one news story, "Titanic Thompson, the well-known sure-thing gambler." Nobody wants to bet against a sure thing. Ti sold his house in Beverly Hills, packed up his Pierce-Arrow and aimed it east on U.S. Route 66.

THE CLOUDS OVER THE ROAD ahead were dead farmland blown into the sky. The Roaring Twenties had led to what newspapers called the "Dirty Thirties," a time of Depression and dust. Almost half the banks in America failed between 1929 and 1932. The price of wheat fell to twenty-five cents a bushel, half what it cost to grow it. A quarter of a million family farms failed. Fifteen million men were out of work. Thousands squatted in shantytowns called "Hoovervilles," named after the do-nothing president. In the Hooverville in New York's Central Park, men dug latrines within sight of the Mayflower Hotel suite where Ti and Alice lived in 1928. The Hooverville in St. Louis had a population of more than a thousand, several churches, a tin-walled bank, and a mayor. Farther west, drought and intense farming exhausted the soil of the Great Plains, turning America's breadbasket into the Dust Bowl by the middle of the decade. People said capitalism had failed. And as they would in later crises, they blamed bankers and Wall Street speculators, two sorts of losing gamblers. That made the early Thirties a welcoming time for outlaws. The frontier spirit lived on in John Dillinger, a grade-school dropout from Indiana whose bank robberies fit the country's anticapitalist mood. Dillinger handed loot to bystanders who cheered as he drove away. A Texan named Clyde Barrow, who started out by stealing cars and turkeys, made headlines sticking up filling stations and grocery stores with his poetry-writing moll, Bonnie Parker (*Their nature is raw, they hate all the law*, she wrote). He and Bonnie shot plenty of clerks and cops but were cordial with hostages and almost always set them free. Dillinger and the Barrow Gang would be dead soon, shot to pieces by the law, while Titanic rolled through the Plains states playing games of chance. A photo from this time shows him in a double-breasted suit and Borsalino fedora, a sharp dresser like Dillinger and Barrow, with a shotgun under his arm. "For self-defense," he said.

After the McManus trial, heisters knew what Ti looked like and knew that he played for tens of thousands of dollars. He hired drivers who also served as bodyguards, providing protection as well as transportation and company on the long empty roads between towns. He terrified some of his drivers by showing off his own driving skills. "He'd take the wheel and zoom around a bend at sixty miles an hour," said one of his traveling partners. "In reverse." Ti's romantic methods could be just as flagrant. Driving past some pretty girls, he would sometimes slow to a walking pace, wave a hundred-dollar bill, and say, "Come for a ride and it's yours." The money was theirs even if they only rode once around the block. By today's standards Titanic was a lecher, but by his lights he was a gentleman. He said he preferred young girls because they were purer and nicer than older women. Cuter too. He never forced his affections on them. He was polite, even courtly, and only slept with girls who agreed. The rest were free to enjoy a luxury car ride as long as it lasted. Traveling with a pretty young thing on his arm enhanced his reputation, and he was starting to enjoy his underground fame. If he could no longer slip into a town incognito, he'd be a high-living good-time gambler, the kind other men want to play, or to be.

In 1932 he motored through East Texas with two dark-haired sisters from Benton, Kansas. The older one, Yvonne Raney, was seventeen. She had agreed to ride in the silver Pierce-Arrow only if her sister Jo Ann went along. Jo Ann was fifteen. The three of them sped east on Texas Highway 80 through brown lowlands dotted with oil derricks. A mile below them lay a black sea of crude, the

East Texas Oil Field, one of the biggest in the world. Near Tyler the oil wells gave way to crisscrossing swaths of color that delighted the girls. After an early-century blight wiped out the local peach crop, Smith County farmers had switched to roses. Titanic and the Raney sisters drove between miles-wide fields of rosebushes, red and yellow blooms that ran to the horizon on both sides of the road.

They took a suite at the Blackstone Hotel in Tyler. Yvonne and Jo Ann drank lemonade and listened to country-western music on the radio—Jimmie Rodgers yodeling his number-one song "Roll Along, Kentucky Moon"—while Ti scouted the local golf course. Chatting up the professional, he said it looked like the kind of track where a halfway decent player could break seventy his first try. The pro puffed out his chest and said he sincerely doubted it. They bet five hundred dollars. Ti picked out a teenaged caddie and had the boy hold the stakes, five hundred from each of them, which the wide-eyed caddie crammed into his pockets. Ti shot sixty-nine, there being no need to do better. He claimed the money and tipped the caddie twenty dollars.

The boy asked, "Mister Thompson, how come you don't play the pro tour?"

Titanic laughed. Few events run by the Professional Golfers Association (PGA) paid the winner as much as he had just earned in one quick round. "I couldn't afford the cut in pay," he said.

That evening—Friday, April 15, 1932—he was sitting in the hotel with the Raney sisters when his car horn sounded. He had rigged the Pierce-Arrow with a rudimentary alarm: If anyone tried to hot-wire it, the horn blared. He stuck his Colt .45 in his belt and went outside.

It was getting dark. The horn had stopped. He looked the car over and was turning back to the hotel when a voice stopped him. "Put up your hands or I'll shoot!"

In one motion Titanic spun and dropped to one knee. He knelt to present a low target, knowing that most shooters are nervous, and nervous shooters tend to miss high. He saw a thief in a ski mask pointing a pistol at him. Ti fired four times. "I shot him over the heart and through the mouth," he remembered. "Then I went to put my foot on his gun, and he talked. He couldn't speak very plain because he was bleeding from the mouth. He said, 'Help, Mister Thompson, I think you've killed me.'"

When the police arrived, they lifted the robber's mask, revealing the face of the caddie who had carried Ti's clubs that day. Titanic told him he had better tell the cops the truth. The boy obliged in a faltering voice: "I tried to stick him up."

The shooting made news. In New York, where readers remembered Ti as the sharp-dressed witness who called Hump McManus a swell loser, the *Times* headlined its story *GAMBLER KILLS A CADDY*: "A.C. Thomas, notorious gambler, known as Titanic Thompson, fatally wounded Jimmy Frederick, 16-year-old golf caddy, when the youth, according to his story, attempted to hold him up last night."

Titanic's fifth killing was the first he regretted. He paced the suite at the Blackstone that evening. "If I knew it was just a boy I'd have given him the money," he said. After a restless night he reported to the police station. He was there for less than an hour. The chief announced that he had no cause to hold Mr. Thomas a.k.a. Thompson given Jimmy Frederick's confession. Privately he urged Ti to leave town and take those two girls with him before he got into trouble on a morals charge.

Titanic lit out with Jo Ann Raney while her big sister Yvonne stayed behind. To keep from running afoul of the Mann Act, which prohibited transporting females across state lines for "immoral purposes," he married fifteen-year-old Jo Ann.

Titanic turned forty that fall—in November 1932, the month Franklin Roosevelt crushed Herbert Hoover in the presidential election. Ti must have thought back four years to the time when Rothstein bet on those two to win the presidency and the governorship of New York, respectively. Now Roosevelt was promising

Americans a "New Deal." Ti took it as a good sign that FDR, an avid stud-poker player, chose a gambling term as his theme. (During the campaign Hoover had scorned Roosevelt's New Deal as a card trick, "a new shuffle.") It was a bad sign, however, that Roosevelt to build wanted a national police force to close in on outlaws of all sorts. Soon the word *Federal* would turn J. Edgar Hoover's Bureau of Investigation into the FBI. Along with the New Deal came another change: The Twenty-first Amendment, ratified in 1933, repealed Prohibition after thirteen years. Titanic didn't care one way or another about that flipflop. It might bankrupt some of the bootleggers he had been playing since 1920, but there would always be men he could part from their money. The urge to gamble couldn't be repealed.

Still a reed-thin 170 pounds, with faint crow's-feet at the corners of his eyes, Ti began recruiting a series of younger golf partners who could shoot par or better, handle a gun, and do most of his driving for him. While the other man drove—Jo Ann rode in the back or relaxed at the hotel in one gambling town or another—Ti devised new propositions and variations on old ones. His weighted-peanut trick became a bottlecap toss. Bottlecaps are too light to throw far, but by hiding a quarter inside and pressing one of the cap's ridged edges down to hold the quarter in place he made a thumbnail-sized discus he could sail a city block and a half. His lemon-throwing con evolved into wagers that saw him hurling pumpkins. In Kansas City he bet a bunch of high rollers that he could fling a pumpkin onto the roof of the Dixon Hotel, ten stories over Baltimore Street, where a ten-foot pennant reading *DIXON* flapped in the breeze. Titanic produced a pumpkin the size of a baseball and threw it to the roof. Then, just to be sporting, he offered double or nothing that he could fling a second midget pumpkin clear over the hotel, which occupied a full city block. Not even Bob Meusel, the cannon-armed Yankee outfielder, could make such a throw. Ti won the wager with help from a partner who hid on the hotel's roof, waiting to grab the little pumpkin and pitch it off the far side.

Watermelons were a bigger task. Hefting a twenty-pounder, passing it around to his betting partners to prove it was real, Titanic admitted he could never throw it to the Dixon's roof. Yet he claimed he could heave it onto the roof of the six-story building next door. Several of his previous victims turned him down. At this point they wouldn't bet against him if he said he could throw a melon to the moon. Ti had to give odds to drum up a couple of hundred-dollar wagers, including one from a man who said it would be worth a hundred dollars just to see how he did it. Whereupon Ti carried the watermelon into the Dixon and rode the elevator to the top floor. From there he climbed a flight of stairs to the roof and pitched the melon down to the roof of the building next door, four floors below.

He and Jo Ann drove through the panhandles of Oklahoma and Texas, where dust storms blurred the air. Ahead of them a dust cloud two miles high rolled through Potter County, Texas, blackening the sky, turning the Canadian River to mud. They detoured to San Francisco, where Titanic phoned the golf pro he had beaten out of fifty-six grand a few years before. Ti said he was thinking about playing some money matches.

Buddy Brainer said, "Not with me."

"Yes, with you—as partners."

Brainer was wary but Ti won him over. They spent a week teaming up against Kingston Club gamblers and other wealthy men who remembered novice-golfer Titanic as a pretty fair stick. Now he was much more than that. Brainer's end of their action amounted to a little over fifty thousand dollars, and Brainer later claimed that his week as Ti's partner proved that Titanic Thompson had a heart, but Ti said it was just business.

Ti and Jo Ann made their way back to Joplin, Missouri, where he had leaped Snow Clark's pool table two decades before. Between the city proper and the zinc mines beyond the city limits sat Oak Hill Golf Club, where the club pro was a hot-tempered, chaw-chewing Arkansan named Ky Laffoon. A gifted ball-striker, Laffoon could barely finish a sentence without pausing to spit a gob of tobacco juice into a Dixie cup. After watching the twenty-five-year-old smash a few balls on the range, Titanic said, "You hit it too good to be working here." He offered a deal: They'd go on the road for a month, play money matches as partners, and split their winnigs fifty-fifty. Titanic would cover their losses, if any, and Laffoon could drive Ti's car. With a glance at the streamlined Pierce-Arrow Silver Arrow in the parking lot, Laffoon agreed.

Ti knew some Oklahoma oilmen who played high-money golf by day and poker all night. In Bartlesville, he and Laffoon beat Washington County's richest golfers with Ti playing right-handed. They doubled the stakes and won the next day with Ti playing lefty. In the evenings Laffoon sat by a brass spittoon watching Ti play cards with John Phillips, heir to the oil empire that had dotted the plains with Phillips 66 stations named for the family and the cross-country highway. The men played seven-card stud, an outgrowth of the five-card game. Poker was evolving—soon a still-more complex game would spread from southeast Texas. Known today as "Texas hold 'em," the new game began as an offshoot of seven-card stud. It was called "hold 'em and fuck 'em," and its strategic and psychic complexities compared to those of stud the way chess compares to tic-tac-toe. But Texas hold 'em was still an occasional sideshow on the night Ti sat at a velvet table dealing seven-stud hands to haggard, half-drunk John Phillips. This new petroleum prince was known for carousing after midnight "holding a half-empty whiskey bottle in one hand and a wad of money in the other," wrote Michael Wallis, John Phillips's father's biographer. John was no match for a predator like Ti, who broke him without mercy, as he did to men he disliked. But the nincompoop still wouldn't quit. "John upped the ante," Wallis wrote. "He put up his house—the one his father built for him and his family. Titanic barely smiled as he dealt the last hand. He glanced down and saw nothing but royal faces and wild cards. . . . John's house with the mahogany railings, the fancy fountain, little Betty's brick dollhouse in the backyard—it all belonged to Titanic Thompson." The next day Ti sold the house back to the Phillipses and rejoined Laffoon at the golf course.

They worked their way south, hustling the best and richest players they could find at country clubs and goat-track public courses north of Dallas. Laffoon would work a few rounds caddying for Titanic, who would lose and then swear, "I'll take this fat caddy and beat you and any pro you want." Laffoon would spit in his hands and shoot sixty-five without so much as a practice swing. Pitted against local champions backed by businessmen, Ti would make heavy side bets with the other golfers, who often fell apart when playing for their own money. During one tight match he and an Oklahoma rancher both hit into bunkers. Ti had Laffoon sneak ahead and drop a ten-dollar bill in the sand near the other man's ball. When the rancher arrived he picked up the money, saying, "Look what I found!" Ti had to point out that moving any object in a hazard is against the rules. "That'll cost you a stroke," he said—his margin of victory. At a lakeside course, Titanic bet club members he could knock a fifty-yard niblick shot into a rowboat. They gave him five tries. He splashed the first four balls and lost the wager when his last shot caromed out of the boat. The next day, swearing he was going to prove himself or go broke trying, he bet ten times as much that he could pull off the shot in only three tries. This time his ball stayed put. He had filled the bottom of the rowboat with sand.

Since Titanic never played tournaments, it is hard to say how good a golfer he was. Several professionals considered him one of the best players of his time. Accurate off the tee if less powerful than some pros, he had a deft, handsy short game that made him deadly around the greens. He was more than a match for his partner Laffoon, who went on to win ten times on the PGA tour and join Walter Hagen and Gene Sarazen on the United States' 1935 Ryder Cup team. The 1958 U.S. Open champion, Tommy Bolt, a teenager when he first saw Ti play, said, "He had a compact swing that didn't require much practice, a gambler's swing. There's no telling how great the guy could have been." Paul Runyan, a Ryder Cup teammate of Laffoon's, called Titanic the best left-handed golfer in the world. Straight-arrow Runyan admired Ti's game but not Ti: "He was crooked and unscrupulous. He was also the most fascinating human being I ever met."

As a partner, he was blunt. When Laffoon left a putt short, Ti needled, "You can't get it in if you can't get it up." Laffoon was a nervous putter who suffered from bouts of the yips, but his tee-to-green brilliance and Titanic's short game made them perfect ham-and-eggers. "We never lost a match," Ti boasted. They emptied pockets from Wichita Falls to Abilene, Waco, and Dallas, but Laffoon soon left to make his name on the tour. Over the next decade he often ranked near the top of the money list—second to Runyan in 1934 with $6,419.22 for the year—while fighting his putter, sometimes literally. Once, after four-putting a green, Laffoon held the club head-down in a water hazard, shouting, "Drown, you son of a bitch!" He would punish the same putter by tying a rope to it and dragging it behind his car, watching in his rearview mirror as it kicked up sparks. And at the 1938 Cleveland Open, his yips led to one of the weirdest finishes in golf history. On the final green, he had a two-stroke lead and a five-foot birdie putt. That gave him three putts from five feet to win. He left the first putt short, then missed again. In a rage he hammered his putter straight down at the ball, which popped into the air about waist high and fell into the cup. He won by a stroke.

Titanic would miss Laffoon but not his chaw. He was tired of finding brown spots on the driver's side of his Silver Arrow after his partner drove. Years later Laffoon's yellow Buick would be famous on tour for the brown racing stripe on its driver's side.

＊   ＊   ＊

MEXICO WAS NEXT. The ponies had foiled Ti's every effort to win money off them. For every hundred dollars he made at other games, he contrived to lose fifty at one track or another. But a mare named Nellie A was going to change his fortunes. She was going to help him break the bank at Agua Caliente, a racetrack in the boiling flats southeast of Tijuana.

Maybe he picked Nellie A because her name reminded him of the girl whose honor he had defended by knocking Jim Johnson off the riverboat *Rambler*. But unlike that Nellie with her scent of violets, Nellie A carried a distinct whiff of glue. The smart money expected her to finish last in the sixth race the day after Ti and his wife arrived at Agua Caliente. He went around the barn introducing himself to the poorly paid jockeys, offering them $500 each to lose the sixth race, more than they'd earn for winning it. They got $250 upfront with his promise of another $250 after they came in second or worse. Only one rider turned him down. The jockey whose mount would be the odds-on favorite refused Titanic's bribe.

That didn't stop Ti. He phoned bookies all over America, distributing bets until he had $120,000 on Nellie A. But that much action wouldn't stay secret. Word got around and Nellie A's odds dropped from twenty-to-one to five-to-one. Ti responded with another round of calls, betting a few thousand on the favorite and a couple of other entries. By post time the odds had bounced up again and he had paid a second visit to the favorite's jockey. "See here, *señor*," he said. "I've got a friend here today. He's on the roof. He's a sharpshooter." Titanic mimed aiming a scope-sight rifle. "*Bang!* He's gonna shoot any jockey comes in ahead of my horse. *Comprende?*"

Nellie A went off at twelve-to-one. Titanic, sitting in a private box overlooking the finish line, watched the starter's flag send the horses on their way. He was less than three minutes from collecting almost $1.5 million. "My horse hit the stretch about a hundred yards ahead of the field," he recalled. "She was so far ahead her jockey could have stopped to light a cigar and still won. I never get excited but I was hollering like a fool, so happy to finally hit the horses a big lick."

Then Nellie A fell. She had broken her leg. As she flailed on the ground, railbirds were treated to the spectacle of seven jockeys standing up in their stirrups and hauling back on their reins, trying not to win. Horses skidded sideways. The favorite's jockey jumped off and ran for cover as his riderless mount cantered across the finish line.

9 OIL, FATS, AND THOMAS THOMAS

THEY PUT NELLIE A DOWN AND TITANIC WAS OUT MORE
than a hundred thousand dollars. "The toughest bet I ever
lost," he called it. Nellie A had broken him for the moment, but
her collapse also gave him a story to tell on himself, to prove how
beatable he was. "Humble-ish" was how he felt.

"But I wasn't broke more than six hours." He promptly wired
Nick the Greek for a loan. The money arrived with a telegram:
Only madmen and drunks bet high on the horses. Ti laughed when Jo
Ann read him Nick's words, since the Greek had blown more at
the track than any hundred common railbirds. He wouldn't have
been surprised to hear that Nick was on his way to Aqueduct at
that very moment, armed with a tip on a sure thing that would cost
him twenty thousand dollars. They both knew the ponies were
for suckers, and yet both lost millions on them. The races were
the one form of gambling Titanic hadn't outsmarted, but he was
sure he would win in the end. In that way he followed the lead of
a great nineteenth-century con man and card sharp, Elijah Skaggs,
who came out of Kentucky in the 1820s. Skaggs beat his family
and friends out of two thousand dollars and parlayed his stake into

a fortune playing faro, America's most popular card game in the pre-poker age. Skaggs retired a wealthy man, running a plantation worked by two hundred slaves, but his luck turned when he invested his three-million-dollar fortune in Confederate bonds. He lost every cent and died penniless.

Titanic may or may not have known the Skaggs story, but he knew its moral: Every real gambler dies broke.

Like the rest of them, Ti thought he was the exception.

He turned Nick the Greek's loan into a new bankroll and moved on. He had liked Texas and figured it was safe there as long as he stayed out of Tyler, where he'd shot and killed caddie Jimmy Frederick. Much of the state was golf country, home to manicured country-club courses paid for with oil money. Titanic motored past pecan orchards where Mexican workers used long cane poles to shake the tree branches, dislodging the pecans, while others followed behind gathering the nuts in bushel baskets. He was headed for Fort Worth because he had heard two youngsters there might make good golf partners, a couple of boys named Hogan and Nelson.

Texans Ben Hogan and Byron Nelson rose from the caddie ranks at Fort Worth's Glen Garden Country Club. Glen Garden was upscale, one of the few courses in the state with grass greens. Other courses made do with brown sand greens where you had to use a rake to smooth a path from your ball to the hole. Golf prodigy Nelson, a lean six-footer with an effortless swing, came from a churchgoing family. Glum runt Hogan grew up scrabbling, often sleeping in sand traps to make sure he was the first caddie in line for a bag the next day. His family had settled in Fort Worth because the city had a hospital where his blacksmith father could get treatment for manic-depression. When Ben was nine years old, Chester Hogan walked home from the hospital and said he wasn't going back. His wife said he couldn't stay home; he still needed help with his "black moods." At that, in full view of his son, Chester produced a .38 revolver and shot himself in the heart. Six years later, fifteen-year-old Ben, five-foot three and 120 pounds, walked seven miles to Glen Garden to play the taller, stronger Nelson in the annual caddie tournament. The winner would earn a junior membership in the club. Nelson knocked in a long putt on the last hole to win by a stroke. He got the junior membership. Hogan was told to find work elsewhere. Bitter, angry, hungry Hogan hiked down the road to practice on courses with sand greens. Titanic found him on a sun-baked driving range in the early Thirties, hitting ball after ball after ball like a mechanical man.

Ti said, "Son, I like your swing."

By then Hogan was a second-year pro who occasionally won a few dollars in local tournaments. He made pure contact nine times out of ten and hooked the tenth ball out of bounds. No one ever practiced harder to perfect his swing, but that hook tormented him. With a tournament or a hundred-dollar bet on the line, Hogan's wrists would turn over an instant too soon, giving the ball too much leftward spin. He blamed his hook on "jumpy nerves" and compared it to a snake. "It nauseates me," he said. Titanic told him to remember the nine pure strikes, not the hook. Then Ti lined up money matches for them to play as partners. Hogan had never seen a golfer as deft around the greens as his new partner, who split their winnings without asking the young man to risk a dollar of his own. With Ti's help Hogan landed late-night work as a blackjack dealer and croupier at the Halfway House, an illegal gambling den midway between Fort Worth and Dallas, raking dice just as the young Meyer Lansky had done in Rothstein's casino.

They encountered another newly minted professional on a road trip. Like Titanic, Sam Snead gulled city folks by playing up his rural roots, describing his honey-smooth swing as "pretty as a red heifer in a flower bed" and claiming falsely that he grew up playing barefoot back in Ashwood, Virginia. Snead played for high stakes and usually came out one stroke ahead. He won proposition wagers by sailing playing cards across hotel lobbies and by leaping up to touch ceilings with his toe—the latter a feat of pure acrobatic skill. On the day they met, Snead asked Titanic, "Just how good are you?"

Ti said, "Play me and find out, pro. I'll take four shots a side."

"Tell you what," Snead said. "I'll play left-handed and *you* can give *me* strokes."

"No thanks," Ti said. "I've heard of that one."

They agreed to stay out of each other's way. Two of golf's cleverest gamesmen, they wouldn't get around to playing each other for twenty years, two decades in which Snead took some of Ti's cons to the tour and regaled other pros with Titanic tales.

Snead and Hogan became stars on the nascent pro tour. Still they often earned more in fifty-dollar side bets than they won in tour events. In those days only the top five or six finishers in a typical pro tournament won anything. The rest lost their entry fees. Only the biggest events, like Bobby Jones's new invitational, the Masters, paid the champion as much as a thousand dollars. Paul Runyan claimed the 1934 money title with total earnings of $6,767. The future U.S. Open champion Lloyd Mangrum reached a New Orleans tournament flat broke and slept in the city jail. Course conditions ranged "from OK to simply goddamned awful," said one pro. In Florida, players stretched their budgets by picking oranges and fishing for dinner. Walter Hagen once unloaded his whole squirming catch, including an alligator, on the clubhouse floor at the Miami-Biltmore Four-Ball, an event players adored because each entrant got a free bottle of White Horse Scotch, plus a tin of Lucky Strikes for every birdie.

Even the most upstanding pros played money matches on the side. In 1934 several members of Fort Worth's Ridgelea Country Club put up two thousand dollars to back Hogan's rival Byron Nelson against Titanic. "I told them I wasn't a gambler," Nelson recalled. "They said, 'We'll do the gambling. You just play.' " The twenty-two-year-old Nelson, who would sweep the Masters and

U.S. Open three years later and be hailed as golf's Lord Byron, one of the four or five best golfers ever, shot sixty-nine to Ti's seventy-one. He thought he had won. "I was pleased with my play." Later he discovered that Titanic had dickered with Nelson's backers before the match and convinced them to spot him three strokes.

Nelson remembered Titanic's "very sharp eyes," he told *Golf Digest*. "Those eyes could look a hole through you."

Hogan, Snead, and Nelson, all born in 1912 and destined to rank among the top golfers in the game's history, admired Titanic's talents. Hogan would recall Ti's knack for working the ball—slicing or hooking a shot around a tree, or punching the ball between bunkers to a rock-hard green—and call him "the best shotmaker I ever saw. Right- or left-handed, you can't beat him." The hustling Snead called Ti "golf's greatest hustler," a title that might have required as much skill as being the game's best tournament player. And Nelson, shortly before his death in 2006, said there was "no question" Titanic could have excelled on tour, "but he didn't have to. He was at a higher level, playing for $25,000 a nine while we played for a hundred and fifty dollars." Twenty years older than the Hall of Fame threesome, Ti was a golfer from another time who still called his nine-iron a niblick and referred to backspin as "English" as if the green were a pool table. He wasn't inclined to report to a course at seven in the morning three or four days in a row in hopes of winning a thousand dollars, even if he could add another thousand in side bets as Snead and Hogan often did. For reasons of temperament and timing—his prime came just before the tour's purses began to grow—Titanic was the last great player to ignore tournament golf.

He seldom trusted skill alone. The great poker player Johnny Moss, who hustled golf on the side, once bet a man five thousand dollars that he could shoot forty-five or better for nine holes using only a four-iron. Titanic appeared out of nowhere and bet three thousand against Moss. "They didn't know it, but I'd practiced for days with that four-iron," Moss remembered. "I'd even given the greenkeeper a hundred to keep the cups where I liked them." On the first hole he missed a three-foot putt. "I wondered how I could miss an easy putt like that." The same thing happened on the next hole—his ball was heading for the cup when it veered off. Moss realized that someone had tampered with the cups. (It was easy, Ti admitted later: "You just reach a pocket knife under the rim of the steel cup-liner and lift it a little.") So Moss sent a friend running to the third green to step on the hole and push the liner back down. "Ti's conniver is on the fourth green raising 'em up and my man's on the third stomping 'em back down," Moss said. "It went on like that for a hole or two, till Titanic stepped out of the crowd. I said, 'So it was you?' Ti just grinned. I told him I'd call off my man if he called off his. I shot forty-one and took all the bets." After that Titanic and Moss teamed up to beat other golfers out of sums ranging up to a hundred thousand dollars. In one legendary match Ti employed a trick that was the conceptual opposite of the one he had used on Moss. He had been thinking about those steel cup-liners, asking around until he found a handyman who helped him rig a car battery and jumper cables to magnetize a few of them. They planted magnetic liners in the last three greens of a course Ti was about to play. He had a twenty-five-thousand-dollar match set up for the following day, and brought a new box of First Flight golf balls.

"Titanic's putts kept sucking right into the hole," said gambler Rudy Durand, who saw the trick years later. "Those First Flight balls had steel centers."

TEXAS HAD BEEN OIL COUNTRY since a fountain of crude gushed a hundred feet into the sky over Spindletop in 1901. Indiana was better known for corn, but the late Thirties brought an unlikely oil boom to the tri-state region where Indiana, Illinois, and

Titanic (*right*) in the early 1930s,
sharply dressed despite the Depression.

(*Family photo*)

Minnesota Fats and Hubert Cokes teamed with Titanic
to fleece suckers from Evansville to Norfolk to
New Orleans in the 1950s.

(*Freddy Bentivegna*)

Titanic left his third wife, Jo Ann, and son Tommy
behind in Evansville after World War II. Tommy wouldn't
see his father for more than fifteen years.

(*Family photo*)

Three years after the hustlers' showdown at Horizon Hills, Lee Trevino eyed the putter he would use to win the 1968 U.S. Open.
(*© Bettmann/Corbis*)

Soon after dueling Trevino at Horizon Hills, became one of the PGA tour's biggest stars.
(*Augusta National / Getty Images*)

Titanic and Jeannette, his last wife, in Texas around 1960.
(*Family photo*)

Long after his prime, Titanic still won more than he lost
in card games around Dallas.

(*Family photo*)

Titanic, at age seventy-seven, cohosted the first World Series of Poker with B-movie actor Chill Wills. In this 1970 photo, WSOP inventor Benny Binion has his right hand on Wills's shoulder, his left on Titanic's, while the game's greats grin for the camera.

(UNLV Libraries, Special Collections)

Actor Chill Wills
handed Titanic his
Living Legend trophy
at the first World
Series of Poker.
(Family photo)

In his dotage,
fighting arthritis,
Titanic won bets
against younger
golfers. "I'll even
play you left-
handed," he said.
(Family photo)

Kentucky meet at a bend in the Ohio River. Evansville, Indiana, had a lunch-bucket labor force that dressed for church on Sunday and kept the local Negroes in line with burning crosses and the occasional lynch mob. There was a red-light district near the train station and a riverbank swamp called "No Man's Land," where men and boys cast dice for dimes and paid up to a dollar for teen whores who dyed their hair platinum blonde like Jean Harlow's. In 1937 a few local farmers noticed oily rainbows in their well water. The following year they struck oil in Posey County, just west of Evansville. Speculators leased the farmers' land, sank wells, and the farmers and speculators got rich together. Gamblers descended on the town, settling in at card tables in the McCurdy and Vendome hotels, playing seven-stud with the farmers and speculators for pots that could reach fifty thousand dollars. According to the *Evansville Press*, "newfound oil was spilling over like a spring flood and riches awaited the soul with the bankroll and the guts" to win at those card tables.

Titanic heard about the action in Evansville from Hubert Cokes, the boy who had helped him pull his cards-in-a-hat trick on Mister Not Enough in Hot Springs twenty years before. Cokes was now a hulking six-foot-two, 220-pound sharp whose specialty was one-pocket pool.

Then as now, most pool players preferred eight-ball, the classic game of college dorms and coin-op tables in which the goal is to pocket stripes or solids and then win by sinking the eight ball. Eight-ball is easier than straight pool, the traditional format for billiards tournaments. Paul Newman as Fast Eddie Felson and Jackie Gleason as Minnesota Fats played straight pool in the 1961 movie *The Hustler*, calling their pockets on every shot. In straight pool each ball is worth a point. Players must earn a certain number of points, usually 100 or 150, to win, re-racking when there's only one ball left on the table. So straight pool can be slow—one famous game lasted 120 hours. Then there's nine-ball, a faster game seen in the *Hustler* sequel *The Color of Money.* Nine-ball calls for the lowest-numbered ball on the table to be struck first until someone pockets the yellow nine. If a player sinks the nine ball on the break, the game's over in a matter of seconds.

In short, straight pool is pocket billiards in its classic form. Eight-ball and nine-ball are pool at its most popular. And in the words of one professional, "They're all for chumps."

As poker Hall of Famer Amarillo Slim Preston put it, "No real gambler plays eight ball. And straight pool, where you can hit any ball in any pocket? That's for people looking to get their picture in the paper. One-pocket's different."

In one-pocket pool, the experts' game, players must sink each shot in a designated corner pocket at the foot of the table. Minnesota Fats called it "the most elaborate, scientific pool game in the world." And Hubert Cokes was one of one-pocket's leading scientists. After getting rich in Evansville oil and investing his winnings during the first years of the boom, he ruled the action at Adolf's Bowling Alley and Pool Hall. Sporting a gray suit set off by a red silk bow tie, Cokes peered down his cue through black-framed glasses that would have made him look professorial if not for the muscles bunched under his jacket. His shaved head earned him the nickname "Daddy Warbucks" after the kindly tycoon in the *Little Orphan Annie* comic strip, but Cokes was as kindly as a pit bull. He would stride into pool halls and announce, "I'll play anybody in one-pocket, or fight anybody, for all the money in the joint." Once, when a stranger tried to cheat him, he grabbed the man by the hair, dragged him outside, and beat him half to death. People said he had won a fistfight with Baby Face Nelson and got away with shooting the sheriff of Garland County, Arkansas, in a fight over a girl. He married the girl.

Titanic and Cokes had crossed paths over the years, two old cronies trading tips on where and whom to play. When Ti hit Evansville in 1939, they teamed up for the first time since their

Hot Springs days. For Cokes, hero worship had ripened into friendship. He helped Ti settle into the McCurdy Hotel, a red-brick palace with Persian rugs and chandeliers in the lobby. Ti and Jo Ann would sleep till noon and go to movies at the Savoy and Orpheum theaters. Jo Ann indulged a growing taste for whiskey sours in the downstairs bar while Cokes showed Ti around town. The local oilmen had heard of Titanic and wouldn't bet much against him. But Evansville was full of gamblers. "Beat the gamblers," Cokes said, "and turn your money into oil leases."

Ti started at the pool hall. He was a nine-ball and one-pocket expert but not a world-class pool player, having spent more time practicing golf because that's where the money was. In Evansville as elsewhere, the swells at the country club tossed around thousand-dollar bills with Grover Cleveland's portrait on them while the hungry characters in the pool hall sweated over fivers. Still there were a few top-dollar cues in most towns. In Evansville, Titanic took them on all at once. "That was his pool M.O.," recalled pool pro Fast Larry Guninger. "Why should he spend all night playing game after game when he could get everybody betting on one trick shot?"

Ti's favorite ploy was the three-rail kick-in. He'd place the eight ball on the foot spot—the dot on the table where the apex ball sits at the start of a game—and put the cue ball six inches away. "I can bank this cue ball off three rails and knock the eight in that corner pocket," he said. On any three-rail shot, the least imperfection multiplies three times until even tournament players can miss the eight ball by a foot. Titanic swore that his three-rail shot was so tricky that even he would need ten tries. After drumming up a few bets from the eager beavers in the room, he gave holdouts a more tempting offer: To beat them, he would have to sink the eight ball in only five tries. Then, after chalking his cue, mopping his brow with a handkerchief, and sinking the eight on the fourth or fifth attempt, he said he felt lucky and gave the losers a chance to get even. "*Three* tries. Double or nothing." His victims whooped and howled as the cue ball traced its path around the table, finally clicking the black eight ball and sending it tumbling into the corner pocket. It wasn't Ti's only trick shot, just the one he'd practiced the most.

COKES HEARD ABOUT A HIGH-MONEY card game in North Carolina—a chance for Titanic to play against men who had never heard of him. Cokes gave him a $2,500 stake and off Ti went, returning a few days later crowing about the $50,000 he had cleared. He gave Cokes $25,000, but Daddy Warbucks wasn't buying Ti's story. "I sent one of my boys down to Charlotte to check out that game," Cokes told a friend, "and he told me Ti won over a hundred thousand."

Nobody got away with cheating Hubert Cokes. "I went to the McCurdy before he woke up," recalled Cokes, who packed a pair of .45s in matching shoulder holsters so he could draw with either hand. "I busted into his room and said, 'Ti, do you have a pistol? Because if you don't, I'll give you one of mine and shoot you with the other.' He was still in bed with his wife. He sat up, all nice and meek, saying 'Hubert, would you kill your best friend lying in his bed?'"

Ti padded to the bedroom closet in his silk pajamas. He pulled a suitcase full of cash from the closet, counted out $25,000 and handed it over. "We're square now, Hubert."

But they weren't. Titanic liked to say every square gambler "has a square A-hole," meaning that squares get screwed. In fact Cokes's informant got the story wrong—Ti's take in Charlotte had been well over $100,000. He was still holding out on Daddy Warbucks.

Cokes found out and swore Titanic was a dead man. He marched through the McCurdy's lobby while the desk clerk, who got a weekly tip from Ti to keep his eyes open, reached for the telephone. The clerk's call gave Ti a chance to grab his .45 and duck down the hall to the stairs. By the time Cokes pounded on his door, Ti was sitting in the lobby, facing the elevator, ready to shoot his friend in self-defense. "I didn't want to shoot Hubert," he remembered, "but if it was him or me it wasn't going to be me."

Minutes bled by on the oversized clock above the hotel's front desk. Ten minutes. Fifteen. Someone tapped him on the shoulder. It was Cokes, pointing a gun at Ti's nose. Too smart to ride an elevator to an ambush, he had slipped down the stairs and sneaked through the hotel's ground-floor restaurant to the lobby.

"Ti, you heartless no-good son of a bitch," he said.

"Yes, Hubert?"

"Let's go play some golf."

They played at Helfrich Golf Course, a ragged municipal layout where Cokes used a modified pool cue as a putter. He got down on his hands and knees and stroked putts into the hole as if the greens were pool tables. Cokes's putter-cue was illegal, but Titanic didn't call him on it. Ti made a point of losing twenty-five thousand—the rest of the Charlotte cut he owed—and then spent a couple months on the road with Daddy Warbucks. As Cokes recalled, "We never lost. We bet high day and night at cards, pool, bowling, golf and propositions. I was better at pool, Ti was better at everything else. He was a genius. He'd give you the odds on bets he made twenty years ago. And what eyesight! We were looking over the river to the Kentucky side when he said, 'Hubert, do you see the little boy hugging his mother?' I could barely make out the buildings over there. I took a pair of binoculars and saw a woman with a child in her arms."

Ti won enough at his various ventures to bid on the oil leases Cokes recommended. He won bowling wagers by rolling games in the 200s and betting other gamblers they couldn't bowl 100. That was a con: When the cash was down he noted that 99 would be a losing score and so would 101—or for that matter, 300. To win the bet they had to bowl exactly 100, which is about a hundred times harder than it sounds.

One night, after betting that a local champion couldn't bowl 100 blindfolded, he paid spectators to keep perfectly quiet after the bowler donned his blindfold. The local champ lost his bearings and rolled one ball at the front door.

Ti invented new coin-tossing hustles too. In one he dropped a quarter on the floor, stepped back twenty feet, and underhanded a fifty-cent piece so that it flipped the quarter into the air and the quarter came to rest on top of the half-dollar. Like his three-rail kick-in, the stunt was the result of many hours of practice. When his marks tried it, they couldn't even hit the quarter with the second coin. They were often glad to offer him long odds or five or ten tries. Then he stepped up and did it on the first try. Those who saw the trick never forgot it, but a hustler who knew him wasn't surprised. "Anything Ti offered to bet on," he said, "he could do in one try."

Titanic had missed out on the first giddy days of Evansville's oil boom, when bean farmers who signed oil leases with *X*s became millionaires. The farmers he met in 1939 wore overalls and dipped snuff while quoting commodities prices from the *Evansville Press* and *St. Louis Post-Dispatch*. They wanted tens of thousands of dollars for the right to poke holes in their fields. Ti needed a way to convince them to work with him.

One stubborn farmer who had turned down twenty thousand dollars for his mineral rights was sitting on his porch when a midnight-blue touring car approached, a 1937 Pierce-Arrow Model 1702 limousine with snow-white sidewalls and a distinctive shallow "V" in the front bumper that made the car look like it was smiling at its owner's good fortune. Titanic, dressed in a summer suit, parked by the porch. He tipped his tan fedora to the farmer and opened the car's trunk. "Got something for you," he said. A bushel basket full of fifty- and hundred-dollar bills. A couple of the bills on top blew away in the breeze. Ti let them go. He put his hat on the rest of the money to keep it in the basket. "Twenty thousand dollars," he said. "I'm hoping to leave it right here on your porch, and we'll be partners."

If twenty thousand dollars had been an abstraction to the man before now, this bushel of money wasn't. The farmer signed over his oil rights

Titanic drove up to other farmhouses with shoeboxes, suitcases, and feed bags full of cash. The gesture worked often enough that he soon had about a dozen wells—what he liked to call his "portfoli-olio"—pumping about two hundred dollars a day in oil revenue. After two years in Evansville he could have retired at the age of forty-eight. But earning by owning never appealed to him. He wanted to win money, not just collect it.

Returning from his oil fields one sticky August afternoon, he passed a truck loaded with watermelons. He flagged the driver and asked what they'd pay for the whole load at the farmers' market in Evansville. Seventy-five dollars, the driver said.

"I'll give you two hundred to drive past the McCurdy Hotel, and you can keep the melons," Ti said.

That evening the gamblers were milling around the McCurdy, sipping coffee from the ground-floor Java Shoppe, watching the big clock over the front desk, waiting for the card games that started around six. Ti pointed at the watermelon truck passing the hotel. "Looky there," he said. "I ain't seen melons like that since I left Arkansas. I used to be real good at counting watermelons when I was a boy. Fact is, I'll bet I can guess how many melons are on that truck, give or take a few." He booked bets that his guess would be within ten of the total. A few holdouts wanted a smaller margin of error. Ti shook his head at what tough customers they were, but he went along. "Okay, within *five*." He tipped his hat back and circled the truck, scratching his head. "Well, hell. I'm going to say there's six hundred and nine." He gave the driver twenty dollars to count the melons—for the second time, since the driver had counted them earlier and phoned Titanic the number. The man dutifully recounted 610 melons. Ti cleared a little over a grand, which was less than his weekly oil revenue but more satisfying.

IN 1942 HE BOUGHT A HOUSE on Stringtown Road, one of Evansville's better addresses. The place had a mansard roof with a weather vane, flower beds full of roses and honeysuckle, and a red-bud tree that turned lavender in the spring. "I'm an oilman now," he told a reporter from the local paper.

His bride, now twenty-four, dressed in the plain skirts and blouses Evansville women wore during the war years. Jo Ann liked the house and the town but she didn't see much of her husband, who spent most of his time with Hubert Cokes. The men played golf all day at the country club or Helfrich municipal course before moving on to shoot pool at Adolf's. One night Daddy Warbucks pointed out a portly visitor who wore alligator shoes and carried his two-piece cue in an alligator-skin case. Despite his size, the fat man was nimble as he stepped around the table to line up spinning bank shots that trickled into a pocket on the last turn. Cokes introduced the two players, then watched tall Titanic and the squat stranger chalk their cues under a green-shaded bulb and play one-pocket for fifteen thousand, or more than two hundred thousand in 2010 dollars, doubling the stakes when Ti began losing.

When Ti threaded a ball down the rail to his pocket, the fat man tapped the butt of his cue on the floor, the pool player's word-less *good shot*. That was the only wordless thing this character did. Whether he was watching Ti play, powdering his pink hands, or running six racks without a miss, the newcomer never quit talking. He rattled on about beating "the world's champeen Willie Hoppe," the difficulty of finding shirts with a size-19 neck, the time he ran a thousand balls in a row, this damned war set off by "the Japs and the Shickelgruber set," how he ate a hundred dollars' worth of chocolates a day—and how hungry he was right now. At which point he sank the last ball and paused for breath.

"Fatty wins again," he said.

His name was Rudolf Walter Wanderone Jr., and he was born in Harlem in 1913 to Swiss-immigrant parents. His father was a plumber and small-time gambler, his mother a knitting-mill worker who earned twenty cents a day. Their coddled "American *bube*" was four when his father won a goose in a picnic raffle. The old man let the goose drink wine and whiskey, and the boy followed the drunken, honking bird around the neighborhood. When the goose staggered into an amusement pavilion, young Rudy saw men playing pool. "I forgot about everything else," he always said. "By the time I was six I could run a rack of balls. At ten I was playing for serious cash."

In 1926 the self-described "thirteen-year-old man" left home. While Titanic and Nick the Greek were fleecing Kingston Club gamblers in San Francisco, Rudy Wanderone was riding the subway from Harlem to Forty-second Street to polish his game at Hoppe's pool parlor over the Roseland Ballroom. He took nickels and dimes off other truants while the sound of big bands playing the Lindy Hop thumped through the floor. Rudy won more in a single game of straight pool than his mother earned in a year. His heroes were the gamblers he saw at Willie Hoppe's and in Broadway's dice dens: Arnold Rothstein, Nicky Arnstein, and Nate Raymond. One day Rudy saw "the greatest proposition man who ever lived." Titanic didn't notice the chubby boy at the edge of the action that day, but Rudy remembered his role model.

Like Ti he spurned tournaments and was never the official champion of anything. "I'm not one of those 'fun players' looking for a trophy," he said. "I play for the gelt." The gold. He beat former world nine-ball champion Cowboy Weston. He challenged straight-pool champ Willie Mosconi and "whacked him out," Rudy claimed. (Mosconi said it was the other way around.) By his early twenties the young man with the Diamond Jim appetite stood five feet nine and weighed 260. He said he followed the formerly poor-boy diet—"steak for breakfast, steak for lunch and two steaks for supper." "New York Fats," they called him, or "Double-Smart Fats" for his smart-guy act. A hustler had to be "a top-notch actor, on account of he plays below his speed until the cash is all aligned, then he shoots out the lights," Fats said.

At Adolf's Bowling Alley and Pool Hall in Evansville, with Hubert Cokes watching the show, the top pool hustler of all time took a thirty-thousand-dollar bite out of Titanic.

Fats mopped his brow with a hand towel. "Want to go again?"

Ti said, "I've had all I want."

Fats looked hurt. "What if I play with one hand?" Ti had met another kindred soul.

He went on the road with Cokes and Fats. Leaving Jo Ann in her big new house, he kissed her and said he loved her. It was probably true. He liked the fire in her. One night when a raging, soused Cokes attacked him at Adolf's, Jo Ann grabbed a bowling ball and whanged Cokes on the top of his bald head, hard enough to knock him out. But now Ti's young wife sat by the fireplace while he and Cokes and Fats went from one gambling town to the next, using gas-rationing stamps they won in pool and card games to fill up the Pierce-Arrow. They made quite a trio, Titanic and Cokes standing in a smoky poolroom while Fats the jowly chatterbox ran ball after ball, crowing that he was so deadly "brave men develop rigor mortis lookin' at me." Lesser players were "mooches, mopes and brokes," he said, while he himself was "part professor, part patron saint and a master of the elocution game." He drank Coca-Cola constantly and gulped fudge-ripple ice cream by the gallon. Of Fats's fifty-five-inch waist, Amarillo Slim joked, "I could've used his belt to rope cattle." Once, shifting his weight on a game-winning shot, Fats felt the floor cave in under him. He caught himself by spreading his arms, catching himself before he fell through to the floor below. "And it turned out okay," he said. "The ball fell, too."

IN 1944, SIX YEARS BEFORE *Guys and Dolls* opened with Robert Alda as Sky Masterson, a surgeon at Memorial Hospital removed Damon Runyon's cancerous larynx. By then Runyon had smoked perhaps three hundred thousand cigarettes. Walter Winchell, the *New York Daily Mirror* columnist who worshipped the man he called the "Grey Ghost of Broadway," led Runyon around town. The mute Runyon communicated by scribbling notes on a pad. One night they were on Fifty-fourth Street outside the Hotel Elysée, where Tallulah Bankhead hailed cabs by throwing open her coat to show she was nude underneath. Runyon, now weighing a hundred pounds in his sharpie suit, smiled at the crowds and hubbub around them. He handed Winchell a note: *Listen to the roar.* After Runyon died, the *Times* reported, "Col. Eddie Rickenbacker, a flying hero of both world wars, scattered his ashes over Broadway." It was a fitting end: Rickenbacker's plane dipping toward Times Square, Runyon's ashes floating toward the guys and dolls below. Let other men lie under the ground, he went out as confetti.

That same year, the FBI followed a lead out of St. Louis: "Alvin Clarence Thomas, alias Titanic," had been caught waving a U.S. Army Colt .45 at a man who refused to pay a dice debt. He went free, but a teletype from Washington, D.C., dated September 11, 1944 (no record of subject being convicted of a felony and no record of gun in national stolen property file), proved that the suspect was of interest at the Bureau's highest level. The teletype was signed, "HOOVER."

Walter Winchell ran a 1944 item datelined *Evansville, Indiana.* In a column syndicated in two thousand papers worldwide, Winchell told his estimated fifty million readers that legendary gambler Alvin "Titanic" Thompson had become a father:

Likely as not, ole Titanic had a sizable wager with his wife on whether their baby would be a boy or girl. And while yours truly isn't too well versed on such matters, it stands to reason that Mr. Thompson, who burst to fame at the Arnold Rothstein murder trial in this city, had the odds worked out so he had a sure thing before he took his wife to the hospital.

Jo Ann gave birth to a boy and named him Thomas. The child's legal name was Thomas Thomas. He wasn't entirely welcome in the house on Stringtown Road because raising a family was feisty Jo Ann's idea, not Ti's. They had argued from the day she told him she was pregnant. He wasn't the fathering type, he said. Kids were loud; they'd disturb his sleep. So he gave her a choice: "You'll have to choose between me and that child. If you want me to stay, you won't have it."

Jo Ann had made her choice. She didn't want to grow old alone. She was going to have the baby. That meant divorce, Ti said, and she agreed. But if he wanted a divorce, she wanted his oil wells. Ti thought about that, then said it sounded like a fair deal. He signed over all his oil deeds, more than a dozen of them. He could probably have kept a couple, but he knew he was no oilman and figured he could always make another million. Miscast as a homeowner and husband, he had been a road gambler with a lawn and flower beds. He packed his suits and ties, golf clubs, bowling ball, Colt .45, a suitcase full of cash, and a picture of Jo Ann and the child, and left Evansville behind.

10 A HOMECOMING

TITANIC WAS TOO OLD TO SERVE IN WORLD WAR II. NOT so sportswriter-turned-war-correspondent John Lardner, who was taking notes on Iwo Jima when a Japanese sniper's bullet whistled past him, struck a pile of rocks, and sent a pebble up to bruise his groin. Weeks later Lardner discovered that the ricochet wasn't a pebble after all, but a small-caliber bullet that worked its way out of one of his testicles as he was taking a shower. He limped to his typewriter to finish a *True* magazine story on Ti. "A fellow gambler who ran across him says that Titanic's pajamas and dressing gowns, always brilliant, are more brilliant than ever," Lardner wrote. "His supply of jewels, rings and stickpins is at high tide. A man like Ti buys jewels whenever he is in the money, to sell or hock when times are hard."

After the war Titanic breezed into Virginia Beach, where sea winds sent hats flying and cooled the bare midriffs of women wearing the latest two-piece swimsuits, some of which showed four full inches of stomach. Three of those women were traveling with him. "He moved into town like a real sultan," Fats recalled. "He was on a brand-new wife, a gorgeous doll named Maxine. And he brought along her sisters, Betty and Bonnie, who were even more fabulous-looking than Maxine." The former Maxine Melton, the fourth Mrs. Alvin Thomas, was sixteen on her wedding day. That made her an "older woman" according to her husband, since Jo Ann had been fifteen when he married her. Fifty-three-year-old Titanic rented an oceanfront villa, where he lived with Maxine and her sisters. Gossips called them his harem. He let people picture him in bed with all three Melton sisters but there is no evidence he slept with Betty and Bonnie, only Maxine. His latest teen bride was "a handful," he said. Maxine wore white dresses that made Fats and other men say she looked "like an angel," but she could handle a gun even better than Alice. Maxine was so competitive she seemed the perfect match for Ti, at least at first. They had a dare: They'd each hold one end of a ripe watermelon, then drop the melon on the sidewalk and see who could be first to grab the heart, the sweetest, innermost part.

They hosted gambling parties that lasted from Friday evening to Monday morning. "All the high rollers would drive out from Norfolk to be on hand for Ti's soirées," said Fats. Titanic won more than enough off his guests to pay for the house and the Melton girls' needs, not that he needed more cash. "He'd made so much money by then, he was just gambling for exercise."

Again he got restless. Bored with the suckers from Norfolk, bored with the bone-chilling wind that blew off the Atlantic when winter came, he also grew less smitten with his child bride as the months passed. So he left Maxine playing house with her sisters while he drove to Texas, where it was 70 degrees in December. He arranged to have a golf partner meet him there. Having outlived the Pierce-Arrow Motor Car Company, a casualty of the late Depression, Titanic drove a silver Cadillac into Austin a couple weeks before Christmas of 1945.

Harvey Penick, the professional at the Austin Country Club, knew a hustle was in the works when a stranger with a booming voice banged through the screen door of his pro shop. "He said,

'I'm Herman,' " Penick recalled. "Then he pointed to the big, hand-some fellow with him and said, 'This is my amateur partner, Mister Thomas.' " The two of them had talked an officer of the club into a money match, Herman and Mr. Thomas against Penick and the club officer. Penick knew all about Titanic Thompson from Ben Hogan, and "Mr. Thomas" fit Hogan's description of him. He told the officer, a past president of the club, to forget about playing these two, but the man pulled rank and said the match had been made. Titanic teed off in street shoes, one with a hole that showed his big toe poking through—part of the act he was using to convince the mark he was new to the game.

Early in the match, Titanic pulled Penick aside. Delighted to be back on the road, Ti was feeling fine about the sure thing he had going. "Give your wife something nice for Christmas," he told Penick, picking a leather pouch from his golf bag.

The club pro peeked inside. The pouch was full of diamonds. "Take a few," Titanic said.

Penick, who would go on to tutor PGA tour stars Ben Cren-shaw and Tom Kite and write the bestselling *Harvey Penick's Little Red Book*, said no thanks. For all he knew the gems were fake. Or stolen. Or a bribe. Maybe Ti thought a grateful Penick would throw the match. Instead he played his best against Herman and Ti, but Penick's best wasn't enough. The visitors took the match—one-up, of course—and the past president started talking rematch. Ti encouraged that line of thinking—"You guys nearly had us," he said—but Penick convinced his partner to quit before they got fur-ther behind. Four months later, in April of 1946, came proof that he had been right: Penick opened his morning paper and saw a picture of the new Masters champion, Herman Keiser—Ti's partner that day in Austin.

Sixty years later Keiser's son said his father came to regret hus-tling golf with Titanic Thompson. "He wasn't proud of it," Herm Keiser said. "He didn't like dressing up as a hillbilly caddie so

Titanic could say, 'Me and that caddie'll beat you.' They'd beat people out of thousands." But the younger Keiser said his father, who died in 2003 after a career in which he won five PGA tour events, was proud of the way he hustled country-clubbers with a ploy he learned from Ti: "You use all your clubs, and I'll just use my putter." The elder Keiser also claimed that Penick was protecting his employers' reputation when he said Ti and Keiser left the Austin Country Club the same day they arrived. In Herman Keiser's account, "We didn't leave that day or anytime soon. We stayed till we broke those suckers."

Titanic's hustling partners included Evansville pro Bob Hamilton, who won the 1944 PGA Championship and seven other tour events, and Lee Elder, who met Ti on a public course in Dallas. Elder was a nineteen-year-old caddie when Ti offered him a chance to make "more money than you've ever seen." To the teenaged Elder, who would go on to be the first black player in the Masters, Titanic's offer was both a great opportunity and a shock. Ti knew it bothered some Texans to see a white man and a Negro traveling together—a detail that served his purposes. "Do you mean to say you're scared to play my colored-boy caddie?" he'd ask, shaming white country-club players into a losing proposition. Sometimes Elder would pose as his chauffeur, dressed in livery, polishing the car before he "tried golf" as Ti's partner. And while Titanic was no civil-rights crusader, he gave Elder the same split he gave his white partners, some of whom were established pros. To Ti, the measure of a man was the stroke he put on a fifty-thousand-dollar putt.

"Every day I learned something from him," said Elder. "He had a gift." Ti fooled even his partner with a trick he played on marks he met on the road. "Titanic would ask you to pick a card from a deck, then bet you his friend the Wizard could name the card—over the phone," Elder said. After the victim chose a card and showed it to Ti, the hustler knotted his brow with telepathic effort while dialing a secret number. "Is the Wizard there?" he asked. At that point

Maxine, at the other end of the line in Virginia Beach, whispered, "Hearts, diamonds, clubs, . . ." When she named the right suit, Ti cut her off: "May I speak to him, please?" Now she named cards: "Ace, king, queen, . . ." and when she hit the right one, he broke in: "Wizard, would you please tell this gentleman which card he holds in his hand?" He handed the phone to the mark, who heard the Wizard's girlish voice identify his card.

Eventually the Wizard left her Virginia Beach playhouse and joined her husband in Tucson, Arizona. She took up target shooting and Ti went along to the range. He enjoyed firing at inanimate targets for the first time since his medicine-show days with Captain Bogardus, and practiced until he could toss an aspirin tablet and hit it with a .22 bullet, turning the pill into a puff of dust.

With Maxine resettled, Ti was eager to travel again. During a spin through Oklahoma he visited an old acquaintance, an oilman named Byron Bennett, who had a brown-haired daughter, Jeannette, eleven years old. Titanic showed Jeannette his best shooting and card tricks. "When you're older, I'm going to marry you," he told her.

BY THE LATE FORTIES, J. Edgar Hoover had spent fifteen years pursuing public enemies of all sorts. Hoover's FBI was most concerned with killers and bank robbers but also kept tabs on illegal gambling, notifying sheriffs and police chiefs when notorious gamblers entered their territory. Ti kept moving but his reputation moved faster. When he hit a new town now, he'd find golfers who wanted to bet with him just so they could say they had taken on the great Titanic Thompson, but they didn't want to bet much. Dice and cards were migrating to Las Vegas, a hitching post transformed into a gambling mecca after Rothstein's protégé Meyer Lansky financed Ben "Bugsy" Siegel's Flamingo Hotel, which opened in December 1946. Siegel had worked as a contract killer for Lansky in New York. Lansky's backing enabled him to open the six-million-dollar Flamingo, which set the standard for modern Vegas with its oversized beds, mirrored walls, and a fountain in the lobby. Siegel's mob ties were no secret but that was no problem: The nearly all-powerful Lansky was said to have J. Edgar Hoover in his pocket because he had evidence that Hoover was homosexual.

Titanic couldn't stand the Flamingo. Siegel's casino was too hard to cheat in. His stiff-wristed toss might help him avoid crapping out on the perfect green felt of the tables there, but not as much as it helped on the shorter surfaces of Broadway dice dens or Army-barracks beds at Fort McClellan. Switching loaded dice into the closely monitored Vegas games was almost impossible. So was cheating at cards. Ti stayed ahead of the house with a secret system for beating casino craps, one of the mysteries he kept to himself. ("An unbeatable mathematical system, as sound as two plus two equals four," one gambler called it.) But the house edge still pinched his profit. In the Flamingo and the other casinos rising on the Las Vegas Strip, gambling was evolving from sport into business. Las Vegas, a boomtown built on consumers' acceptance of the house's relentless rake, a place where every bet's a sucker bet, was no place for him.

When gamblers of his generation dealt cards, they said they were "peddling the papers." In Vegas, paid dealers distributed plastic-coated cards that were harder to mark than the old paper cards. Soon only old-school sharps would say a dealer was "peddling the papers." Still worse for Ti was the fact that he couldn't be new in this town even once. On his first visit to the Flamingo, all the pros and some of the pigeons knew who he was. A few asked to shake his hand.

Ti and other old-timers saw the rise of Las Vegas as the end of their era. "Before Vegas," Johnny Moss said, "we were all road gamblers." After Vegas they were endangered. Journalist Jon Bradshaw, calling every true gambler "an outlaw traveling along back roads," lamented his heroes' fate: "Times had changed, the country had aged, become somehow tame and uniform. The high wild players were now extinct or imprisoned in a zoo."

Titanic, alive and free, detested the casinos but saw opportunity on the golf courses springing up all over town. He helped pioneer a few ploys Vegas golfers still use, including thumbing a dab of Vaseline on the face of his irons. The jelly reduced the spin on the ball, which flew farther and straighter when "greased." Some credit Ti with inventing another local rule: "I'll spot you strokes, but I get to tee my ball up on any shot." It didn't sound like a big edge until he hit a ball into the rough or a bunker. Sometimes he hit into a creek just to see the look on his opponent's face when he picked his ball from shallow water, placed it on one of the six-inch tees he kept in his golf bag, and slapped it toward the green.

One day he bet Moss he could make four out of five putts from twenty feet—a wager Tiger Woods couldn't win. After Ti sank four in a row, Moss offered a hundred dollars for his putting secret. "Easy," Ti said. "I came out last night and put a garden hose twenty feet from the hole. Ran the hose for a couple hours, made the grass lie down. You can't see it, but there's a little trough runnin' right to the cup."

He made a killing with professional skeet-shooter Dick Shaughnessy as his unwitting accomplice. "Titanic was friends with L.S. Pratt, who won the first National Skeet Shoot," Shaughnessy told a reporter for *Trap & Field* magazine. Pratt arranged a big-money Calcutta in which gamblers "bought" shooters at auction after the first round. A bettor won if his man downed the most clay pigeons overall. Shaughnessy recalled Ti's arriving with "two beautiful babes" on his arm. Neither one was his wife. "I was at the top of my game, a big favorite to win," said Shaughnessy, who somehow failed to break four of the fifty clay pigeons in round one.

"After that the auctioneer sold me cheap. Titanic bought me and made a pile of money when I broke the last fifty straight." Ti had sneaked four solid wooden targets into the first batch.

MAXINE THOMAS OF TUCSON, now eighteen, won the Arizona women's trap-shooting championship in 1950. Her husband topped her by winning the men's title from 1951 through 1954. Competing for trophies was as novel to Ti as returning to the same home base for five years. "Hell, Ti, you're plumb respectable," golfer Herman Keiser told him when he stopped by in the early Fifties. "Next thing you'll be joining the Jaycees."

By 1954 Maxine was twenty-one and pregnant. As in Evansville, pregnancy and birth led to divorce and a settlement. Maxine named her son Robert. "No hard feelings," said Ti, who moved out, rented a house in Tucson, and threw a stag party to celebrate the divorce. He hired three young girls to act as hostesses for him and his friends. Late that night the Tucson police, following a tip from an anonymous caller—possibly Maxine—raided the party and found one of the girls in bed with the sixty-one-year-old host. After another hostess claimed she had been pawed by one of his guests, Alvin Clarence Thomas was booked on multiple counts of contributing to the delinquency of a minor. He tried greasing justice's skids with a thirty-five-thousand-dollar donation to police charities, but after a prosecutor described his long, shady career, the jury found him guilty. Titanic must have struck the jurors as the worst sort of old coyote. Forty-five years after he came out of Rogers as a rawboned boy with an appetite for gambling and girls, his sheer consistency of character was working against him. While men like Shaughnessy still saw him as one of the last of the old-time sharps, a likable rogue at a skeet shoot with a babe on each arm, each one as pretty as the diamonds on his fingers, ordinary folks saw the graying defendant as a dirty old man. Pale and natty in his tailored suit, he stood to hear the judge sentence him to two years in the Arizona State Penitentiary in Florence.

Titanic had something to do before he served his sentence. While out on bail, he drove to Missouri, where his oilman friend Byron Bennett lived. Bennett's daughter Jeannette was eighteen now. She had learned typing and shorthand at William Woods College in Fulton, Missouri, before her father's wells across the Oklahoma border dried up. There was no money for tuition after that, so she was at home when Titanic drove up in a silver Cadillac.

"I've come back to marry you," he said.

Jeannette Bennett barely knew the man who had come to propose. She remembered seeing him with Maxine, a striking brunette in a white dress. Her father's friend was polite, tipping his hat and holding doors for Maxine. Now he did the same for Jeannette. He was supremely self-assured. "He turned my head," she said years later. "I think I knew he didn't love me, but he liked me." And he seemed to be rich. As for his age, Jeannette made a clear-eyed calculation. If he lived to be eighty she would be thirty-six when he died, with time for a whole life still ahead.

Titanic and the Bennetts drove separate cars to Arizona. He led the way in his silver Cadillac. Nervous Jeannette rode the thousand miles in the backseat of her parents' car. The mini-caravan led to Tucson, where Ti would soon need to report to the county jail. What was he thinking during that twenty-hour drive? To judge from what he said and did later, he must have wanted to change at least a little, to get marriage right for once. Jeannette, leaving her parents behind in Tucson, got into Ti's Cadillac and rode two hours north to Mesa, where they were married by Mesa's justice of the peace on August 6, 1954. There was no honeymoon. Ti went out gambling that night. He may have hoped to get this marriage right, but he wasn't going to change his stripes.

In the end he avoided the Arizona State Penitentiary. He turned himself in at the Pima County Jail, where John Dillinger was held twenty years earlier. Dillinger, caught hiding out in Tucson, got shipped home to serve time in Indiana, where he promptly escaped. Ti's strategy was less daring. He complained of stomach pains before the state's One-Way Wagon arrived to transfer him to the prison at Florence, and wound up serving eight months in the relative comfort of the county jail before the state set him free, trimming fourteen months off his sentence for good behavior. He rejoined Jeannette as if nothing had happened.

AMARILLO SLIM PRESTON WAS in Tucson, playing one-pocket pool with a mobbed-up New Yorker named Ira. Titanic leaned on the wall watching, clucking like he couldn't believe what he was seeing.

"Slim, he stinks," Ti told Preston. "You can't let this son of a spaghetti-eater beat you."

"Ti, knock it off. Let the man play."

Preston figured Ti had an agenda. He usually did and it was usually bad news for anyone but him. In Preston's words, Titanic was "not the most docile cat in the world." They had teamed up a year or so earlier to fleece a pair of Texas millionaires at high-stakes dominoes, another of Ti's sidelines. Preston must have done something to irk Titanic—he never knew what—and found himself in a cutthroat card game on the train ride home. Ti wound up with his own share of their dominoes haul plus every dime of Preston's share. Now he was wedging his way into Preston's game with Ira.

"Let him *play*? He can't play." Titanic waved his arms, letting them see the .45 tucked into his pants, the Colt with the adhesive tape around the barrel.

"Fuck off," said Amarillo Slim, but Ti lit into Ira again, calling him a girl, a fool, a monkey, and more until the mobster waved his cue stick.

"Sure, you can talk when you're all rodded-up," Ira said. "What can I do when you've got that big-ass pistol?"

As Preston wrote in his book, *Amarillo Slim in a World Full of Fat People*, "This is where it got interesting. In a room full of people who had *seen* that gun, myself included, Ti said, 'Man, I ain't never carried a pistol in my life.' "

Ira had $2,800 in his wallet. He bet it all that Titanic was packing. Ti rounded up a couple thousand in side bets from other onlookers who had seen the .45. "I was tempted to make a wager myself. But I'd been around Ti long enough to know better," wrote Preston.

"Now we'll search you," Ira said.

According to Preston, Ti said, "Well, *suuuuuure!*" He took off his jacket. They patted it down. "Then they made him take off his pants. Then his socks—everything! After they'd stripped him stark naked, we looked in all the pockets around that pool table, under that table, all over the damn place, and the gun wasn't there. He couldn't have thrown it in the wastebasket; there wasn't one. We never did find that gun, and Ti never did tell me how he did it. I reckon if he did, I could have made a lot of money making things disappear. But that was Ti—he took some of his best secrets to his grave."

Ti and Jeannette headed west, stopping in Long Beach, California, where he shot dice, played seven-stud and hold 'em and hustled golfers half his age. When the action dried up they moved on to New Mexico to cash in on a short-lived oil rush there, then returned to Tucson, where Ti found himself sitting home two or three nights a week, dealing poker hands for practice. He was good company, full of jokes and songs and tales of his adventures on the road. He told Jeannette her shapely underarms reminded him of Myrna Loy's, and her skin was lots better than Harlow's.

She liked to help him practice. Her husband's love of numbers was contagious. "They're all you can count on," he said. He taught her the arithmetic of coin flips, dice rolls, and poker hands. And the odds hadn't blinked since his days with Professor McAlley. One weekend he dealt 5,000 five-card hands. Jeannette wrote the results in a notebook:

Straight 19
Flush 10
Pair 2461
No pair 2539
Difference 78
Price 103–100

Fifty years later she still had the notebook. Its pages were yellowing but the numbers were clear, and if you reach for a deck of cards right now and deal five thousand hands, your results will be nearly identical. The odds are immortal.

Titanic felt immortal too. At age sixty-five he would stand on the porch of their rented house while Jeannette carried a deck of cards across the street. When she was forty yards away she turned and held up a card. From that distance most people can barely tell a deuce from a king.

"Ten of clubs," he said.

She held up another card: the king of hearts with his sword sticking into his head.

"Suicide king!" Ti never missed.

He was a grouch in the mornings, so jealous of his sleep that Jeannette learned to slip out of bed without making a sound. One morning she woke doubled over with pain. Afraid to disturb him, she drove to the hospital. She had a ruptured appendix. "They told my mother I might die," she recalled. Jeannette spent two hours in the operating room and a week in the hospital. Her husband never darkened the door of her hospital room. She didn't blame him. "He didn't like illness," she explained. "It was hard for him to deal with people's imperfections."

In 1959, when Jeannette was twenty-three and her husband was sixty-six, she gave birth to a son, Ty Wayne Thomas. Titanic promptly packed up and left. She found a shoebox full of cash in the closet where his suits had hung. Alone with her baby, she waited up for the husband who had seemed such a charmer when she was eighteen.

FOUR DECADES AFTER HIS first visit to French Lick, a new road led to the Indiana resort town. This road was more than twice as wide as the old one, with a concrete median down the middle. The Federal Highway Act of 1956 had authorized twenty-five billion dollars, a figure that impressed even Titanic, to build forty-one thousand miles of interstate highways. For now, modernization meant occasional traffic jams as construction crews turned dirt roads and two-lane blacktops into rivers of smooth cement. Ti's Cadillac crept north and east to French Lick and the French Lick Springs Hotel, where he had once kayoed a cocky prizefighter with his newspaper-in-the-doorway gambit. He was back in town to ruin another boxer, Joe Louis. The famed "Brown Bomber" was a two-handicap golfer who considered himself a potential touring pro. Celebrity golfer Louis had won heavy wagers with Bing Crosby and Bob Hope as well as Al Jolson, who was no more inclined to keep his fly zipped on the golf course than he'd been with Roaring Twenties hookers in his limousine—Jolson made it a condition of golf bets that if he won, he got to piss on your shoes. But Louis, who had been heavyweight champ as recently as 1949, was down on his luck a decade later, owing the IRS more than a million dollars in back taxes and tumbling deeper into debt playing golf. He was a dream mark for Ti, who had picked up his Evansville accomplice

Bob Hamilton, the 1944 PGA champion, on his way into town. They teed it up with the ex-champ for five thousand dollars, then ten thousand and twenty thousand. At each stage Louis came tantalizingly close to winning his money back. After each stage they offered him a chance to get even. They left him penniless. *Broke him*, in gamblers' parlance, and moved on when he was broke. The *Washington Post*'s Shirley Povich made a point of keeping Titanic's name out of his account, which read, "Joe Louis was taken by hustlers, guys who were better golfers." A friend of Louis's blamed the game itself, saying, "That little white ball took his money away."

Ti rolled from there to Robinson, Illinois, eighty miles of back roads from French Lick. He was planning a long con to multiply his profits.

On the day after a high-school golf phenom named Don Stickney upset eighteen-year-old Jack Nicklaus in the Ohio Amateur, the phone rang at the Stickney home in Columbus. A Mr. Thomas asked to speak to Don. When the boy came to the phone, Ti asked if he'd like to join him on the road for a month or two. "You'll make more money than your daddy makes in a year."

Don's mother told him to stay home. "He's a no-good crook." But the youngster thought he knew better. Within a week he was driving Ti's Cadillac, staying in the only good hotel in Robinson, a town so remote that Titanic went unrecognized. He and Stickney skinned some rich old men at the local country club. Among their marks was Bayard Heath, heir to the Robinson-based Heath Candy Company, who handed them each a Heath Bar on the first tee. Stickney wasn't privy to the stakes, but after they broke Heath, Stickney's junior-partner split amounted to five thousand dollars. He was still counting his money when Titanic handed him a pair of overalls and told him to report to a farmhouse the next morning. "For the next month you're not a golfer. You're a farmer," he said.

Ti had taken out a thirty-day lease on the farm beside the golf course. Stickney's job was to drive a tractor back and forth across a bean field. He did this for three weeks. Titanic wasn't even in town half the time. Dressed in bib overalls and a straw hat, Stickney drove the tractor, watching golfers come out of the clubhouse and gather at the first tee to bicker over their bets. Finally Titanic and Bob Hamilton appeared one afternoon, shaking two club members' hands, belting their drives and moving off down the first fairway. Ti was playing right-handed.

Titanic and Hamilton lost two thousand dollars. From his tractor seat Stickney saw Ti kick his golf bag. The next day was worse. Titanic and Hamilton lost three thousand. The day after that they lost five thousand. Now Ti was apoplectic. "You skunk! Get out of my sight," he yelled at Hamilton, who slinked away with his head hanging.

Ti turned to the winners. "You got lucky," he said, still steaming. "Tell you what. Forget that guy. You've got me down ten thousand. I'll play you for fifty thousand. I'll play left-handed. And you know how sure I am? You can pick my partner."

The other men couldn't resist. They looked past the hackers on the practice green and the caddies loitering by the clubhouse and chose the tractor driver they'd seen working that bean field for weeks. "There's your partner," they said, laughing.

Stickney climbed off the tractor and fired a sixty-six, probably the best round ever by a golfer wearing overalls. He and Ti won in a rout and split their loot three ways. The fifty-thousand wager minus the ten thousand Ti had "lost" baiting the hook left ten thousand for Stickney, ten thousand for Hamilton, and twenty thousand for Ti, enough to keep him going for at least a week.

Johnston City, Illinois, was a mining town an hour and a half from Robinson. The main road branched into dirt roads that led through piles of slag to the mouths of boarded-up coal mines. Rocking-horse oil rigs sucked a few last barrels of crude from old wells. The liveliest place in town was Jansco's Cue Club and Show Bar, a cement-block box with a pink neon sign blinking *Members*

Only. Titanic stopped in at Jansco's to play cards and back pool players in games arranged by Fats, who lived thirty miles away in Dowell. In the late Fifties more and more road gamblers were doing the same. Professional pool was struggling so much that there were no world championships in 1960 or 1961. So the top players convened on their own to play the gamblers' own game. At the end of '61, Titanic joined a row of men carrying leather pool-cue cases into Jansco's for the first-ever Hustlers' Jamboree.

"Titanic Thompson, put up your hands. *You're under arrest!*"

It was Fats, aiming a chubby finger at his old friend. Fats chuckled and carried his Coca-Cola to the pool table where he was holding court. Fourteen of the country's finest players were on hand for the three-week event, officially known as the World One-Pocket Billiards Tournament. Ti saw "Daddy Warbucks" Cokes, Johnnie "Irish" Lineen, Marshall "Tuscaloosa Squirrelly" Carpenter, Bill "Weenie Beenie" Staton, and "Connecticut Johnny" Vevis, who would take the trophy while Fats spouted about his lousy luck ("I put a million dollars' worth of spin on that ball and only a nickel's worth took hold"), his IQ ("I'm so intelligent I could spot Einstein the ten ball"), and that lying new movie *The Hustler*. Fats called the film "my life story" and threatened to sue everyone connected with it, while writer Walter Tevis claimed that the Minnesota Fats character Jackie Gleason played in the movie was fictional. In time, though, as the press and public lionized him as the "real" Minnesota Fats, a name he had never used, Fats would adopt it and become more famous by that name than he had ever been as "New York Fats." He saw the Johnston City one-pocket tournament as a lark, a pretext for the more serious action that earned the event its nickname, the Hustlers' Jamboree. While Vevis collected the trophy and his measly five grand, with Cokes coming in third and Fats fourth, the hustlers scrapped over more than one million dollars in unofficial games. Titanic got more than his fair share while making only a token appearance at the tables.

"Titanic was going on seventy," said Fast Larry Guninger, who saw him at Jansco's, "but he looked a lot younger, tall and skinny with slicked-back hair. After a couple trick shots he let Fats do his playing for him. Ti stood at the bar booking bets. He'd keep more side bets in his head than you could think up."

JEANNETTE CAST A LINE INTO brown water. Titanic's last wife was sitting in a lawn chair beside a shallow canal in Corpus Christi, Texas, fishing for trout and Texas drum. Her parents had driven down from Missouri and rented a bungalow nearby, to give their twenty-five-year-old daughter a place to stay and help her look after little Ty Wayne. They all knew Titanic wasn't coming back. Until he did. Jeannette was fishing when she heard footsteps behind her and there he was. After a year without a word, he was tipping his hat to her, saying, "I'm back."

He rented a house in San Antonio and they resumed their old routines. Jeannette kept three-year-old Ty Wayne quiet in the mornings while Titanic slept late. Titanic made occasional forays to high-stakes hold-'em games in Dallas or Shreveport or New Orleans. When a phone call came inviting him to play cards, he asked, "Paper or plastic?"

Most days he hustled golf for a few hundred dollars. No longer a big hitter off the tee, he relied on his short game, which he practiced every day, indoors and out. He could still chip a ball into a shoe or a drinking glass. One evening he was chipping balls in the front yard when a sports car pulled up at the curb, a low-slung blue Jaguar convertible, dusty from the road, with Indiana plates. The driver climbed out, a skinny bearded beatnik-looking kid.

"Are you Titanic?" the kid asked.

"Who wants to know?"

"I'm Tommy. I'm your son."

11 TITANIC'S LAST STAND

TOMMY THOMAS, EIGHTEEN, HAD HUGGED HIS MOTHER and set out from Evansville the night before. It was a little more than a thousand miles to the address in Texas he had gotten from a relative. He made the drive in half a day, pushing his Jaguar's speedometer as high as 180. A state trooper pulled him over near Dallas, but Tommy had slowed down by then. He got a ticket for doing 140.

The kid who got out of the car in San Antonio was as tall as his father. Titanic didn't think much of the boy's bushy beard and black jeans or the gold chain around his neck. But he liked the car, a Jaguar XK150, midnight blue with red leather seats. "How'd you pay for a car like that?" he asked.

"I'm a gambler," Tommy said. "Just like you."

"You got any money on you, son?"

"I've got four hundred dollars."

"Well, come on in the house."

Titanic led his boy to the kitchen table and brought out a deck of cards. As he shuffled and dealt, Tommy talked about how his mother, Jo Ann, Ti's third wife, had married a plastics executive and become a women's golf champion back in Indiana. He said his mother drank too much and his stepfather was as stiff as the toothbrushes his company made. He said that in the years when he was growing up, eighteen years during which Titanic never visited him and his mother, never phoned or sent a birthday card, he had read every newspaper and magazine article about Titanic that he could find. He had taught himself to mark cards and cheat the rubes at the Elks Club out of their poker money.

Titanic cleaned him out in half an hour. Then he stood up and pushed the boy's four hundred dollars across the table. "I'm giving you your money back," he said. They played another hour. He broke Tommy again and pushed the money across the table again. The house was quiet except for the ticking of a wall clock. It was after midnight; Jeannette and little Ty Wayne were sleeping down the hall. Ti said, "Son, do you shoot dice?" They switched to dice and he won Tommy's money for a third time. This time he kept it.

Tommy recognized this scene from clippings he had read. Some of the stories told how the young Titanic had tracked down his own father and beaten him at poker in Oil City, Louisiana. This was the same scene with one crucial difference: This time the old man won.

Tommy moved into an extra bedroom in Ti and Jeannette's house. He stayed up late playing cards with Titanic and practicing the card cheats Ti showed him. Tommy proved to be less of a sportsman than his father, more of a thief. He became a brazen card mechanic who could slide an ace from his sleeve to his hand fast enough to fool gamblers who were watching to see if he'd try it. "Tommy was the absolute best at kickin' coolers," said a famous Vegas gambler, using the experts' term for slipping a prearranged "cold deck" into a poker game. Tommy limited his losses with one of the oldest cheats of all, palming a chip while shoving a pot across the table to the winner. (A dot of adhesive called "check-cop glue" in the palm made it easy.) In his first months in San Antonio, Ti's son won several thousand dollars in local games. He relished the role of badass gambler, dressing in shit-kicker boots, black jeans, and a leather jacket, letting other players see the pearl-handled .38 Special tucked in his belt. If a poker pot mounted into the tens of thousands, he'd place his gun on the table, reminding other players that they'd better not cheat. And from the start, Tommy cut his father in on his winnings. He even improved one of Titanic's tricks: After Ti showed him how to glue a chip of mirror under a fingernail, so he could see the cards' corners while he dealt them—a trick that can get the dealer shot if the mirror reflects a telltale sliver of light—Tommy paid a contact-lens maker for tiny strips of nonglare mirror-finished glass.

With his new, improved fingernail mirrors, his gun, glue, and a growing bankroll, Tommy joined his father on the road. He proved himself by keeping his head when pots grew far bigger than any he had played for on his own. One gambler said, "Titanic's son got to be a real master at all forms of cheating." Still Ti needled him, reminding Tommy which one of them was the legend and which was the sidekick. He never said what it meant to him to have his son find him after so many years, if anything. Letting Tommy "tag along," as Titanic put it, worked fine as long as Tommy didn't disturb his sleep or cost him money. When Ti ran short of cash, Tommy sold the Jaguar and gave his father the proceeds. All the while, Ti was keeping a secret from him.

The old man slept late while the others—Ty Wayne, Tommy, and Jeannette, who was only eight years older than Tommy—tiptoed around the house. Around noon Titanic would pad to the dining room in his house slippers and say, "Every dog has his day!" Jeannette warmed up the foods he liked: boiled ham, green beans, and scalloped potatoes. He drank water or Dr Pepper. He still ate nothing fried, packed no more than 160 pounds on his six-foot two-inch frame, and crackled with energy. Both boys liked to watch their dad practice hopping the cut—a sharp's way to cut a deck without really cutting it, leaving the cards in the same order as before—or chipping golf balls off the carpet into one of Ty Wayne's baby shoes. "Everyone thought he was the coolest man in the world," recalled Ty Wayne, whose first memories include seeing his father roll a stack of quarters back and forth through his fingers, the coins moving like a silver snake.

A year later they moved to Dallas. "More money there," Ti said. By now Jeannette, like Alice and Maxine before her, was an ace target-shooter herself. The family made frequent trips to a rifle range where they fired at playing cards. After her husband shot the six pips out of the six of hearts from twenty paces, she'd put six bullets through the same holes in the card. One day Tommy stood by their backyard fence like a firing-squad victim and lit a cigarette; Jeannette raised her pistol and shot the ember off the tip. Ty Wayne recalls an evening when Titanic loaded the family in the car and drove to the state fair. The boy was dazzled by the crowds, music, and flashing lights but most of all by his parents. Titanic threw darts at balloons and fired baseballs at stacks of milk bottles. Ti and Jeannette shot air rifles. "They beat every game on the midway," Ty Wayne said. "We left with armloads of teddy bears."

In Dallas, seventy-year-old Titanic hustled golf most afternoons and came home for supper when it got dark. Too antsy to sit through TV shows, he sometimes joined the others on the couch if there was an old movie on. One night they were watching one of his favorites, *The Wizard of Oz*, with Judy Garland singing "Over the Rainbow," and Jeannette saw tears in his eyes. It was the only time she ever saw him weep.

The family often followed his night-owl schedule, going bowling after the eleven o'clock news. Ty Wayne, still too small to bowl, watched his father's left-handed delivery send a twelve-pound ball toward the pins at a walking pace. It took forever to get there but always seemed to find the one-two pocket. The Thomases were regulars at the Cotton Bowling Palace, a mammoth all-night alley near Love Field airport whose forty-four lanes, barbershop, and beauty parlor served a seedy clientele after midnight. One late-night regular was mobster Jack Ruby, who would gun down Lee Harvey Oswald at Dallas police headquarters in November 1963. Ruby ran the Carousel Club burlesque house up the road and often took his strippers for bowling and beers after the club closed at two in the morning. Ruby was a big fish in a Dallas underworld teeming with bottom-feeders. One night Jeannette carried sleeping Ty Wayne to the Bowling Palace parking lot while Titanic lagged behind, chatting with the cashier and maybe watching Ruby's strippers roll a few balls. She was almost to the car when a man in a ski mask stepped in front of her, waving a pistol. "Give me your wallet!" he said. Jeannette turned her back to shield her child. She saw Ti strolling toward them, carrying their his-and-hers bowling-ball bags.

Titanic made no move for his own gun. Still holding the bowling bags, he told the robber, "You'd better find a softer spot to land"— meaning an easier target. "I don't particularly want to kill you, but I will." While the masked man watched, Ti opened the car door for Jeannette, walked around to the driver's side, got in, and drove away. Jeannette was surprised by the look on her husband's face on the way home. He didn't look angry, or worried that his wife and son might have been shot. "He looked insulted," she recalled. "Like he couldn't believe someone pulled a gun on *him*."

The next day a nervous, unshaven man tapped their screen door. He apologized for bothering them, saying he had no idea it was Titanic Thompson he had held up the night before. He was a gam-bler on a bad run, not really a robber, he said, and went on to give such a sad account of lame racehorses and river cards running dry that Titanic wished him luck and gave him twenty dollars. Ti said he was glad he hadn't shot the guy the night before. He was still nagged by thoughts of killing teen caddie Jimmy Frederick thirty years earlier.

Tommy loved seeing gamblers treat his father like a celebrity. The Falstaffian Fats, who now saved time on autographs by carrying a *Minnesota Fats* stamp pad in his pocket, paid his respects when he was in Dallas. Fats had four cue cases, one each in lizard, alligator, crocodile, and python skin, and shoes to match each case. Poker greats Johnny Moss, Doyle "Texas Dolly" Brunson, and Amarillo Slim Preston stopped by, as did the occasional FBI agent asking about reports of illegal gaming. Ti and his wife made the FBI men stand on the porch and talk through the screen door. Jeannette disliked the stone-faced agents as much as she distrusted the petty thieves and their girlfriends and wives who hung around her husband—people who couldn't stop at a filling station without shoplifting something. But Titanic welcomed them all, handing out twenty-dollar bills like ten-cent tips, and from time to time they repaid his generosity. One scraggly sponger came back months after getting a handout to say he was going to hijack a Texas hold-'em game Ti often played in. "Mister Ti," he said, "you ought to stay home that night."

The card-game hijackers of the 1960s tended to be better organized and more heavily armed than the door-busting heisters of old. Ti and Johnny Moss were in Beeville, Texas, draining some oilmen at Kansas City lowball, a game in which the "worst" hand wins—the nuts is two-three-four-five-seven unsuited—when their eyes started itching. Moss heard tear gas hissing under the door. "We looked outside and there were five or six thieves carrying scatter guns, wearing fatigues and gas masks," he recalled. "They looked like men from space." Titanic hid his bankroll in the freezer compartment of a refrigerator, then turned to Moss and said, "Johnny, let's stroll out and get us some clean air." The thieves found the money but Ti seemed not to mind. He had his health, plus a proposition or two in the works.

One of his most talked-about propositions involved a rock garden near Kansas City. The mark was a high-ranking member of the

Civella crime family that ruled the city's underworld, a man who was puffily proud of the rock garden behind his mansion. When the Mafioso and his wife went on vacation, Titanic hired a team of quarry workers. They drilled holes in the biggest boulder in the garden, hollowed it out, plugged the holes with cement and smoothed them over. When casino night at the mobster's house rolled around, Ti bet he could roll another, smaller boulder downhill to the driveway. That rock may have weighed five hundred pounds. He pushed, cursed it, failed. Kicked it. He picked out a slightly bigger boulder, doubled the wager, and failed again. Now he was riled. This was vintage Titanic—pushing the mark, if not the rock, until this looked like the biggest, easiest score in the world, and the most entertaining. Ti rubbed his hands together. He pointed to the biggest boulder. "*That* one," he said. He would roll that eight-foot-high rock, but not for a few pissant grand. "For twenty thousand." The don and his friends added side bets while Ti made as if to shake the tension out of his wrists. He placed his hat on a smaller rock. He took a deep breath, put his shoulder to the boulder and sent it flying down the driveway.

Nobody moved. They watched the hollow boulder roll, bouncing off saplings. All eyes turned to the hoodwinked don, who stood silent for a moment. Then he began to applaud. A gambler lost face if he whined when he had been conned. That was the code. The don paid up like a good sport and got a Titanic Thompson story to tell for the rest of his life.

In those days some of the best poker in the world was played at Redman's Club, a Dallas card room run by a burly, boisterous fellow named Ace Darnell. Redman's was a dingy joint up a set of wooden stairs in a rough part of central Dallas. A plastic cooler full of ice held a couple bottles of Dr Pepper for Ti and beers for other players. There were tables for limit games and a back room with a bigger table for no-limit poker, Ti's old sky's-the-limit style. The old-timers called it "scoot," since you could scoot all your chips

into the pot. Greenhorns like Tommy weren't welcome in the biggest games at Redman's, where even Ti was a second-tier player. "Ti
had to cheat to keep up," said poker Hall of Famer Doyle Brunson.
"He'd peek at the top card when he dealt. We let him do it because
of who he was. We'd let him win that pot and beat him on the
next." The hustler-for-all-seasons may have been a notch below
Brunson, Moss, and Amarillo Slim at poker, just as he was a world-
class but not Fats-class pool player, but he could beat them all at
golf, bowling, horseshoes, coin-pitching, skeet shooting, and just
about anything else, as they all knew. They also knew better than
to make him mad. "You could see by the look in his eyes that he'd
kill you. Everybody knew he'd killed five men," Brunson said. "We
were in a pool hall one night when a hijacker comes in. This was
known to be a real bad guy. The rest of us back off. The guy's got
his gun out. Ti goes up to him and says, 'I hear you're the blankety-
blank likes to steal money. Try to take mine.' And he's got that
dead-eyed look. The guy with the gun looks at him for a long time.
Ten seconds, maybe. It seemed longer. And then the guy left."

Dallas dentist Jim Hill met his hero the day Ti turned up at Hill's
office with a toothache. Hill, who had heard about Titanic through
the golf grapevine, was ready when new patient Alvin C. Thomas
opened his mouth.

"Bet you double or nothing on my fee I can pull that tooth in
ten minutes," Hill said.

"Sorry, Doc, but I like your end of that one," Ti replied. But
he accepted Hill's offer to join him at Glen Lakes Country Club,
where the dentist and his friends played a weekly game. Ti bet them
twenty dollars each and beat their best ball. They were reaching for
their wallets when he said, "Keep your money, boys. You don't hit
it good enough to bet with me." That annoyed a couple of them,
but Hill listened when Titanic took him aside and said he could
play better. To prove the importance of striking down on the ball,
he had the dentist use his wedge to chop a waist-high bush to bits.

"Keep swinging!" Hill swung until his wrists felt like noodles and the bush was a nub of root. Next Ti talked percentages. Thirty years before statistics like driving distance and putts-per-green entered golf's lexicon, he had Hill keep track of how many fairways he hit off the tee in each round, how many greens he hit in regulation (one shot on a par-three hole, two on a par-four hole, three on a par-five), how many putts he took. "If you hit less than nine greens in a round, practice irons for an extra hour. If you take more than thirty putts, spend an hour on the putting green." Soon Hill shot seventy-three in the club championship, but the best score of his life didn't impress his tutor. Watching Hill hit a few balls after his seventy-three, Ti said, "Goddamn, Doc, would you develop some dexterity?"

Titanic played most of his golf at Dallas's rough-and-tumble Tenison Park, where the city maintained a pair of sun-blistered public courses flanked by thousands of pecan trees. Gamblers called it "Hustlers' Park" because the action never stopped. "You could always find a money game at Tenison," said a PGA tour pro who knew the place. According to one tall Tenison tale, a hustler mocked the "scaredy cats" huddling in the cream-colored club-house one morning as a tornado approached. He said he could bogey the first hole in winds that were bending trees sideways and whipping pecans through the air like bullets. After booking a few bets, he ran outside, whacked his driver at the roaring funnel and was never seen again.

Titanic spent long afternoons on the practice-putting green. At seventy he was too creaky and weak off the tee to break par anymore, a condition that irked him. He had the aging athlete's conviction that he could still do everything he used to, but in him that common delusion dueled with the numbers running through his mind: how far his drives traveled, how many fairways he hit, how many greens, how many putts. And his numbers were getting worse. He kept busy by betting he could break eighty left- or right-handed, and by standing around flipping silver dollars at a hole in the practice green. When someone stopped to watch, he'd offer to bet he could sink one silver dollar out of three. "I might possibly make two," he'd say, trying and missing, "or even three in a row." Of course he could make twenty in a row if he tried.

Around this time Titanic and a few others invented cross-country golf. Teeing off from one course, he and some Texans known as Moron Tom, Cecil the Parachute, and Magoo played across streets, fences, front yards, parking lots, and the odd highway ramp, holing out after thirty or forty or a hundred swings on a different course two or three miles away. Ti always won. Some said he went part of the way by bus.

He also crossed paths with hustlers he dismissed as gimmick golfers. One was LaVerne Moore, a three-hundred-pound con man who had joined Titanic on the road thirty years earlier. Moore followed Ti to Los Angeles in the Thirties and skinned movie-colony golfers. Calling himself "The Mysterious Montague," he made his name by hustling two-handicapper Bing Crosby for five dollars a hole. Crosby used his full set of clubs while Moore played with a baseball bat, a shovel, and a rake. On the last hole he raked in a birdie putt. Moore was briefly famous for what *Washington Post* writer Shirley Povich called "Titanic Thompson stuff—tricks he learned from Titanic when Thompson was the biggest sure-thing gambler on Broadway and Moore was his stooge."

Scammers abounded in the Fifties and Sixties. The next best after Titanic was probably Martin "Fat Man" Stanovich, who looked like a hippopotamus crouching over the ball and had a hippo's short-armed backswing, but whose steel nerves and miraculous short game made him more than a match for touring pros. After Ed Furgol outlasted Hogan and Gene Littler to win the 1954 U.S. Open, Stanovich drained Furgol of every dollar he had won. Later, finding himself leading a PGA event on the last day, hustler Stanovich avoided publicity by making a deal with his closest pursuer, Al Besselink. Stanovich finished double-bogey, double-bogey, took home second-place money, and split Besselink's paycheck. (As if to prove cheating pays, Besselink's victory got him into the Tournament of Champions in Las Vegas, where he bet a thousand dollars on himself at a hundred-to-one odds, and won.)

Another mystery man went by "Count Yogi." The Count, who played in a turban and silk cape, said his full name was Harry Hilary Xavier Frankenberg. He swore he had made fifty-five holes in one and could drive the ball four hundred yards but couldn't prove either claim. Another trickster, Ray Hudson, beat crooner Dean Martin in a thirty-five-thousand-dollar round in which each man had to down a bottle of vodka. Martin never bothered to check Hudson's Smirnoff bottle, which was full of water. Tennis pro Bobby Riggs, who would challenge Billie Jean King in the "Battle of the Sexes" in 1973, spent the Fifties and Sixties hustling golf, often using only a four-iron. Riggs won tennis bets by using a frying pan as a racket while playing with an open umbrella in his other hand and a poodle leashed to each leg.

The most alluring golf hustler was a Las Vegas mob moll who belted 220-yard drives while wearing high heels and a bikini. Gamblers distracted by Jeanne Carmen's 36-25-36 figure missed the pure *thwack* she put on the ball. A generation later she might have been an LPGA star; instead she tucked hundred-dollar bills into her bikini top after stacking three balls on a tee (a tricky task in itself) and lacing the middle ball 220 yards while the top ball popped up into her hand and the bottom ball sat untouched on the tee. Carmen and mobster Johnny Roselli employed a Ti-style scam at Vegas country clubs: Jeanne lounges around the pool until Johnny comes off the course telling a pigeon, "You're no golfer—that girl in the bikini could beat you!" Jeanne shoots sixty-nine in her swimsuit. Roselli, movie-star handsome in his Italian suits, a fat diamond on his pinkie, owned the Tropicana with backing from silent partners Lansky and Sam Giancana. In 1960 he and Giancana allegedly colluded with the CIA on a plot to kill Cuban president Fidel Castro. Nobody proved anything, but Johnny wound up stuffed into a steel drum that was discovered bobbing in the surf off Miami in 1976. Jeanne and her bikini wound up in Los Angeles, starring in B movies (*Untamed Youth, Striporama*). She befriended Marilyn Monroe, taught her to play golf, and claimed they had shared bedfellows including John F. Kennedy, Robert Kennedy, and the famously well-endowed Milton Berle.

The trick-shot artists steered clear of each other. They couldn't compete except to see which one looted a particular country club before the members grew wary of traveling sharps. Titanic might admire Jeanne Carmen's three-ball stunt as well as her figure, but he dismissed Carmen, Moore, and the rest as his imitators. "Bush-leaguers." Anyone with eye-hand coordination could work up a trick shot. There was a better breed of golf hustler around Dallas in those days, including one or two who might be of use to him.

Lee Trevino grew up poor near Glen Lakes Country Club, dentist Jim Hill's home course. Trevino was illegitimate and never knew his father. Raised in a dirt-floor shack with no plumbing and no windows, he worked in his tenant-farmer grandfather's cotton and onion fields from the time he was five. He helped his grandfather earn a few extra dollars digging graves. The boy did some caddying at Glen Lakes, where the caddies smoked cigarettes and gambled at dice, cards, and golf. Sharing cast-off clubs they played a makeshift three-hole course behind the caddie shed. "We had as many as sixteen guys playing for quarters," Trevino remembered in his book *They Call Me Super Mex*. "I'd hit a shot and throw the club to another guy so he could hit. As soon as he'd hit, he'd throw the club to another guy. It might take thirty minutes to play one hole with clubs flying around." After a stint in the army, he took a job at Hardy's Driving Range. He and owner Hardy Greenwood built a par-three course, digging bunkers, welding drainpipes, and putting up stadium-style lights so the course could stay open at night. It was there that Trevino worked a few hustles with Titanic Thompson.

Like any Dallas golfer with any gamble in him, Trevino knew his way around Tenison Park. He'd work at Hardy's till midnight, go out drinking till dawn, and turn up at Tenison at six in the morning dressed in Bermuda shorts and a sloppy T-shirt. In his early days he played barefoot. In July and August, when temperatures rose past 100, he'd walk through the creek on Tenison's second hole to coat his feet and legs with mud that kept the bugs away. Trevino often bet more than he had in his pocket. Titanic liked the kid's spirit. He also liked Trevino's unorthodox swing, a self-taught slash that sent the ball on a beeline toward the flagstick. Trevino was living—squatting—in a condemned motel with his seventeen-year-old wife. They had dated at the Cotton Bowling Palace, where a robber had drawn a pistol on Ti's wife Jeannette a few years before. Lee wooed his girl at the Bowling Palace and hustled grocery money on the night shift at Hardy's. "It was win or don't eat," he recalled. During this time he developed his trademark hustle, using a thirty-two-ounce Dr Pepper bottle as his only club. He would flip a golf ball straight up and swing the bottle like a fungo bat, knocking balls to Hardy's par-three greens. He putted croquet-style. Breaking par with a Dr Pepper bottle wasn't a talent Trevino just happened to have—like Ti he spent hundreds of hours preparing what seemed to be a crazy proposition. "I practiced almost a year before I got into a match with my Dr Pepper bottle," he said. "Then I played with it for three years and never lost." The key to the hustle was that it seemed to make him an underdog. Players he thumped nightly were suddenly giving him strokes. At first he'd win ten or twenty dollars, betting his own money. The stakes improved when Titanic got involved. Ti would flatter golfers who thought they could beat Trevino. "That's a fine swing you got," he'd say. "See that little Mexican? He's got no golf clubs. Too poor. He'll play you with a bottle. What'll you spot him, ten to one?" Trevino's split would be a hundred dollars, sometimes two hundred if Ti was feeling generous.

Trevino dreamed of playing the PGA tour with Arnold Palmer and Jack Nicklaus. "Forget that," Titanic said. He urged hungry Trevino to make thousands—tens of thousands—on the hustlers' tour with Ti. Instead the young pro took a job on the game's lowest rung. He agreed to be the assistant pro at Horizon Hills Country Club near El Paso. His pay was thirty dollars a week. Twenty-four-year-old Trevino drove his battered 1958 Oldsmobile 650 miles from Dallas to Horizon Hills, a desert course on a shoulder of the Rio Grande, and Titanic had to look for another kid worth backing.

Raymond Floyd, twenty-two, was a second-year touring pro with a look of satisfaction in his eye. Like Trevino he would go on to a Hall of Fame career—Floyd would win the 1976 Masters, 1986 U.S. Open, and two PGA Championships. Like Trevino he was a member of the last generation of touring pros who came up as serious gamblers, betting more than they could earn in tournaments. "In those days gambling was part of what made a good golfer," Floyd recalled. He was in his element at Tenison Park, where he beat Ti's friend Ace Darnell, the card-room proprietor, in a money match for a thousand dollars. The next day they played for twice as much, with Floyd handicapped: "He played straight-up and I played two-ball worst-ball." That meant Floyd hit two drives off the first tee, picked up the better-situated ball, and played the worse one. After hitting that ball, he dropped another, swung again, and played the worse of the two shots. If one hit the green and one plugged in a bunker, he had to hit two from the bunker and use the one that wound up farther from the hole. If he made one putt and the other rolled off the green, he played his next two from off the green. Most pros struggle to shoot eighty-five playing two-ball worse-ball. Floyd broke eighty to beat Darnell again. All the while Titanic watched from the shadows. "You couldn't help but notice him," Floyd said. "An older man in the background, tall and very thin. Quiet, observant. After the round he came up to me and said, 'Young man, I'm impressed with the way you gamble. I'm Ti Thompson.'"

Floyd said, "*Titanic* Thompson?"

"That's me."

"I've heard a lot about you."

"You and me could go on the road," Ti said. "You'd make more than you'll make on the tour."

Floyd said no thanks. He knew pro golf was changing. Ti might have been right if they were talking about the old-time tour with its $1,500 first-prize checks. As recently as 1959 the leading money-winner had earned $53,000. But now Arnold Palmer and television were enriching the game. Palmer had won $128,000 in 1963, Floyd's rookie year. Jack Nicklaus would bump that to $320,000 by 1972. Floyd would have enjoyed hustling tens of thousands with Titanic but chose to chase future millions on the televised tour. He turned Ti down, then began worrying that the great Titanic thought less of him for it. A couple days later Ti and Jeannette were eating at Denny's when Ray Floyd approached their table. Floyd leaned down over their breakfasts, looked Ti in the eye, and said, "I am the greatest golfer in the world."

Jeannette was impressed. She had thought her husband and Minnesota Fats were the cockiest men alive. Titanic, watching Floyd walk away, said he didn't mind the kid's bragging—he might even give him a chance to back it up.

It would need to be soon. The gamblers' road map was folding in around Ti's little house in Dallas. He was driving a Lincoln Continental, no jalopy but no Pierce-Arrow either. Playing cards with Tommy was fun and profitable, but Tommy spent more and more time on the road alone, trying to prove he was more than his father's sidekick. Dallas was proving to be a dry hole for Ti; the poker lords at Redman's knew all his tricks. He had outlived the Broadway heyday of craps, a game tamed and corporatized in Las Vegas. Poker was going the same way. Pool was so moribund that Fats was reduced to hawking discount cue sticks and playing against Zsa Zsa Gabor on a syndicated TV show, *Minnesota Fats Hustles the Stars*, soon cancelled. Nick the Greek, broke, sat in a bingo hall in Gardena, California, playing for five cents a game. "Hey, it's action," he said.

Fats had socked some money away, but Titanic and the Greek were purists. Asking why men like Ti and Nick don't save some of their winnings is like asking why wolves don't bury their kill. They live to hunt. Putting some money away—a squirrel's approach—wouldn't work for such men because then the hunt *wouldn't matter.* To matter it has to get your nostrils flaring if you win and hurt if you don't. So they bet until they were broke and then started over.

There wasn't as much action for Ti after Floyd left Dallas to rejoin the PGA tour. On a good day he hustled up five hundred dollars. He needed a boost.

He made a scouting trip to El Paso and found that Trevino had galvanized the money men on both sides of the Rio Grande. The wealthy cotton farmer who founded Horizon Hills loved the chatty Mexican-American pro, and so did his friends, including a few prosperous Mexicans from Ciudad Juárez, across the river. Trevino's backers were staking him against all comers. Titanic stuck around, getting comfortable in El Paso. He paid $250 to join the club. "After a week he had robbed our members of so much money—pitching coins, blackjack, poker, playing golf right- and left-handed—they asked real nice if he would leave," Trevino recalled. The club's owners got a call from the Texas Rangers asking if the notorious Titanic Thompson was gambling on their property. The answer was no—they had just missed him. He had left town after shaking hands with Trevino's backers, saying they'd all have a hell of a time next time.

●   ●   ●

"Ever hear of a little Mexican named Trevino?"

Floyd shook his head.

"Want to play him for money?" Ti asked. "Down in El Paso?"

Floyd liked the sound of that. "Anybody I never heard of, I'll play anywhere."

Titanic, Floyd, and Ace Darnell flew a turboprop from Dallas to El Paso. Ti was sparing no expense. He expected to finish the week a hundred grand to the good, with help from Darnell.

The golfers weren't told how much they were playing for. This was standard procedure. Gamblers had several reasons to keep the numbers to themselves when they financed money matches. Straight-arrow golfers like Byron Nelson felt that playing in such blissful ignorance kept their hands clean, while others got nervous if they knew the stakes were high. The backers, for their part, figured the players had no more need to know than a racehorse does. A fifty-thousand-dollar win might be better for Ti if Floyd thought the stakes were two thousand. What the golfers knew for sure was that they would be well paid for winning and not so well paid—tipped a few thousand—if they lost. To Trevino the difference was something like wealth. Even Floyd stood to match the five-thousand-dollar first-place check he had won at the PGA's St. Petersburg Open. But no one had more at stake than Titanic, who had called in IOUs and borrowed money from Darnell to fund what might be his last stand. He had about twenty-five thousand in his pocket.

Floyd sat by the window on the plane to El Paso, watching the fields and pecan groves of central Texas give way to desert. When they landed, Ti rented a car for the drive to Horizon Hills. At the course, the self-styled "greatest golfer" climbed out and yawned, squinting at fairways that showed as much dirt as grass.

"Welcome to Horizon Hills, Mister Floyd," said a clubhouse attendant. "Let me get your clubs for you."

"Who'm I playing?" Floyd asked as the attendant hauled his clubs to the curb.

"Me. I'm Lee Trevino."

Trevino, who served as Horizon Hills' assistant pro as well as part-time locker-room attendant, bartender, and range-ball retriever, lugged Floyd's golf bag into the clubhouse. Ace Darnell clapped Floyd on the back and asked if he wanted to look over the course. "I don't need to look over a thing. I'm playing the locker-room boy," Floyd said. He bought into a clubhouse card game and called for a drink.

Titanic saw a little of the youthful Derby Kid in the preening Floyd but saw more of himself in the tough, self-made Trevino. Still he told Darnell they had the odds on their side. They were backing one of the top young players in the world against an assistant pro who still washed golf carts and was now in the locker room brushing and shining Floyd's golf shoes.

That night Floyd stopped by Ti's hotel room. "He was sitting on the bed, throwing cards. Had his hat upside down in the corner, twenty or twenty-five feet away, and he flipped fifty-two cards into that hat, one after the other. Not on a bet, just to show me," Floyd said. "I remember his hands. Ti was seventy-something, but he had the hands of a twenty-five-year-old. It's an odd word to use about a man's hands, but they were beautiful."

The players and their backers met at the course the next day. A few locals came out to watch. Titanic bet nine thousand dollars for starters. Darnell added another nine thousand. Floyd threw down a thousand of his own. Trevino's backers put eighteen grand on their man, with side bets on birdies, chip-ins, and other extras. There were whistles and hisses as Floyd out-drove Trevino off the first tee. The game was on.

There were no caddies. The players rode golf carts between shots. Trevino had a souped-up cart he liked to drive at top speed, getting airborne as he barreled over humps and through gullies. Six-foot-one Floyd, who towered over his five-seven opponent, was twenty to thirty yards longer off the tee. Floyd had a deft, pinpoint short game, but so did the underdog, whom sportswriter Jim Murray later called "a young Mexican with a putting stroke you could set to music and the guts of a train robber." They played conservative golf on the first few holes, matching pars, feeling each other out. Then the birdies began. With its dry, hard fairways, Horizon Hills would play short to any golfer with tour-level power. "The course was wide open, with no irrigation. I was driving it 350 yards," Floyd recalled. He could reach the par-five holes in two shots and would birdie almost all of them. "But Lee was long enough. His low hook was perfect for those fairways. At that time he couldn't hit the ball over a two-story house, but his hook would hit the ground and run 150 yards." More important, Trevino knew every inch of Horizon Hills. Early in the match, after Floyd missed a putt that seemed to break the wrong way—uphill!—Trevino knocked in an uphill-breaker of his own. He was proving the old saw *Don't play a good player on his course.* According to Trevino, "Desert greens are the toughest. On an ocean course, everything breaks toward the ocean. In a mountain region you look for the highest mountain and everything breaks away from that. But in flat desert a putt on one hole will break east, on the next hole south and the next west. I liked my chances against Raymond Floyd."

The first day went down to the wire. On the back nine, Trevino sank another tricky putt. Floyd, eyeing the way Trevino's putt moved, played the same quirky break and matched Lee's birdie. Trevino had a one-shot lead—the stroke he had gained with his first local-knowledge birdie. He nursed that edge all the way to the eighteenth hole, where Ti and Darnell followed the action from their golf cart, zipping ahead of the Mexican contingent and parking on the fringe of the green. The Mexicans whooped when their man rolled in a clinching putt.

No scorecard survives from that day's play. Floyd guessed he shot sixty-five to Trevino's sixty-three. Trevino was never sure. Some accounts credit him with a seven-under-par sixty-five to Floyd's sixty-six. One thing is certain: The home team won. Titanic lost his nine thousand dollars. "But he was calm as could be," said Jesse Whittenton, a former Green Bay Packers cornerback who co-owned Horizon Hills. "Titanic never called attention to himself, but people were drawn to him. When he wasn't on the golf course or playing some high-money poker game he'd sit in the clubhouse with a deck of cards. Pretty soon he's surrounded by little kids, entertaining them with card tricks."

Trevino's backers agreed to play for the same stakes on the second day. They thought they had an added edge this time, having treated Floyd to a trip across the border the night before. "They told Ray, 'Hey, let's go to Juarez, see some women, drink some booze,' " Trevino recalled. After a night of *taberna*-hopping, they took him dove-hunting. Floyd and his new friends huddled in the dark for hours, waiting for something to shoot at, but there were no doves. Finally one of the men decided Floyd's hunting cap looked like a dove.

"I'm not hunting with those crazy bastards again," Floyd told Trevino the next day. "One of them shot my hat off!"

If they thought a hung-over Floyd would be easy prey the following morning, they were wrong. Floyd could hold his liquor. He could sleep for an hour, wake without knowing what town he was in, and break par on any course anywhere—which he did on his second full day in El Paso.

"Word had gotten around that Raymond Floyd was at Horizon Hills and the crowd picked up," Trevino said. With another nine thousand dollars on Floyd, Titanic kept an eye on Trevino to make sure the assistant pro didn't try anything slick. They both knew how to hide a dab of ChapStick under the bill of a golf cap and thumb a bit on the clubface before a key shot; the stuff acted like Vaseline, taking spin off the ball. But Trevino didn't need to cheat. His hooking drives found every fairway. Again he took a one-stroke lead and hung on. He shot sixty-three to Floyd's sixty-four.

Titanic was livid. "We bring a sports car to race a Model-T and get run over!" he told Darnell. Their one hope was to talk Trevino's backers into a third round for still-higher stakes, a real showdown. But first Ti had to take his man's measure. He sat Floyd down in a corner of the clubhouse. Floyd hung his head, griping about the cement fairways, the unreadable greens, and the wind.

"Listen here," Ti said. "You forget all that. There's times you get yourself down to two choices. You can lose. Or put your head down and *play*."

"I can beat him," Floyd said.

Trevino's camp agreed to one more round. Titanic wanted to play for fifty thousand dollars. The Mexican moguls agreed to twenty thousand, not knowing he couldn't cover even that. Down eighteen thousand already, Ti would be in a fix if Floyd lost. He would have to offer his marker for most of the last twenty thousand dollars and scramble to pay the debt. Losers who were slow to make their markers good sometimes "woke up dead," as he put it.

The final day was a golf fiesta. "There were pickup trucks bouncing down the fairway full of guys drinking beer and watching our match," Trevino recalled. Truck radios provided a Spanish-music soundtrack as Floyd fired a thirty-one on the front nine that had Ace Darnell thumping the steering wheel of Ti's golf cart. Titanic, riding shotgun, had yet to crack a smile. "Got a ways to go," he said. Sure enough, Trevino made a late birdie to cut Floyd's lead to one shot. He birdied again to pull even. They were deadlocked as they stepped to the tee box at the eighteenth hole, a 556-yard par-five that was reachable in two shots, thanks to a hard-baked fairway that sent Floyd's drive bounding and rolling to a stop in a patch of brown grass within 250 yards of the green. Trevino's shorter drive left him farther back. That meant he would hit next. He lashed a fairway-wood shot that sizzled audibly as it passed Floyd, who was standing by his tee shot twenty yards ahead. Trevino's ball zipped past at head height, curled from right to left, and bounced to a stop fifteen feet from the hole. The *muchachos* in their pickup trucks pumped their fists and honked their horns. Floyd was surely snake-bit; if Trevino made that eagle putt, Floyd stood to lose even if he birdied the last hole.

He reached for his one-iron. He settled over his second shot. Head down, Floyd pictured the target, a flagstick with another ball too damn close to it. He swung and struck a low, near-perfect approach that bit the green, skidded, and stopped—a tour-level shot, almost as good as Trevino's. Moments later the eighteenth green was ringed with golf carts, pickup trucks, Horizon Hills golfers, course workers, and other locals who had heard about the match, a rowdy gallery of perhaps a hundred spectators. Some were drunk, others just festive, but everyone and everything—every gambler, dog, crow, and cowboy-hatted truck driver—went quiet as Floyd studied the green between his ball and the cup. After three days at Horizon Hills he knew which way his twenty-foot putt would break. He started his ball toward the hole. It rolled for four long seconds and curled into the cup. An eagle!

Those four seconds turned the match upside down. Trevino would have to sink his own fifteen-foot eagle putt to match Floyd's sixty-three. If he missed, he would have outplayed the tour's golden boy for fifty-three holes only to lose on the fifty-fourth. Trevino stalked the putt, eyeing the line from every angle. When he chose his line, he didn't hesitate; he took his stance, rapped the putt.

The ball horseshoed around the hole. Floyd blinked. "I can still see that putt in my sleep," he said later. "It went down in the cup, went around, came back out and stuck on the lip." Trevino looked at his ball in disbelief. Titanic sat up straight in his golf cart. After more than a minute of waiting, with Trevino walking around the hole, peering down from every angle, the ball still refused to drip in. Ti and Darnell clambered from their cart and hugged Floyd. Trevino's supporters surrounded him, commiserating in Spanish. Their assistant pro had fought Floyd to a three-day standoff. They loved him more than ever.

Floyd worked his way through the crowd to Trevino. The players shook hands as Floyd deployed the only Spanish he knew. "*Adios, amigo*," he said. "I can make easier money on the tour."

Almost half a century later, golf insiders still talk about Floyd and Trevino's three-day war. Veteran pro and CBS golf announcer Gary McCord calls it "secretly famous—the last of the great money matches." Floyd's eagle and Trevino's in-and-out putt meant that Titanic lived to bet another day. It gave Ti the poker stake that was his real reason for setting up the golf match in the first place—not to beat Trevino's backers out of twenty or even fifty thousand dollars on the golf course, but to cheat them for much more playing cards in Juárez. His plan would have fizzled had Trevino swept the golf match, but as it turned out Trevino may have helped him. Despite their last-day loss, the Mexican moguls had had a good week. They were flush, happy—ready to cut the cards.

Titanic was in a buoyant mood as he and Darnell walked the crowded streets of Juárez. He approached a policeman and said, "Let's see your gun. *Pistola*. I don't think it works." He snatched the shocked cop's revolver before the man could react. Ti aimed at a storefront window and pulled the trigger. *Click*. The gun didn't fire. Smiling, he handed it back.

Darnell couldn't figure it. "How'd you do that?"

"Give me your piece, Ace."

Darnell handed over his .45. Titanic aimed it at Ace's foot and pulled the trigger, his free hand flashing over the firing pin like a Wild West gunslinger's.

"Wait!"

Click.

"Jesus, Ti, you could have shot me!"

Ti handed back the pistol. "Only if I did it wrong." Darnell checked it. The gun was still loaded. He never found out how Ti had made it misfire.

That night, playing hold 'em in an underground card room in Juárez, Ti quickly doubled his twenty thousand. He marked the cards as they came through his hands, so he knew what Darnell and the Mexicans held at all times. Darnell's job was to follow Titanic's instructions, raising when Ti scratched his cheek, folding when he coughed or smiled in a way that showed teeth. They changed the signals whenever they stepped outside to stretch their legs. "It's our night," Ti crowed. "We'll be up a hundred grand before we're through."

Titanic began playing possum, complaining about his luck, building the others' confidence. After hours of biding his time, he looked around the table. The cards were arrayed the way he wanted them. Ti held the mortal nuts, the perfect hand. The Mexicans had strong cards too and raised, building the pot. Ti signaled Darnell to raise, but Ace hesitated. Most of the light had drained from the smoky room. He didn't believe Ti could still see the tiny crimps and nearly invisible touches on the cards he had been reading all night. The pot was growing fast; Darnell didn't want to screw up. He hesitated, then folded. So did the others.

On the next break Ti pulled Darnell aside. "I ought to shoot your sorry ass," he hissed.

"Ti, come on. I couldn't see my hand in front of my face in there."

Titanic put his hand on the butt of his Colt. He said, "Do that again and I'll kill you."

They returned to the game, but the all-in moment had passed. Trevino's backers began betting less, checking their watches. In the end Titanic came out ahead, but he never forgave Ace Darnell for ignoring the signal that might have turned Juárez into El Dorado.

Trevino went on to join Floyd on the PGA tour. Titanic returned to Dallas. He worked solo at Tenison Park, flipping silver dollars on the putting green or playing nine-hole matches, and haunted poker parlors at night, sitting behind short stacks of ten- and twenty-dollar chips. He was civil to Darnell when he saw him at Redman's, but more and more he chose his son Tommy as his partner. Tommy never second-guessed Ti's signals, and Ti started thinking the bond between the two of them might mean more than any split he could offer a man like Darnell. Maybe blood was thicker than money.

12 LIVING LEGEND

A YEAR AFTER THE FLOYD-TREVINO MATCH, A CRAGGY man in a fedora sauntered into the *Golf Digest* offices in Norwalk, Connecticut. "He was introduced as Mr. A.C. Thomas of Texas," recalled staffer Ross Goodner, who knew the visitor's other name. "Titanic Thompson! The name evoked memories of tales we'd all heard. It was as if Merlin himself had walked in."

Titanic flipped cards at a filing cabinet across the room. According to Goodner, "Each card hit the same spot on the cabinet. It had to be seen to be believed." Ti pitched quarters and half-dollars, making one hop onto the other. He told stories about Hogan, Nelson, and Snead. He had come to sell his life story to the magazine, but *Golf Digest* didn't meet his price and he left without a deal. His departure reminded Goodner of another time Ti's skills went to waste: "I had seen Titanic years earlier, at a small golf club where he was standing on the putting green, idly stroking the ball left-handed, scanning the clubhouse, the parking lot, the home green." Looking for a pigeon. "But he was known, and the club manager came out and told him to leave. Titanic Thompson had been one of the world's most talented men and perhaps one of its loneliest."

Was he lonely? His wife didn't think so. "He liked having people around, but all he *needed* was people to gamble with," Jeannette said. "And then it wasn't for the company or even the money. It was for the sport—to show another gambler who was smarter, who was who." Titanic's fifth wife was certain her husband wasn't lonely on the road. She knew Ti slept with more than a few of the young girls who caught his eye. One of his sidekicks said he knew "for a fact Ti slept with a Miss America contestant when he was in his sixties— not Miss America, but one of the states." Jeannette, who recalled Ti as a vigorous lover well into his seventies, forgave his infidelities.

In his way, he was a good father. He let young Ty Wayne tag along with him at the Rockwood Park par-three course in Fort Worth. The boy found golf boring. "He'd hit the ball up, it came down near the hole, he made his birdie or settled for par," Ty Wayne said years later. "I thought golf had to be the easiest game in the world." Titanic played with cronies at scruffy Tenison Park and with his dentist friend Jim Hill at Glen Lakes Country Club. Hill marveled at the way the old dog kept inventing new tricks. Once, comparing aches and pains with a muscle-bound opponent, Ti offered the man a bottle of pills. "Try these Anacin. I always take three or four." They were sleeping pills. An hour later the mark's slow-motion swing resulted in a one-yard drive.

"I met Titanic in Palm Springs," said high-stakes golfer Rudy Durand. "He had a wind-chiseled face and an aura, like you wouldn't want to cross him. He looked like Clint Eastwood. The hustlers would all be hanging around Canyon Country Club, hoping to get a game with Frank Sinatra or Glen Campbell, and they'd step aside to let him go by." Big-money gamblers sometimes arrived by limousine from Las Vegas or Los Angeles to play cash games for five thousand dollars a hole. The older ones feared Titanic, but his aura was dimming. Durand, who knew all the hustlers' tricks, saw Ti resort to one of the simplest in a match against a Rolls-Royce– driving member of the club. Ti's ball was plugged in a bunker. He palmed another ball, holding it flat against the grip of his sand wedge. He stepped on the first ball to make it disappear and swung hard, spraying sand, releasing the palmed ball while the sand flew so that it looked like an explosion shot. "It didn't seem worthy of him, but he'd do anything to cheat rich guys," Durand said. "Arrogant CEO types were his meat. 'They think they're tigers, but they're squirrels,' he told me. And he said he was an alligator, waiting for a squirrel to step between his jaws and then—*snap*."

Hill helped Titanic manage what was left of his money. "He had gone through at least ten million dollars, and he had nothing," said Hill. No investments, no checking or savings account, no insurance. The hustler who had driven through the Holland Tunnel with a satchel stuffed with $960,000 in cash now counted on a monthly Social Security check for $109.20 to get him through the lean months. He needed to dope his marks with sleeping pills or fool them with lame golf gaffs to come home a winner. One Tenison Park regular who watched him play a thousand-dollar round with Dick Martin, a hustler half Ti's age, felt sorry for Titanic: "His flexibility was so limited that he couldn't raise the club above waist level, and I don't think he hit a shot that traveled two hundred yards." Too proud to ask Martin to spot him strokes, Ti lost. Now he was the one with an East Side bankroll, an inch-thick wad of singles inside a hundred-dollar bill.

IN 1969 TI GOT A CALL from Benny Binion, a former bootlegger and mob boss with two murder convictions on his rap sheet. Binion, who had once worked for Lansky, fled Dallas for Las Vegas in the Forties and opened Binion's Horseshoe casino, pioneering the sort of hospitality that became the town's gold-plated standard. He promised patrons "good food cheap, good whiskey cheap, and a good gamble." The Horseshoe was the first Vegas casino with carpet on the floors instead of sawdust. It was the first to ply players with free drinks. And in 1951, the year it opened, Binion's Horse-shoe was the site of a five-card-stud showdown between Nick the Greek and Johnny Moss, the genesis of modern big-time poker.

Nick Dandolos was sixty-eight in 1951. Age had hollowed his cheeks and made his nose more prominent. He dyed his gray-ing hair jet black. The Greek had won and lost tens of millions on his road to eventual ruin, but in 1951 he was still riding high, winning enough five-figure poker pots to offset his horse-racing losses. Moss, forty-four, was probably the best poker player alive. Now bald, he peered at his cards through thick Clark Kent spec-tacles. Moss had won some black hundred-dollar chips in games they both played but had never gone against the Greek mano a mano. The format of their showdown, a heavyweight champion-ship of five-card stud, was Binion's idea. One card down, four up. At Benny's invitation Nick and Moss squared off at the Horseshoe for weeks that stretched into months, playing five days a week while surrounded by crowds that gathered under Binion's trademark, a giant golden Plexiglas horseshoe filled with a million dollars in cash. "They were crowdin' around that table with their eyeballs hangin' out," Moss recalled. He and the Greek pushed chips back and forth from Sunday noon through Thursday night, when Moss would sleepwalk to his room and fall into bed for a day and a half. When he returned to find Nick playing craps, the Greek said, "Johnny, you're going to sleep your life away." Marathon poker had a long history—the pros were so accustomed to playing for three or four days at a stretch that the thirty-hour game that got Arnold Rothstein killed was thought of as a short one. Even in the Forties and Fifties, before cocaine became the stimulant of choice, poker players gobbled speed like long-distance truckers. A few could play for a week with nothing more than bathroom breaks, and none was longer-lasting than Nick the Greek. After Sunday-through-Thursday sessions at the Horseshoe he would nap for a few hours before he woke, shaved, donned a fresh suit and tie, and returned to the casino while waiting for Moss to come back to the poker table. During one of those breaks their match was eclipsed by a celebrity sighting: Albert Einstein was in Vegas. The great scientist, a faculty member at the Institute for Advanced Study in Princeton, New Jersey, was in town for a physics symposium. Nick knew him—the Greek knew everybody—but doubted many gamblers had heard of Einstein, so he introduced him around as "Al from Princeton—he controls a lot of the action around Jersey."

The Moss-Dandolos marathon lasted five months. In its most famous hand, with about $150,000 in the pot, Moss had six-nine-two-three showing. As the Greek suspected, his hole card was a nine. The Greek had eight-six-four on the table, followed by the final card: a jack. Moss raised. Nick pushed in all his chips, saying, "I think I've got a jack in the hole." And he did—the last card had vaulted him from broke to $520,000 ahead. By the end, however, Moss was up by at least that much. Some accounts put his advantage as high as two million—tantamount to twenty million dollars today. Whatever the difference, the Greek was finished. After tossing in one last losing hand, he stood up and uttered one of the most famous lines in gambling lore. "Mister Moss," Nick said, "I have to let you go." His graceful exit proved immortal; card players still quote him when quitting a game.

Almost two decades later, when Binion phoned Ti in 1969, the Horseshoe's future was in doubt. Las Vegas crowds were leaving Glitter Gulch, the downtown home of Binion's Horseshoe and the Golden Nugget, to flush their money down more opulent drains at Caesars Palace and Kirk Kerkorian's International Hotel on the Vegas Strip five miles to the southwest. Benny needed to recapture the excitement of *Moss v. Nick the Greek*. He told Titanic he was putting together a tournament, the first-ever World Series of Poker, and inviting the best players around. Ti was not asked to play. "But I want the legends there," Binion said. "That means you."

Ti had his doubts. He had gone to Las Vegas with Tommy, who

beamed with a son's pride when gamblers recognized his father and called out, "Titanic, you're the greatest!" But the plastic cards and the house advantage wore Ti down. You can't cheat in Vegas, he said—the casinos beat you to it with their 1½ percent edge in some games and a 5 or 6 percent rakeback in poker. He left broke and nobody said goodbye.

"We had to pay him to get him to come," recalled Benny Binion's son Jack, who ran the first World Series of Poker at the Horseshoe in 1970. No fan of the great Titanic, Jack called him "a cheap son of a bitch" who demanded an appearance fee despite the fact that "the public didn't know who the hell he was." Ti's hair was going from gray to white and the skin under his chin sagged, but his beautiful hands were as quick as ever. He impressed the Binions and the players with his card tricks, coin flips, and other feats. Then they rolled their eyes when he tried to cheat them. He didn't understand that times had changed. People were more suspicious than they used to be—not just sharps but regular folks watching TV stories about Vietnam and the Nixon administration. The charmer who had gotten his start with a traveling medicine show was out of step with the 1970s. "His act was corny," Jack Binion said. "He'd say, 'Betcha I can flip this card right on top of your hat,' rather than work the conversation around to hats. Who'd take that bet?"

The first World Series of Poker featured seven players: Johnny Moss, Doyle "Texas Dolly" Brunson, Amarillo Slim Preston, and four others. Titanic served as cohost with Chill Wills, a movie-actor friend of Benny Binion's. The cohosts smiled and shook a lot of hands. Wills signed autographs and hee-hawed for fans in the voice of his most famous film character, Francis the Talking Mule. Titanic lifted a Dr Pepper as the Binions and the players toasted the event's future, none of them dreaming of the more than six thousand entrants and $8.5 million top prize the World Series would boast in 2009. In later years Binion would introduce a freeze-out

format—everyone gets a certain number of chips and play contin-
ues until one player has all the chips. In that inaugural year, though,
the champion was chosen by polling the players. The first ballot
ended in a seven-way tie when they all voted for themselves. Benny
broke the logjam by asking them to vote for the second-best player.
Johnny Moss won in a landslide and was given first prize—the title
"World Series of Poker Champion" and a handshake.

The trip to Vegas was shaping up as Titanic's best road trip in
years. Hill had given him a thousand-dollar grubstake; Ti turned
it into ten thousand playing hold 'em. The most challenging poker
game was a perfect match for Ti's mathematical bent and his eye
for others' weaknesses. In hold 'em, two hole cards are followed
by three face-up community cards called the "flop," shared by all
players. After the flop comes a fourth up card, called the "turn,"
and a fifth, the "river." The game's four rounds of betting and
ever-shifting odds have made hold 'em—particularly the no-limit
version in which players can go all-in, risking everything to bully
or bluff an opponent—a popular subject of academic study. "For
many years chess served as the [fruit fly] *Drosophila* of artificial-
intelligence research, but poker, as an experimental test-bed for
exploring AI, is a much richer domain," reads a report in the International Computer Games Association journal. In 2008 a hunk of
software dubbed Polaris 2.0 defeated a team of poker professionals in a hold-'em match with betting limits, but no computer has
come close to beating any top player in the more complex no-limit
game, for one reason: Computers aren't devious. Unfortunately for
Titanic, his heyday was over before hold 'em reached its peak.

He cashed in his ten grand in chips and stuck the cash in a
suitcase. That night, someone slipped into his hotel room using
a key—an inside job. Heavy-sleeper Ti didn't know he had been
robbed until he woke the next day. He flew home to Texas on the
Binions' dime with the clothes on his back and a trophy inscribed
World Series of Poker—Living Legend—"Titanic."

As Ti neared eighty, he began to feel as run-down as the aging Runyon, who wrote, "I long ago came to the conclusion that all life is six-to-five against." Ti grew preoccupied with blood. "I haven't got enough blood in me to keep a grasshopper alive," he said. But he could still get his back up. Playing nine-ball with Tommy in a Dallas pool hall, he did a slow boil as a couple of toughs at the next table taunted him. "Hey old man, whaddya got?" They said they were thinking about robbing him. He set his two-piece cue on the table and opened his jacket, giving them a look at the .45 in his shoulder holster. "I don't particularly want to shoot you, but I wouldn't mind," he said. The men backed away. Ti nodded at Tommy as if to say, *See? The old man's still got it.* He didn't know the toughs were afraid of his son, not him. Tommy was twenty-eight, bearded, broad-shouldered, and as badass as they come. He'd had his pearl-handled .38 trained on the chump who said "old man" long before Titanic made his speech, and back in his belt before Ti ever saw it. Tommy had his father's back but never told him so.

Ti's son, who had his father's deep-set eyes and lightning fingers, stood six feet two and cultivated a baleful, intimidating glare. Tommy had always emulated his father, from gambling and gunslinging to marrying young. No prize as a husband, he had three ex-wives by the time he turned thirty. "All I wanted to do was sit in a straight-back chair around a poker table and smell the cigar smoke," he said. Now, however, he was wondering if he had chosen the wrong route the day he went looking for Titanic. Regrets tugged at him more often after he survived a card-game shootout. Tommy and Bill Douglas, an old traveling partner of Ti's, had gone to Memphis to cheat a pair of marks at high-stakes poker. Douglas was a ruthless, dangerous man. He braced a two-by-four under the doorknob to foil hijackers and played with one eye on the door. But that night he wasn't quick enough. Two men kicked the door down. They came in shooting. Douglas lay dead on the floor as the gunmen turned to Tommy. He raised his hands as if to ward off bullets. "Don't shoot," he said. And they let him live. According to Tommy, he felt God's presence in the room. Already doubting his chosen path, he began to wonder if he was cursed to be a gambler like his father and grandfather.

In the Seventies, Ti, Jeannette, Tommy, and little Ty Wayne lived in a small white house in Colleyville, Texas, near Dallas. Not long after they moved in, Titanic was unpacking a box when he told his son about a time he was getting settled in a hotel room in some town or another, unpacking stacks of money tied with rubber bands. Ten thousand here, twenty over there. The numbers had clicked in his head and he realized he was looking at a million dollars in cash.

"What happened to it?" Tommy asked.

Ti shrugged. The gambler who had packed all that cash now picked coins from a dish in the kitchen so he could take his wife out for ice cream. They both liked root-beer floats but couldn't always afford them. Ti's eyes were failing—he couldn't tell an ace from a king when Jeannette held them up across the street—but he claimed his vision was better than ever. He would peek at the kitchen clock on his way to his favorite living-room chair, then plop down and point at the clock as if he could read it from fifty feet away. "We better go, it's 7:08!"

One day he phoned Doyle Brunson. "He said he had a proposition for me," recalled Brunson, who drove to Colleyville to find Titanic waiting with a deck of cards. Ti wanted to sell his best hold-'em techniques. Dealing hand after hand, he expounded on the game's complexity. To show how hold-'em odds defy intuition, he dealt two pairs of hole cards. One was the ace and king of spades. The other was the ace of clubs and the suicidal king of hearts. Players believed the off-suited cards were better because they offered two chances to complete a flush. But Titanic said it wasn't so. The suited ace-king was a far better bet.

"Hell, Ti, everybody's known that for ten years," Brunson said.

Titanic looked crestfallen. He had nothing to sell but couldn't bring himself to ask for a handout. After a minute he brightened. "Doyle, do you pitch horseshoes?"

"Not well enough to bet you."

They went to the backyard, where Ti took a few throws to warm up his spindly arm. Then he began making ringers. With each toss the shoe made a three-quarter turn in flight before clanking the stake forty feet away. "Ringer after ringer after ringer," Brunson recalled. "Not for money. He just wanted to show me."

In 1972 Jim Hill called Ray Cave, an editor at *Sports Illustrated*, offering to sell Titanic Thompson's life story. Hill had better luck as a salesman than Ti had. Cave said the magazine didn't pay subjects for stories but could pay Ti five thousand dollars to be coauthor of a first-person piece. All Titanic would have to do was talk to writer Edwin "Bud" Shrake.

"Tell him to come, we'll play some gin rummy," Ti said. That invitation led to a unique provision in the contract Cave mailed out. Along with the usual legal boilerplate, the contract read, *Under no condition will Sports Illustrated be responsible for Bud Shrake's gin rummy losses to Titanic Thompson.*

Shrake pulled up at the house in Colleyville to meet a tall, white-haired man in corduroys and a sweater vest. Ti had let the stubble on his chin grow into a short, scraggly beard. Shrake thought he looked like Uncle Sam. They spent the rest of the week at the house, the local bowling alley, and the par-three course, where the writer saw Titanic shoot "a respectable score, three or four over par, just enough to hustle some guy." Ti spoke of Carlo the rock-fetching water spaniel, the Bogardus medicine show, Capone, Rothstein, Nick the Greek, and that broken-legged nag Nellie A. The magazine's fact-checkers would confirm almost every detail. Ti said little about his personal life other than to emphasize how he had tracked down his father. "See, that's one of the main stories you can write about," he told Shrake. "I found my father and beat him out of sixteen hundred dollars. I said, 'Well, I'm your son from Rodgers, Arkansas.' That was at Oil City, Louisiana."

The story, "Soundings from Titanic," ran in the October 9, 1972, issue of *Sports Illustrated*. Shrake considered it one of his favorites. He went on to write eighteen books and seven movies and became, as Governor Ann Richards's companion, the unofficial "first gentleman of Texas." Shortly before his death in 2009 he talked about Titanic: "He was tall and thin and leathery, with a quick grin and eyes that had a mischievous twinkle. I think he told me he was sixty-five. His wife was much younger. They lived in a rather ordinary small house, certainly not a mansion that would befit someone who won all the money he got away with, but of course his salad days were way behind him. I would call him proud, certainly not regretful, an extraordinary athlete who got the best of everyone. And he was a genius of sorts, computing the odds on any proposition in an instant. He gave me a long lecture about odds, but I barely understood it."

Shrake solved the riddle of the Mexican misfires of 1965—when Ti took a policeman's revolver and shot at Ace Darnell's foot— by adding a detail that didn't make his *Sports Illustrated* story. "The main thing I remember happened in his living room," Shrake recalled. "Titanic pulled out a pistol, cocked it, handed it to me, and told me to shoot a hole in the sliding glass door that led to the patio. I protested. He said, 'Don't worry, just do it.' So I pulled the trigger—and somehow he stuck the meat of his palm between the hammer and firing pin so fast there was no shot fired."

Ti and Jeannette waved to Shrake as he drove away. Then they went out for root-beer floats.

ARTHRITIS CURLED TITANIC'S HANDS until he winced gripping a golf club. By 1973 he could no longer drive his car, a 1971 Ford LTD that topped out at about sixty. Jeannette drove him to the par-three course and walked along while he played. He could still play nine holes around par, sometimes better, popping Anacin tablets to ease the pain in his hands. In his last month as a golfer she saw him make three aces. "That's quite a run—three holes in one," she told him.

He said, "Well, that's what I was aimin' at."

There came a time when she couldn't take care of him anymore. Tommy was out on his own, living the road-gambler life he had dreamed of. Someone had to pay for the groceries, so Jeannette took a job at the Tarrant County Department of Motor Vehicles. She was gone all day, helping motorists fill out license-plate forms for three dollars an hour while Ti knocked around the house. He couldn't cook for himself and had dizzy spells when the Texas sun blinded him. "We need to find you a rest home," she said.

With help from Tommy and Hill they found an affordable nursing home in Euless, a chip shot from the Dallas–Fort Worth airport. Titanic didn't want to go. "He was madder than hell," says Hill, who drove him there. Ti perked up when he saw card tables and a pool table in the day room and a horseshoe court outside. "Doc," he said, "I'll beat these geezers out of their last nickel."

There was a legal obstacle to his staying. As a married man whose wife had a job, he didn't qualify for Medicaid. "I told him I loved him as much as the day we were married," Jeannette recalled. "I cried and cried." Some couples have marriages of convenience; on August 30, 1973, Alvin and Jeannette Thomas got what she called a survival divorce. After that, Medicaid and Social Security eased the pinch. She gave him a few dollars to bet with and Tommy kicked in when he was flush. Hill added an occasional contribution even after Ti conned another patient—Hill's elderly father—out of his last dime on a Dallas Cowboys football game.

The big man in the nursing home paid young nurses ten dollars apiece to rub his feet. He offered the prettiest one eighty dollars to parade around in the nude for a few minutes. She agreed, and when she was finished he asked if he could touch her. Not in a lecherous way, he swore, and it wasn't. His once-beautiful hands were creased but gentle. After a second he thanked her and said her skin was soft like Nora's and Alice's and Jo Ann's and Maxine's and Jeannette's. He had only married girls with soft skin.

Thunderstorms still scared him. Jeannette came home from the DMV in a storm one night and fell into bed, exhausted. The next thing she knew Ti was standing in the doorway. He had paid one of the nurses to drive him. "I want to come back," he said. "I want to come home." Jeannette said, "Honey, it's impossible." She drove him back to Euless but didn't follow him inside. She was thirty-seven—still young, she told herself—and the nursing home was a dimly lit, troubling place that smelled of Lysol and decay. When a nurse called to say Ti was complaining he was cold, Jeannette left a blanket at the front desk. She couldn't bring herself to go to his room.

Titanic turned eighty-one in November 1973. He chipped golf balls outside the nursing home while planes going to and from the airport roared overhead. He pitched horseshoes from half the regulation distance. Mostly he played poker—five-card stud, because hold 'em was too complicated for some of his fellow patients. His fingers were too stiff to deal the cards, so he dealt by pressing a knuckle to the top of the deck and pushing a card across the table. He bet more aggressively than he used to. When Tommy asked why, Ti said he wanted to get ahead while he still had the brains to do it. Raise, raise against the dying of the light.

Tommy stopped in when he was in town. The two sharps sat up late playing for five or ten dollars while the TV played soundlessly in the corner. As the months passed—Patty Hearst kidnapped, Watergate burglars indicted, Hank Aaron breaking Babe Ruth's home-run record on the mute TV—Tommy noticed something different about his father.

"All his life he entertained and fooled people and never needed anyone," Tommy said. "But at the end he did." The interactions of numbers had always been plain to him; in his dotage he began feeling his way toward warmer human connections. And in the end he told Tommy the truth about finding his own father in Oil City, Louisiana: It never happened. Ti had made it up. Yes, he had left home at sixteen in 1909. Yes, he had asked after a gambler named Lee Thomas in every town from Tulsa to New Orleans. But he never found him. When Tommy showed up that day in San Antonio and Ti took his four hundred dollars and gave it back, they were reenacting a story Ti had invented to make sense of his life story. To make him more than an abandoned boy. To suggest he had proved to Lee Thomas which of them was smarter, who was who. Over the years he had told his lost-father story so many times it seemed real even to him. But now he'd thought it over and didn't want to con Tommy anymore. He said he guessed he had set out to find a father all those years ago and wound up finding a son.

Tommy blinked tears. He said he had a little secret of his own to share. "I've been cheating you."

Titanic didn't believe it until Tommy showed how he had been switching cards on the deal. Not that it mattered much—Tommy gave back what he won. Ti was just sorry he never spotted the trick. He looked at the floor. "I guess I'm going to die here," he said.

Tommy felt his father's bony arms around him, an awkward hug. Titanic said, "I just want to tell you I love you, son."

TOMMY THOMAS WAS PLAYING a high-money game in Cincinnati when the call came. His father had suffered a massive stroke.

Jeannette hung up the phone and drove to the nursing home. She sat in the LTD for a moment, steeling herself, and then hurried inside to find Titanic thrashing in bed while doctors and nurses clapped electrode paddles to his chest. He was trying to speak, but his voice didn't work. He kept pointing to the dresser beside the bed. Jeannette tried to read his lips. Was he trying to say *pajamas*? She looked through his dresser drawers and found a roll of twenties in a pocket of his silk pajamas. Almost four hundred dollars. She held the money up where Ti could see it. He nodded. It was the same signal he had given Nate Raymond when they agreed to double-cross Rothstein in 1928. Jeannette wasn't sure how to interpret his nod. Was he saying yes, he was glad she'd found it for him, or yes, she should keep it? She thought the money might belong to Hill or Tommy, but she could surely use it. She slipped Titanic's last bankroll into her purse.

Alvin Clarence Thomas died on May 19, 1974, and was buried under a shade tree in pancake-flat Bluebonnet Hills Cemetery in Colleyville. Seventy-five mourners attended the service. Jim Hill, Ace Darnell, and Doyle Brunson attended along with fifteen-year-old Ty Wayne and thirty-year-old Tommy, who got what amounted to an inheritance through his mother, Jo Ann, Ti's third wife. The Evansville oil wells Ti gave Jo Ann in exchange for his freedom back in the Forties were still producing, and would produce royalty checks of $1,000 to $1,500 a month "to the order of Thomas Thomas" through 2010 and beyond. Tommy also got the *Living Legend* trophy Benny Binion had given Ti for cohosting the first World Series of Poker.

Jeannette, a widow at the age of thirty-eight, with time for a whole life ahead, got the roll of twenties and twenty years of memories. She wished Titanic had left her a shoebox full of cash instead of a handful of medical bills, but she didn't regret marrying him. "Here was a man who came out of Arkansas with nothing but the spirit in him," she said decades later. "He rose up and made more money than most people ever see. I thought he was the sun and sky."

When the service was over, the mourners dispersing, a young nurse went up and placed a rose on the coffin.

●　　●　　●

THIRTY-FIVE YEARS LATER, a sharp-suited hustler stepped onto Broadway to thunderous applause. It was opening night: the debut of a new multimillion-dollar production of *Guys and Dolls*. The gambler who told Damon Runyon he didn't want publicity was getting his latest revival, one of countless performances of the musical since it first opened in 1950. The theater was only eight blocks from the gamblers' old haunt. The original Lindy's closed in 1957—it's now the site of a huge, busy restaurant called Ruby Foo's—but the sidewalk scene was the same, with crowds and traffic as loud as when the voiceless Runyon wrote Walter Winchell a note: *Listen to the roar*. On opening night, billboards, buses, and taxis were plastered with blowups of the actors playing Sky Masterson and Nathan Detroit. Crowds streamed down Broadway to the foot of Times Square, where Titanic may have stood in 1928, eating an ice-cream cone, looking up at the lights.

In the show, Sky Masterson thinks back to his youth "when the dice were my cousins." He talks about sucker bets ("As sure as you stand there, you're going to wind up with an earful of cider") and love affairs. "The companionship of a doll is a pleasant thing," he says. "But for a close relationship that can last through all the years of life, no doll can take the place of aces back to back."

Alvin "Titanic" Thompson couldn't have said it better himself.

Late in the second act the spotlight falls on Sky. Dressed in a felt fedora and purple silk suit, he's shaking the dice. He's made the ultimate gamble, a bet he can't cover. His soul is at stake and he's got one last do-or-die throw. He rolls 'em and the lights go out.

POSTSCRIPTS

Hyman "Gillie" Biller, the bag man who killed Arnold Rothstein—according to Titanic—came out of hiding in 1930, when New York vice cops caught him booking bets at Yankee Stadium. They kicked Biller out of the ballpark. There is no trace of him after that.

In 1973 **Benny Binion** said he hoped his World Series of Poker might someday have 50 entrants. In 2006 the WSOP had 8,773 entrants. After Binion died in 1989 his friend Amarillo Slim Preston suggested an epitaph: "He was either the gentlest bad guy or the baddest good guy ever." Binion's sons, Jack and Ted, ran the Horseshoe until 1997, when their sister Becky bought them out. Ted Binion died the next year—murdered by his stripper girlfriend and her lover, prosecutors said. The lovers were convicted, then granted a new trial and acquitted. Jack Binion, who became chairman of Steve Wynn's casino empire, is one of the richest men in America.

Poker legends **Doyle "Texas Dolly" Brunson** and **Amarillo Slim Preston** still pluck pigeons. Brunson, seventy-six, a two-time World Series of Poker winner with $2.8 million in career WSOP earnings, is the author of 1978's *Super System*, the most influential poker book ever published. He sometimes regrets writing *Super System*—he probably cost himself millions by sharing his secrets—but the book cemented his status as king of his era. Preston, eighty-one, won the 1972 World Series of Poker and earned $436,000 in WSOP events. In 1992 he followed Brunson into the Poker Hall of Fame.

Three months after Rothstein's murder, according to mob lore, **Al Capone** celebrated Valentine's Day 1929—the day gunmen massacred six members of Bugs Moran's rival gang, plus a luckless optometrist who happened by. The killers riddled their victims with so many bullets that some were nearly cut in half. Scarface Al attended a subsequent meeting in Chicago's Blackstone Hotel, where the pock-faced "Lucky" Luciano, one of Rothstein's former lieutenants, defined the territories of the nation's crime families, set rules for how many "made men" each family would have, how they would deal with each other and the police, and whom they could kill. A decade after serving as a croupier at the Brook, Luciano was what crime writer Selwyn Raab called "the designer of the modern Mafia."

Capone's influence waned. Imprisoned for bootlegging and tax evasion from 1932 to 1939, his health ruined by syphilis, he died in 1947.

Hubert Cokes was charged with murder in Evansville, Indiana, in 1964. The sixty-six-year-old Cokes had killed Richard Kallio, forty-six, after losing a golf bet. "I owed him $380," Cokes testified. "He figured it at $526, and he grabbed for my [bank]roll. . . . I picked up a gun. It was a .357 Magnum. The gun went off accidentally." Cokes was cleared of all charges on a verdict of "defense of property." He died peacefully fourteen years later in an Evansville nursing home.

"Nick the Greek" Dandolos died broke in Los Angeles on Christmas Day 1966. By his own estimate he had won and lost more than $500 million. When word of his death reached Las Vegas, some of the town's high rollers dispatched a hearse to bring the Greek back to Vegas, where he was buried in a golden casket in Woodlawn Cemetery, just off the Strip. His headstone features a pair o' dice, the gamblers' pun on his destination.

Jack "Legs" Diamond, wanted for murder, fled the United States in 1929. Denied entry into England, France, and Germany, he was shipped home on a freighter carrying 4,500 canaries. The following year he was sitting in bed in a New York hotel ("A chorus girl was tubbing in the bathroom," *Time* reported) when two gun-men burst in, shot him, and left him for dead. Diamond dragged himself to the elevator "with the help," he said, "of a coupla shots of whiskey." Rushed to the Polyclinic Hospital, he recovered in the same room where Rothstein died. By then A.R.'s former henchman had survived so many attempts on his life he was called "the clay pigeon of the underworld." His rival Dutch Schultz said, "Can't nobody shoot this guy so he don't bounce back?" Somebody did: A week before Christmas 1931, Diamond was sleeping off a night of drinking in Albany, New York, when he took three shots to the back of the head. His killers were never caught. His widow was the only mourner at his funeral.

Nightclub queen **Mary Louise "Texas" Guinan** starred in a Wild West roadshow—forty showgirls and a horse—in 1933. After a bout of dysentery during a gig in Vancouver, she died at age forty-nine and was buried not in her native Texas but in New York.

Twelve thousand people filed by her casket in a Broadway mortuary. The casket was open per her instructions, "so the suckers can get a good look at me without a cover charge."

Texas golfers **Ben Hogan** and **Byron Nelson** went on to win 128 PGA tour titles between them, including fourteen majors. Nelson won eleven consecutive tournaments in 1945, golf's equivalent of Joe DiMaggio's hitting streak, a record that will never be matched. The kindly "Lord Byron" retired at age thirty-four to run his cattle ranch in Roanoke, Texas. He became a beloved TV commentator, and died in 2006 at the age of ninety-four.

The glum, tightly wound Hogan nearly died in a 1949 auto accident. On a foggy highway near Van Horn, Texas, his Cadillac collided head-on with a Greyhound bus. An instant before impact he threw himself onto his wife, Valerie, to protect her—an act that may have saved both their lives. Police examining the wreckage noted that the steering wheel had punctured the back of the driver's seat. Hogan spent two months in the hospital. Doctors doubted he would play golf again, but four years later he had a miracle year. "Bantam Ben" entered six tournaments and won five, including the 1953 Masters, U.S. Open, and British Open. He died in Fort Worth in 1997.

Howard Hughes quit golf. Badly burned in a 1946 plane crash, he became addicted to painkillers and obsessed with germs. Over the next thirty years he moved to Las Vegas and became a recluse, living in a penthouse at the Desert Inn, which he owned. By the late 1960s the once-handsome, vigorous Hughes was padding around his penthouse wearing tissue boxes for shoes, getting his hair and fingernails and toenails cut once a year, storing his feces in glass jars. He died in 1976 at age seventy, weighing only ninety pounds, with broken-off hypodermic needles still stuck in his emaciated arms, leaving an estate of $2.5 billion.

"Shoeless" Joe Jackson had survived three heart attacks by 1951, when supporters mounted an effort to clear his name. Jackson, sixty-three, was to appear on Ed Sullivan's TV show that winter, but died of a fourth heart attack the week before the show.

Titanic's golf partner **Herman Keiser**, who edged Ben Hogan to win the 1946 Masters, regretted his road trips with Ti. "I have got nothing good to say about him. He was a *thief*," Keiser told *Golf Digest*'s Dave Kindred in 1996. "Then one day, he's got to be 80 years old, he shows up at my house in Ohio, with a partner and two young girls. He says, 'Herman, I've got a plan that's going to make you rich.' Here's Titanic after all these years and he's trying to hustle me. 'Give me $5,000, Herman. . . .' I tell him, 'Ty, stay here, I'll be right back.' I go in the house and get my .22 pistol. I come out and tell him, 'Get outta here right now or I'm gonna shoot you.' Last I ever saw of Titanic Thompson." Keiser died in 2003.

Meyer Lansky, Arnold Rothstein's protégé, was called "the inspirer and controller of American organized crime." In 1982 *Forbes* magazine pegged Lansky's net worth at $100 million, but *Forbes* had it wrong. Lansky's investments in Las Vegas and Cuba went south; he reportedly said of his Havana losses, "I crapped out." He died in Miami Beach in 1983. According to his granddaughter, his estate was worth thirty-seven thousand dollars.

Little Rock, Arkansas, police chief **O. N. Martin**, who jailed Titanic on New Year's Eve 1929–30, became the subject of a corruption investigation. On New Year's Day 1947, he ordered his chief lieutenant, Oscar Deubler, who was heading the investigation, to join him in North Little Rock. Chief Martin killed Deubler with a sawed-off shotgun, then used his service revolver to shoot himself to death.

The year after he was acquitted in the Rothstein's murder trial **George "Hump" McManus** learned that his wife had died in a car wreck. He collapsed with a heart attack. McManus recovered and went back to work. After multiple arrests for gambling and bookmaking, he died in Sea Girt, New Jersey, in 1940 at the age of forty-seven.

Jack "Machine Gun" McGurn, the best golfer in Capone's circle of criminal sportsmen, entered the PGA tour's 1933 Western Open at Olympia Fields Country Club, near Chicago. On the seventh hole, policemen surrounded him. A lieutenant told McGurn he was under arrest. The charge was "criminal reputation," due in part to his alleged involvement in the St. Valentine's Day Massacre four years before. McGurn's wife, Louise—a.k.a. "The Blonde Alibi"—waved her three-carat diamond ring and asked, "Whose brilliant idea is this?" McGurn asked the cops if he could finish his round. Amused, they agreed and joined the other spectators. The badges in his gallery seemed to unnerve McGurn, who shot eighty-six, sixteen over par. But he beat the rap in court. Less than three years later McGurn was machine-gunned to death by three assassins in a Chicago bowling alley.

In his 1966 autobiography, *The Bank Shot and Other Great Robberies*, **Minnesota Fats** called Titanic his hero and role model, "one of the highest rollers and top action men of all time." Ti, wrote Fats, pulled off "fantastic phenomena that not only defied all known laws of science, but made Sir Isaac Newton look like a bellhop." Fats was inducted into the Pool Hall of Fame in 1984. He died in Nashville in 1996, at the age of eighty-two, and was buried under a brass marker reading "St. Peter, rack 'em up."

Lee Trevino and **Ray Floyd** went on to win fifty-one PGA tour titles and ten majors between them. In 1986 the forty-four-year-old

Floyd became the oldest U.S. Open winner ever. Trevino, struck by lightning during the 1975 Western Open, had surgery to remove a damaged spinal disk and struggled to regain his form before winning the 1984 PGA Championship at age forty-four. Trevino was inducted into the World Golf Hall of Fame in 1981, Floyd eight years later. Both men still compete occasionally on the Champions Tour for players over fifty. "We still trade old Titanic stories," Floyd says.

Ty Wayne Thomas, Titanic's younger son, lives in Dallas. A musician and entrepreneur, he helped lead a pop-rock band, The Crossing, to regional fame in the 1990s. Now fifty, Ty Wayne entered 2010 fired up about Windows on Rockets, a Christian band he's backing. "Check out windowsonrockets.com," he says.

Tommy Thomas quit gambling in 1996. A strapping man with a booming voice and a silver-gray beard that makes him look like Moses in a Stetson, Tommy, sixty-six, is an evangelist for the Light of Life Ministry in Dallas. Remembering the night he and his poker partner were ambushed in Memphis, he says, "God kept his hand on me." His partner died; Tommy lived to rethink his path in life.

"Biblically, there are curses that pass down through generations," he says. Tommy believes his father's "chasing for silver and gold" was a curse that passed down to him from Titanic. "All I ever wanted was to be like my dad. But that was the wrong path. So I cut a deal with God."

Twenty years after Ti's death, one of the best card mechanics Texas ever saw traded cold decks and his Colt Cobra .38 Special for a life of preaching in prisons. You can follow his progress on his website, Howtobeattheodds.com.

Jeannette Thomas Miller, Titanic's last wife, remarried in 1985. She lives in Texas's Rio Grande Valley with her husband, Max. Now seventy-four, she says she wishes she'd had the confidence to make a career of her own fifty years ago rather than counting on Ti to support her. She would have loved to have had a couple of those valises full of hundred-dollar bills, but she's not complaining about her twenty vivid years with the handsome, charming genius who swept her off her feet in 1954.

"We all live with our choices," Jeannette says.

For further information about Titanic Thompson, this book and its author please go to **http://titanicthompson.tumblr.com**.

ACKNOWLEDGMENTS

First, thanks to Jeannette Miller, whose kindness and wisdom I will not forget. Tommy Thomas, an inspired card mechanic who became a spokesman for his faith, comes next. Tommy and Ty Wayne Thomas are, in their ways, as impressive as their father. I'm also glad I met Dr. Jim Hill, an invaluable friend to Titanic who helped me understand the man we'd both love to beat on the golf course.

Many thanks to Gary McCord, who helped me understand Titanic, and Gary Foster, who provided valuable background material. I'm also grateful to Carlton Stowers, Doyle Brunson, Jack Binion, Bill Walters and the late Bud Shrake, Lee Trevino and Ti's favorite young hotshot, the great Ray Floyd. The family of Frank Loesser kindly allowed me to use a line from *Guys and Dolls*.

I was delighted to talk golf and gambling with Don Stickney, Herm Kaiser, Paul Bondeson, Dewey Tomko, Rudy Durand, Larry Guninger, Eddie Merrins, Duke Evans, Mal Elliott and Jeanne Carmen's son, Brandon James. Others who supported my work include Dr. Patricia Cook, Jim Herre, Starr Bennett, Ken Kubik, Steve Randall, Scott Gummer, Walter Bingham, Miriam

Marseu, Terry Heeg at *Trap & Field* magazine, Darin Tennyson, Bill Skrzyniarz.

I'm grateful to Picador's Paul Baggaley for publishing *Titanic Thompson*, as well as to Kris Doyle for his support and Nathan Burton for his striking cover design. At W.W. Norton in New York, Starling Lawrence turned his sharp eye to my work, which got a boost from a terrific young editor, Tom Mayer. Thanks also to my agent, Jim Levine, and to Kerry Evans and her colleagues at the Levine Greenberg Agency.

And to my dad, Art Cook, who had a big heart and a lot of gamble in him.

A NOTE ON SOURCES

Many of Titanic Thompson's deeds are a matter of public record. Multiple sources reported his roles in Damon Runyon's New York, Arnold Rothstein's death, pool's Hustlers' Jamboree, and the first World Series of Poker, along with his marriages, divorces, and arrests. After the Rothstein murder trial of 1929 made him semifamous, to Ti's chagrin, newspapers noted his comings and goings. Journalists including Runyon, John Lardner, Shirley Povich, Jim Murray, Jon Bradshaw, and, most important, Bud Shrake recorded their encounters with Titanic. My research also benefited from the published recollections of Minnesota Fats, Sam Snead, Hubert Cokes, Lee Trevino, Amarillo Slim Preston, Harvey Penick, Oscar Fraley, John Scarne, and many others. Most crucial of all were the hundred-plus interviews I conducted with people who knew Titanic, from Shrake, Ray Floyd, Don Stickney, Jack Binion, and Doyle Brunson to Titanic's sons, Tommy and Ty Wayne, and his last wife, Jeannette.

Many of the quotations I attribute to Titanic come from the sixty-nine-page transcript of the interviews Shrake recorded on his trip to Colleyville, Texas, in 1972. Other dialogue is taken from Titanic's recollections, published sources including contemporary news accounts and the books in my select bibliography, and, particularly in the latter part of the book, my interviews with participants.

My research made it easy to establish the framework of Titanic's life. But how to tell fact from lore in some of the old Ti stories told by gamblers, golfers, and other liars? It helped that Titanic himself wasn't much of a fabulist. It did him no good to claim he could do things he couldn't. A man could lose bets that way. Ti's game was to claim he could do the seemingly impossible, then do it. So almost all of the most sensational Ti tales came from others. Some were verifiable and turned out to be true. Others were clearly false or embellished, like an old canard that said Ti got his nickname by dressing up as a woman to escape the *Titanic*. (He was riding Missouri riverboats at the time.) Some details conflicted with others; some were beyond even Ti's considerable powers. (He couldn't flip cards around corners or roll dice so that they came to rest with one on top of the other.) In the end I used material that was clearly true plus stories I believed to be true because they jibed with other facts and came from disparate sources.

The *JOPLIN 20* road sign is an example. That story has been told by gamblers all over the country for at least half a century, with variations including *TULSA 10* and *CHICAGO 100*. There are two reasons for that. The first is that gamblers telling Titanic tales are unconstrained by fact-checking departments. The second is that Ti used his best tricks wherever he went until his pigeons got wise. I chose Joplin because the most-told version of the story featured Joplin gamblers Beanie Benson and Hickory McCullough.

In most cases I signaled judgment calls with phrases like "he may have" and "he probably." Occasionally, in the interest of keeping the narrative train rolling, I let my best guess stand for itself. Those cases amount to far less than 1 percent of the book.

SELECT BIBLIOGRAPHY

Anonymous. *The Education of a Poker Pigeon*. New York: Lyle Stuart Books, 2008.

Asinof, Eliot. *Eight Men Out: The Black Sox and the 1919 World Series*. New York: Holt, Rinehart & Winston, 1963.

Berliner, Louise. *Texas Guinan: Queen of the Nightclubs*. Austin: University of Texas Press, 1993.

Bigham, Darrel E. *Evansville: The World War II Years*. Charleston, S.C.: Arcadia, 2005.

Bradshaw, Jon. *Fast Company*. London: High Stakes, 1975.

Breslin, Jimmy. *Damon Runyon*. New York: Ticknor & Fields, 1991.

Charyn, Jerome. *Gangsters and Gold Diggers*. New York: Thunder's Mouth Press, 2003.

Collins, Marilyn. *Rogers: The Town the Frisco Built*. Charleston, S.C.: Arcadia, 2002.

Crump, Leon, and John Stravinsky. *Drive for Show, Putt for Dough: Memoirs of a Golf Hustler*. New York: HarperCollins, 1997.

Dobereiner, Peter, ed. *The Golfers*. London: William Collins, 1982.

Dodson, James. *Ben Hogan: An American Life*. New York: Doubleday, 2004.

Eisenberg, Dennis, and Uri Dan. *Meyer Lansky, Mogul of the Mob*. New York: Paddington Press, 1979.

Fowler, Gene. *Beau James: The Life and Times of Jimmy Walker*. New York: Viking Press, 1945.

Gosch, Martin, and Richard Hammer. *The Last Testament of Lucky Luciano*. New York: Little, Brown, 1975.

Jay, Ricky. *Dice: Deception, Fate and Rotten Luck*. New York: Quantuck Lane Press, 2003.

Kahn, Roger, ed. *The World of John Lardner*. New York: Simon & Schuster, 1961.

Katcher, Leo. *The Big Bankroll: The Life and Times of Arnold Rothstein*. New York: Harper & Brothers, 1959.

Keeler, O. B. *The Bobby Jones Story*. Chicago: Triumph Books, 1953.

Kobler, John. *Capone*. New York: Putnam, 1971.

Lears, Jackson. *Something for Nothing: Luck in America*. New York: Viking Press, 2003.

McManus, James. *Positively Fifth Street*. New York: Farrar, Straus & Giroux, 2003.

Minnesota Fats. *The Bank Shot and Other Great Robberies*. Guilford, Conn.: Lyons Press, 2006.

Novak, Joe, and Al Stump. *Bel-Air Country Club: A Living Legend*. Bel-Air, Calif.: Bel-Air Country Club, 1993.

Painter, Nell Irvin. *Standing at Armageddon: A Grassroots History of the Progressive Era*. New York: W. W. Norton, 2008.

Penick, Harvey, with Bud Shrake. *The Wisdom of Harvey Penick*. New York: Simon & Schuster, 1997.

Pietrusza, David. *Rothstein*. New York: Carroll & Graf, 2003.

Preston, Amarillo Slim, with Greg Dinkin. *Amarillo Slim in a World Full of Fat People*. New York: HarperCollins, 2003.

Raab, Selwyn. *Five Families*. New York: Thomas Dunne Books, 2005.

Runyon, Damon. *Guys and Dolls and Other Writings*. New York: Penguin Books, 2008.

Scarne, John. *The Odds against Me.* New York: Simon & Schuster, 1966.

———. *Scarne on Dice.* Harrisburg, Pa.: Stackpole Books, 1962.

Schwartz, David G. *Roll the Bones: The History of Gambling.* New York: Gotham Books, 2006.

Snead, Sam, and Jerry Tarde. *Pigeons, Marks, Hustlers and Other Golf Bettors You Can Beat.* New York: Golf Digest Books, 1986.

Solomon, Brian. *Southern Pacific Railroad.* Osceola, Wisc.: MBI, 1999.

Stowers, Carlton. *The Unsinkable Titanic Thompson.* Santa Barbara, Calif.: Palmer Magic, 1982.

Thomas, Tommy. *God and the Gambler.* Hurst, Tex.: Light of Life Ministries International, 2002.

Trager, James. *The New York Chronology.* New York: HarperCollins, 2003.

Trevino, Lee, and Sam Blair. *They Call Me Super Mex.* New York: Random House, 1982.

Wallis, Michael. *Oil Man: The Story of Frank Phillips and the Birth of Phillips Petroleum.* New York: St. Martin's Press, 1988.

INDEX